# Iconography in Medieval Spanish Literature

# ICONOGRAPHY
## in Medieval Spanish Literature

JOHN E. KELLER AND RICHARD P. KINKADE

THE UNIVERSITY PRESS OF KENTUCKY

Publication of this book has been assisted by a grant
from the National Endowment for the Humanities.

**Library of Congress Cataloging in Publication Data**

Keller, John Esten.
    Iconography in medieval Spanish literature.

    Bibliography: p.
    Includes index.
    1. Spanish fiction—To 1500—History and criticism.
    2. Spanish fiction—To 1500—Illustrations.
    3. Art and literature.  4. Narration (Rhetoric)
    I. Kinkade, Richard P.  II. Title.
    PQ6141.K44  1983     863'.1'09      83-2478
    ISBN 0-8131-1449-7

# Contents

[Color plates follow pages 40 and 104]

# Preface

question has haunted us from the outset of this work and indeed was partially responsible for our undertaking it: how many scholars of medieval Spanish literature have ever seen the illuminations or other illustrations commissioned by the patrons of the works studied in their classes? Even the great critics of medieval Spanish fiction—Menéndez y Pelayo, Amador de los Ríos, Bonilla y San Martín, to name but three—did not consider it worthwhile to describe the narrative art found in such books as the *Cantigas de Santa Maria, Calila e Digna,* and the *Libro del Cavallero Cifar.* Nor have we until recently made any effort to synchronize the two mutually compatible art forms—the written word and the narrative art that visualized it for medieval man. This fault, committed in even the best handbooks of literary history, is a serious omission in the presentation of literary history, since illustrations greatly enhance textual presentation and can even alter it or color it with novel concepts.

When an educated English-speaking public was wont to read the *Divine Comedy* and could view simultaneously Gustave Doré's compelling and often terrifying engravings, this great book took on a vivid life not quite present in English translation, or indeed in the original Tuscan. The connection between the medieval poet and the nineteenth century artist was powerful enough to reshape in the reader's mind the sequences illustrated so long after Dante's time. This is an extreme case, perhaps, but it is illustrative of the influence of visualizations on the reader's perception of a text. Illuminated medieval texts, both ecclesiastical and secular, were more esteemed and more memorable than texts of the same works without illuminations. Consider miracles of the Virgin, for example.

These were written in Spain from the time of Gil de Zamora, who wrote in Latin; Gonzalo de Berceo, who used good Castilian; and King Alfonso X, who wrote or caused to be written the largest collection or anthology of Marian miracles in Galician-Portuguese rather than in his native Castilian. Those who have compared the manuscripts of the *Cantigas de Santa Maria* and their gorgeous illuminations with the unillustrated collections of miracles by these other authors can best comprehend what we mean. The illuminated miracles are memorable, for their miniatures cling to the minds of those who have seen them and serve to intensify the stories they illustrate.

Literary historians and art historians have too often gone separate ways, the former stressing text, the latter illustrations, leading to a regretable lack of communication and a mutual misunderstanding of interdisciplinary possiblities for study. Students of literature (and we among them, we confess) have labored in considerable ignorance of atelier traditions and the possibilities present in their development. And students of art have overlooked or studied only superficially the illuminations found in the medieval secular books we treat. Some of these illustrations have never been reproduced anywhere, while others have entirely escaped the notice of both literary scholars and art historians.

This leads us to a second question: Must the two disciplines—art and literature—continue their separate and therefore limited progress toward knowledge? Surely the answer must be in the negative. Communication is as possible as it is necessary if comprehension of the kind we envisage is to be attained. As historians of literature and of literature's narrative techniques in verbal form, we believe this book can assist art historians, although we concede it is not written with the competence in art possessed by those who have made medieval art their life's study.

How, then, can comprehension and communication be brought about, if we may ask still a third question? The answer, we believe, is through the comparative study of literary content and artistic content. The iconography and narrative art of these pictures, that is, the visualization of the written work, can be indispensable to literary scholar and art expert alike. Some investigation, though not a great deal, is being made with regard to text and visualization of ecclesiastical works, as we shall show in the course of this book. We hope that through this study of the narrative techniques of visualization found in five repositories of secular Spanish fiction, including both brief narratives and more novelesque pieces, we can accomplish two goals: first and foremost, to lead literary historians and critics of literature (primarily of Spanish literature) to some new insights into the interplay of influences between literature and illumination; and secondly, to open a virtually unexplored area of Spanish art to art historians, both peninsular and foreign, in order to increase the communication so often lacking between students of literature and those of the fine arts.

Our approach thus seeks to be interdisciplinary, though perforce more literary than visual, since we are students primarily of literature and its history. With each literary sequence which we summarize or translate, we offer a parallel discussion of its visualization, since we see the two art forms as working mutually and simultaneously.

What we write is our own interpretation of each picture or set of related pictures in their alliance with text, and our conception of the narrative devices or techniques both artists and writers employed. Insofar as possible, we attempt also to indicate how artists and writers accommodated the nine elements generally regarded as making up the structure of narrative: plot, conflict, setting, characterization, theme, style, effect, point of view, and mood or tone. Obviously not every story, and certainly not every miniature can contain every one of these elements, but we hope to demonstrate that more of these nine elements than has been suspected do indeed appear in both media of medieval Spanish story telling—the verbal and the visual. No one, to our knowledge, has attempted this in the field of medieval Spanish secular book illustration.

We are most grateful to the National Endowment for the Humanities and the University of Kentucky, through whose matching funds we were able to spend the summer of 1978 traveling through most of Spain, especially along the Way of St. James, and to photograph in museums, palaces, libraries, churches, and other places the various art works needed for the completion of our books. Without this aid, and a semester's leave of absence for one of us, we could hardly have made more than a start on our project.

We render deepest appreciation to Don Agustín Cano, Ministro Encargado de Asuntos Culturales of the Embassy of Spain in Washington, whose letters of introduction brought great success to our investigations. Don Carlos González Echegaray of the Cuerpo Facultativo de Archivos Bibliotecarios y Arqueológicos and Subdirector General de Bibliotecas, smoothed our path in various museums. The Director of the Museo del Prado, Don José Manuel Pitandrade, as well as the Subdirector, Don Javier Morales, have sent us most excellently prepared transparencies of a significant part of the Prado's medieval collection. Don Manuel Sánchez Mariana of the Cuerpo Facultativo de Archiveros y Bibliotecarios of the Biblioteca Nacional, made it possible to obtain magnificent color transparencies of numerous miniatures. Special mention, too, must go to Father Eduardo Torra de Arana, Canon of the Santa Eglesia Metropolitana de La Seo in Saragossa, whose kindness in securing for us photographs of the famous collection of fourteenth- and fifteenth-century tapestries will greatly enrich our studies. Thanks too, are owed to Father Pascual de Galindo, whose definitive study of the tapestries preserved in the La Seo collection has proved invaluable; and to Carlos Sánchez García, who has generously pointed out much about these art works. We are greatly indebted to Dr. Kathleen Kulp-Hill of Eastern Kentucky University for permission to print her translations of the *Cantigas de Santa Maria*. Spain's Consul General to New Orleans, Don Enrique Iranzo, has also helped with his encouragement and support. From the University of Connecticut came a handsome grant to aid in the cost of publication, and due thanks are made here. We offer grateful acknowledgment, too, to Don Ramón Bela, Secretario Ejecutivo and the Comité Conjunto Hispano-Norteamericano para Asuntos Educativos y Culturales: these scholarly persons through their assessment of our book's contribution to the diffusion of Spanish culture in the United States made possible a munificent grant toward publication.

Very special thanks are rendered to Bruce F. Denbo for his encouragement and constantly good advice as this volume was developed. Last, but not least, we owe a great debt of gratitude, as does our profession, to the correct dating of the illuminated manuscripts of *Castigos e documentos* and the *Cavallero Cifar* to Doña María Elena Arizmendi, whose knowledge of medieval dress and coiffure is deep and recognized internationally.

# Introduction

oday scholars are conscious more than ever before of the relationships between the literary, the graphic, and the plastic arts. With greater frequency literary scholars are traversing borders once rarely crossed, and are, in the process of such exploration, discovering fascinating and important concepts. Within the past few years iconography and literature have moved into parallel orbits, if the general meaning of the former is accepted without the more specific connotations established by art historians. It is necessary here that we make quite clear what we mean by iconography.[1] *Webster's New World Dictionary of the American Language* (second edition, 1970) defines iconography as "the art of representing or illustrating by pictures, symbols, images, etc.," and goes so far as to state that iconology is the same as iconography. *The Oxford Universal Dictionary on Historical Principles* (1955) considers iconography to be "a pictorial representation; a drawing, a plan; the description of any subject by means of drawings or figures; any book in which this is done; also a branch of knowledge which deals with representative art in general."

We hope that we do not stray too far from the definitions used by professional art historians. The *McGraw-Hill Dictionary of Art,* for example, defines iconography as "a discipline concerned with the meaning of symbols and themes of works of art," and goes on to state that "The traditional discipline of iconography has expanded to include iconology." It also avers that "while iconography proper deals mainly with the identification and classification of visual symbols, iconology seeks to discern the intrinsic meaning of these symbols and their broader interrelationships as

themes." Probably we cleave to a concept closer to K. Wietzman's, which states that "Iconography is the science that deals with the forms and recensions of images." Wietzman uses recension in the sense of textual revision as in Biblical and later literary studies.

We have attempted to ply a course which does not stray far from either the more general or the more specific concepts of iconography. While we concentrate to a greater degree upon narrative art, that is, the means employed by medieval artists to illustrate brief narratives as well as novelesque narrative sequences, we nevertheless do not neglect symbols and their meanings.

Since so little has been written about narrative techniques in medieval Spanish secular books, and since apparently no one has explored the iconography and narrative art devices used by medieval Spanish artists, or by artists imported from abroad,[2] we here attempt to describe and interpret these techniques.

Our studies of medieval Spanish fiction were nearing their end when we realized that much still remained to be done to make clear the ways in which medieval Spaniards came to know the stories of their times. After all, a majority of the populace was illiterate. Yet a world of visualized knowledge surrounded the ignorant and taught them much of what they needed to know about the great folk of history, of the Bible, of literature, both past and current, foreign and domestic, and also about folklore. When medieval people went to church they gazed upon stained glass windows, at least in the larger churches and cathedrals. There in gorgeous colors they could view scriptural and other pietistic events depicted in detail; occasionally historical personages glowed in stained glass;

and from time to time, especially in Spain along the Way of Saint James, local miracles appeared. Inside churches, too, in elaborate or simply carved choir stalls, on *misericordias* beneath the seats, in pulpits, on columns, and on walls and ceilings, they could view a multitude of stories. From tapestries and frescoes, sculptures, carvings in wood and ivory, stucco, painted or unpainted, a host of visual images instructed the viewer at every turn. Frequently during important seasons of the ecclesiastical year the clergy displayed tapestries, paintings, and sculptures representing such important incidents as the Nativity, Ressurection, and events from the lives of the saints, some life-sized, some smaller, to rival the presentations dramatized in mystery and miracle plays and in *autos* and *pasos.* The exteriors of churches and palaces were similarly rich in visualization of Scripture, history, and sometimes literature and folklore. Sculpture, statuary, bas-reliefs, columns, lavishly carved facades, and beam paintings joined to elucidate and perpetuate for medieval people the lore of past centuries. Castles, guild halls, civic buildings, fortresses, and private dwellings of the rich and poor (though of the latter virtually nothing is known) were also repositories of this visual heritage, while emblems, blazons, and various heraldic imagery constantly appeared. In sum, medieval people could not escape the vast visual array proffered by the Church, royalty, and the nobility to attract and instruct them.

Visual, too, of course, were the great mystery and miracle plays and sacramental *autos,* as well as other religious dramatic productions, and folk dramas and secular plays such as those censured by King Alfonso X in his *Siete Partidas,* or *Seven Divisions of Law,* which were apparently widespread enough to merit legal prohibition.[3] In Spain much of the graphic, plastic, and dramatic art from the Middle Ages survives to this day, particularly in the displays of Corpus Christi during Holy Week.

Ecclesiastical visualization predominated in all areas of medieval art, supported by the powerful church with frequent directives such as those of Gregory the Great to the effect that visual representations should be used to instruct the illiterate masses in matters of the Gospel. Secular narrative art offered considerable rivalry, however, since the classical past—Aesopic fables, Roman and Greek myths, and the heroes of Antiquity—all played persuasive roles in the medieval symphony. Indeed, ecclesiastics also made use of personages, events, or stories from the Ancient World, from popular lore, or the plethora of oriental apologues and tales, either adding virtuous exhortations or cleaving to the original interpretations, since many

of these tales belonged to a kind of universal morality satisfying to Christians and non-Christians alike.

Popular or folkloristic themes were also preserved throughout the visual media. They varied in content, dealing with particular local saints or containing miracles of the Virgin and other religious figures known across all Christendom. Frequently, too, purely Spanish miracles of Our Lady as well as those of Spanish saints were the inspiration of both literary and artistic treatment. Another source for both written and visual representation was the deeds of foreign heroes like Charlemagne and Arthur, together with Spanish personages like the Cid and Fernán González. Still others depicted folktales and regional superstitions exemplified by the remarkable *alfarjes,* or beam paintings, recently discovered in a church in Los Balbases, a tiny village near the monastery of Santo Domingo de Silos, or by the innumerable and artistic *alfarjes* of that great monastery itself.[4]

Spain, then, is rich in visualizations of many varieties. In the Iberian Peninsula respect, devotion, and deep interest in what is hispanic have always been powerful mainsprings, sentiments that contributed forcefully to the rise of realism in medieval literature and art. Spanish writers, for example, consistently avoided the impossible or the exaggerated in epic poetry, a genre which in other cultures often stressed these very elements. Even in the realm of miracles, which were considered as perfectly factual, this realism prevailed, so that one finds unusual portrayals of the real world in such works. Similarly, we believe, to a degree Spanish artists, particularly in the case of miniatures, went beyond the realism found in much of European Gothic art in order to depict elements peculiar to Spanish life. Visualization thus provided the greater part of the medieval Spaniard's education and recreation. Sermons in stone, as well as in stained glass and ivory and paper, were sermons indeed. This does not mean that books like the *Cantigas de Santa Maria, Castigos e documentos,* and the *Cavallero Cifar* were available to the populace. Their content, however, reached the people in song and story in churches, palaces, plazas and streets, and instructed them.

Analogies can be found in our own century. If one were asked how the average person of today learns about events of the past, about history, the lives of prominent people, the Bible, great literature (classical, historical, or national), the answer might be from reading. But a moment's thought would surely correct this, for what the average American (alas, even the average college-trained American) knows of such matters may stem, as in the Middle Ages, from visual media—television primarily, and after television the cinema. Probably more people learned something of the life and times of the Emperor Claudius through the televised version of Robert Graves's biographical novel than by reading the book itself or the history from which Graves drew it. So, too, for the lives of Henry VIII, Queen Elizabeth, the Churchills, the Adams family, and other televised dramatizations of the past. Great literature, the Scriptures, significant religious and civic events, though often badly curtailed or altered, also reach the public through these same media. Perhaps it is just as well, for the Middle Ages and its ignorance perforce come to mind when we reflect upon the large segments of the contemporary population who never read a book or have not learned how to read one.

In the Middle Ages the word miniature, today meaning "diminutive," had another connotation due to its derivation from the Latin *minium,* meaning "red lead" or "vermillion," the color used for the borders of pages as well as for the initial capital letters, into which smaller pictures or pictorial scenes and events were often introduced. Later these red initials were known as rubrics, and when entered in the Church calendar to mark a saint's day or festival, these days came to be known as red-letter days. In time the term miniature was applied by extension to most vignettes or decorations limned with the red border. Minature by this time also drew upon the French *mignature,* "small," so a miniature is a "small painting" because the paintings within the red border were small. The word illumination comes from Old French *iluminer* from the Latin *illuminare,* "to paint," so medieval representations in miniature are also called illuminations.

Miniatures appeared in books for the most part, but they were present too in a wide variety of painted *objets d'art.* Our present study of miniatures includes only those found in books. Later we plan to treat miniatures in enamel, ivory, and those carved in other materials. Fortunately, miniatures in books are generally accompanied by verbal accounts which describe or refer to the visual representations, thus greatly contributing to an understanding of them and permitting us to comprehend better these two parallel narrative techniques, the verbal and the pictorial.

We have often been surprised at the very real differences which frequently exist between verbalization and visualization in some of the books we have studied, most markedly in the *Cantigas de Santa Maria.* We have wondered, too, at the marvelously close relationship achieved between these two expressive media on other pages. How the variations came about is a subject for speculation. These questions and

others, as well as the entire process of visualized presentation in Alfonsine illuminations, may suggest areas of further study to those more expert than we in the history of art.

Spanish secular miniatures, particularly in books of fiction which have survived the ages, are not numerous. For this reason we feel confident that we have fairly well encompassed the primary artistic repositories in the few volumes we treat, and that these volumes portray a majority of the narrative techniques utilized in the Peninsula before the Renaissance. Like Emile Mâle when he assembled materials for his monumental study *The Gothic Image: Religious Art in France of the Thirteenth Century,* we can best and most effectively treat one representative block of time. Mâle preferred to focus upon thirteenth-century France with only a few references to earlier and later periods. We treat the thirteenth, fourteenth, and part of the fifteenth centuries, entering the fifteenth century only where necessary to round out the development of secular miniatures and other art forms found in books. This time span in Spain formed a somewhat homogeneous period in art and letters. This homogeneity may reflect that "Spanish belatedness" so well described and exemplified by Curtius in *European Literature and the Latin Middle Ages,* in which he makes clear how reluctantly Spanish culture relinquished many of its medieval characteristics. This belatedness in literature was reflected also in medieval art in the Iberian Peninsula. Of course, no one can with real authority draw the limits of a cultural period, but as far as seems feasible and sensible we feel that the period we have described is a logical one. In the volumes in which we plan to treat frescoes, stained glass windows, and other art media, we must venture deeper into the fifteenth century because some of the best examples of these art forms belong to this later time and because fewer survive from an earlier period.

The representative art works we have selected correspond to the acme of the illuminator's art, to an excellence in line drawings and fine woodcuts in books that we consider to be monuments of Spanish literature. Apparently it was neither fashionable nor customary to have books of fiction illustrated, making the ones we study unique. One may search in vain for art work of any kind in Don Juan Manuel's famous collection of moralized tales, *El Conde Lucanor,* although one of its manuscripts mentions another copy which contains illustrations. The three extant manuscripts of *Barlaam e Josafat,* important in the development of prose narrative, are unillustrated. Spain's earliest version of the *Book of Sindibad,* known as the *Libro de los engaños,* a work sponsored by no less a personage than Prince Fadrique, brother of Alfonso X, and the purveyor of many tales to become famous in peninsular fiction, is without miniatures or other illustrations, at least in extant copies. Nor do any of the three copies of Juan Ruiz's famous *Libro de buen amor* contain any art beyond a few rudimentary illustrations which might best be described as capricious scribal sketches.[5]

We must therefore resort to some five books in which one may profitably witness the rise and development of secular illustration. Most are royal manuscripts or copies of royal manuscripts, and this no doubt explains why they have survived virtually undamaged. We know of no illustrated secular literature before the thirteenth century. We study the few in the period we have chosen to investigate, and we marvel at the dearth.[6]

The thirteenth-century book chosen happens to be the most lavishly illustrated and perhaps the most exemplary specimen of narrative art. The *Cantigas de Santa Maria* of King Alfonso X survives in four manuscripts, three of which are justly renowned for their exquisite illuminations and calligraphy. Two of these, the Escorial codex and a similar but much shorter codex preserved in the National Library of Florence, when viewed as a whole, contain nearly three hundred full pages of illumination. Insofar as we can ascertain, these two volumes of miracles and hymns to the Blessed Virgin embody almost all, if not all, artistic devices known or employed in medieval Spain up to their time and perhaps even until as late as the fifteenth century. The influence of this thirteenth-century work on literature, music, and art has been incalculable, though until recently scholars have not recognized its importance. Though *cantigas* is indeed the plural of *cantiga,* or "canticle," we shall write of the *Cantigas* as a unified work and mention the separate manuscripts upon which we base our study only when necessary to indicate to which one a particular narrative belongs.

The anxiety of King Alfonso (who ruled from 1252 to 1284) to render into Castilian the world's greatest corpus of knowledge, to produce a code of laws fit to cope with the needs of his kingdom, to provide his people with a history of the world and another of their own land, to attempt to gather together encyclopedic works in the sciences, literature, games and recreations, makes his reign a veritable treasure trove of medieval information. Given his ecumenical curiosity and insatiable penchant for detail, it is no wonder that he embarked upon Europe's most ambitious collection of Marian miracles. Nor is it surprising that he may have sponsored the translation (as we believe he

did) of one of Arabic literature's finest works, the book of *Kalilah wa-Dimna,* known in Spanish as *Calila e Digna,* a compendium of oriental wisdom, precepts, and moralized tales some of whose origins may be traced to the Hindu *Panchatantra.* The three extant manuscripts of the Spanish translation are believed to date from the fourteenth or early fifteenth century. One of them is illustrated in lively fashion with clear line drawings.

The thirteenth century also witnessed the creation of another important work, written at the behest of King Sancho IV, son of Alfonso X and his successor to the throne. It bears the title *Castigos e documentos para bien vivir,* or Teachings and Treatises for Right Living. Sancho, who surely was conversant with his father's literary achievements, and who had been reared under the tutelage of the king himself, knew the value of visual story, and yet the manuscripts of *Castigos* penned in his reign do not have illustrations, and his son, for whom the volume was designed, had to read it without the beautiful pictures a later manuscript contained, the details of which will be given in the chapter devoted to this work.

We offer no book illustrations from the fourteenth century. Not even the *Cavallero Cifar,* purportedly finished in 1301 (a date not accepted by all scholars) contains illustrations in its earlier manuscript. Not until the fifteenth century was there an illuminated *Cifar.* It is a pity that the original manuscript was not as rich in pictures as the later version, for had it been, we would possess a valuable pictorial account of thirteenth-century life and custom, since the author was a thirteenth-century man. The same ideals of religion and chivalry, the same aspects of daily life, the same customs, the same credulity, and similar concepts of law, philosophy, and government, ran like a steady stream through the thirteenth century and the greater part of the fourteenth. The authorship of *Cifar* is not known, but it was probably composed by Ferrand Martínez, archdeacon of the Church of Toledo. Its plot is not original in its entirety but part of it is a rather clever adaptation of the famous and widely dispersed story of the life of St. Eustace, or Placidus. But here we are interested primarily in its wealth of more than 200 miniatures from the fifteenth-century manuscript, and in their place in the history of peninsular narrative.

From the fifteenth century also we have selected an incunabulum dating from 1489, among the first of its kind to be composed primarily of brief narratives. The illustrations of *La vida del Ysopet con sus fabulas hystoriadas,* or *The Life of Aesop with Its Fables Illustrated,* are in the form of woodcuts taken directly from a similar book of fables first printed in Germany. The narrative art in this instance came from outside Spain, but a German printer in Saragossa seemed well aware that these stories, gleaned from Aesopic fables and other apologues and stories from both European and oriental sources, would likely turn a profit. Its narrative techniques must have been well designed to suit Spanish tastes, for it fast became Spain's richest single volume of fabulistic story and the most influential fable book in the Peninsula. In fact, no fable collection for the next four hundred years failed to draw heavily upon its content, and it continued to be published with surprising frequency until the eighteenth century. This book provided later writers—Cervantes, Lope de Vega, Calderón, and many others—with most of their knowledge of fables. It has been greatly neglected and seldom appears in histories of Spanish literature.

On five books, then—the *Cantigas de Santa Maria, Calila e Digna, Castigos e documentos,* the *Cavellero Cifar,* and the *Vida del Ysopet*—we base our study of the devices and techniques employed in miniatures, line drawings, and woodcuts.

# Las Cantigas de Santa Maria

ing Alfonso X, who ruled from 1252 to 1284, was a much-misunderstood monarch, and in his own time bore the brunt of heavy criticism. His unflagging interest, monumental curiosity, and ambitious pursuit of knowledge in all areas made him a focal point for such attacks. Yet somehow, in the midst of wars, of disputes with the Pope over his claim to the title of Emperor of the Holy Roman Empire, and his traumatic family difficulties, he managed to be the thirteenth century's most noted bibliophile, one of its greatest musicologists, a knowledgeable student of literature, law, history, and the sciences, and—what interests us most in the present study—its greatest patron of pictorial art. He was, in short, a man universal in space and time, and this of itself rendered him incompatible with his subjects at most levels of the social hierarchy, for they could not grasp his successful efforts to create what we have come to regard as a thirteenth-century Renaissance.[1]

Some of those he governed must have realized what he was attempting to accomplish, and understood the difficulties of the task. Few of his people could read Latin, the language of religion, of science, and of knowledge in general. Alfonso understood this, and knew that most Spaniards were illiterate even with respect to their own language. But, he reasoned, if they could understand what was told them or read to them, it would be worthwhile to embark upon encyclopedic projects to put before them a collection of the knowledge available to man. Therefore he caused to be written a great legal code, the *Siete Partidas,*

finished in the late thirteenth century and so lengthy and detailed as to rival the great codices of the past, even the *Code of Justinian.*[2] Read aloud, it was within the reach of his uneducated subjects, and read by the literate it could serve, and did, as an uncommonly successful corpus of jurisprudence which, though not promulgated in his lifetime, nevertheless was taught in universities and shaped the legal thinking of his reign.

With high ambition, Alfonso embarked upon two great historical projects: a history of the world from the Creation onward and a history of Spain. But he got no farther than the birth of Jesus in the case of the former, and the death of his father, King Ferdinand III, in the latter. Of Alfonso's works on the sciences, the *Libro de astronomia* and the famous *Los lapidarios*[3] contain illuminations of surpassing interest and fine quality, demonstrating once again that the king's interest lay not merely in books, but in books made beautiful and more practical by the addition of illustrated examples.[4]

Though some of the miniatures in these works are worthy manifestations of narrative art, they are but a pale shadow when compared to the brilliance of the lavishly illuminated *Cantigas de Santa Maria,* or *Canticles of Holy Mary.* These collections of Marian lore are in themselves encyclopedic, not surprisingly, for Alfonso was one of Our Lady's most devoted patrons and her self-proclaimed "troubadour." Early, probably even before his coronation in 1252, Alfonso began to gather her miracles from every available source. As a king who refused to be deterred by financial restrictions, he could create in her honor a copious outpouring of praises, extolling her virtues in three media, poetic, musical, and pictorial. Not content with those accounts to be found in the pan-European collections of Our Lady's miracles and hymns, Alfonso introduced many from Spain's unique hagiographic lore, including several contemporary miracles which he himself was able to document by traveling to the sites of these occurrences and questioning people who had been present at the time. A few *cantigas* illustrations actually depict him at the scene of such miracles, and of course one can read the appended verse accounts corroborating these wondrous events.

The body of the *Cantigas* consists of over four hundred miracles and hymns, all composed in verse in Galician-Portuguese, the language considered by contemporary Spanish poets to be the most musical medium for lyric verse. It exhibits a remarkably large number of poetic meters, easily comprising the most comprehensive collection of poetic forms in the Peninsula. All the forms of verse known until the seventeenth century, with the exception of the sonnet, appear in the great Alfonsine song-book. Each of the four hundred or so poems required a separate melody, and the *Cantigas* is therefore Spain's richest anthology of medieval song. Many believe that King Alfonso was himself the author of several poems with their attendant melodies, and it is possible that he was the author of them all.[5]

Apparently the various codices of the *Cantigas de Santa Maria* were to grow and expand throughout Alfonso's life and reign. From the outset, though he may have been cognizant of the vast scope of this undertaking, he could not have known the exact number of miracles and hymns which would eventually be incorporated into the work. We are certain of this because Alfonso inserted miracles which he believed to have taken place in some particular connection with himself, his family, or his courtiers, and several of these occurred many years following the initiation of the *Cantigas* project. Thus the encyclopedic proportions of this monumental enterprise grew with the years.

While the *Cantigas* is at the same time a superb florilegium of poetry and music and the most comprehensive assemblage of Marian miracles known to date, other noteworthy and encyclopedic characteristics quickly emerge. No other medieval text embodies or presents so graphically the sociological patterns of its time, for through the illuminated pages of the *Cantigas,* as if through a myriad of magic windows, we may view the vast variety of facets which inform the panorama of the Middle Ages. All the masses and classes unfold before us through the miniatures, from kings and emperors and popes and cardinals to the lowest serf in the field. Here one can observe in unbroken succession a multitude of miracles whose background is the farm, the hunt, travel on land and sea, battles between armies, squabbles between commoners, or the more formal jousts of knights. Moors and Jews play frequent roles, while the clergy, along with a host of angels, saints, and demons, engage in still another kind of war. Rural life present and past (since some of the miracles take place in previous centuries), scenes of urban life in all its diverse forms—in short, the complete landscape of the Middle Ages—meet the viewer's eye as he examines these magnificent illuminations.[6]

Encyclopedic, too, is the representation of the illuminator's art, with its wealth of devices employed to express on paper such a variegated world of man and beast, nature and the supernatural. Here experts and students of medieval art may study both pigments and the manner of their application in a work reflecting the entire gamut of iconography during the Spanish Middle Ages, for the *Cantigas* drew upon a fund of native Spanish art enriched by foreign contributions across the centuries.[7] And certainly the substantial artistic techniques involved in visualizing elements of plot and scheme in each miracle provide a practical means of studying some basic concepts of the production of narrative art.

Most authorities believe that contemporary French Gothic art exercised a dominant influence on Alfonso's artists, especially in miniatures. But if the art of the *Cantigas de Santa Maria* is to be viewed as Hispanified French Gothic art, one must also be aware of the departures from French art. France was one of the great centers of Gothic illumination and its techniques, both undisputed and authoritative for artists everywhere, thus prompting Dante's observation in the *Paradiso* that Paris was indeed the focal point of miniatures. Yet, although Alfonsine illuminators drew upon the art of their trans-Pyrenaic neighbors, they clearly diverged from their models. While preserving a certain French grace, they added numerous distinctive touches—a Spanish gravity, a deeper religious atmosphere, a violence foreign to their models,[8] and a realism far from anything found in French art of the same period. The *Cantigas de Santa Maria* frequently reveals this modification in the form of new departures and original concepts and subject matter, as well as in variations in technical presentation. Originality, we believe, is sufficiently well demonstrated in the Alfonsine miniatures to reveal the rising success of a new school of illumination.

Jesús Domínguez Bordona, a truly great historian of Spanish illumination, states that though Spanish artists often accepted and utilized time-honored iconographic concepts, at other times they were obliged to develop first-hand interpretations and render ideas in a personal way.[9] He considered Spanish artists' use of gold, and to a lesser extent, of silver, to be not so lavish as that of their French counterparts, leading us to wonder, in view of the superabundance of gold in the *Cantigas,* just how much gold French manuscripts contained. More perceptive, perhaps, is his statement on the use of white space in the *Cantigas* to obtain effects of light and shadow.

Paul Durrieu noted that whereas the number of human figures in a French miniature never exceeds five or six, in the *Cantigas de Santa Maria* great numbers of people are often portrayed. He was intrigued, too, by the well depicted human figure, carefully executed to achieve the effects of movement in a most natural way.[10]

Books as meaningful and excellent as the *Cantigas* demanded the best artists, leading one to wonder who these artists may have been. While the names of a few of Alfonso's craftsmen are known, it cannot be proved that any of them actually illuminated his Marian miracles. One likely candidate is Pedro Laurenço, actually named in *Cantiga 377* as a man who "painted swiftly and well in her books," that is, in the *Songs of Holy Mary.* He is also described as "the king's man." The miracle relates that as a reward for his art the monarch bestowed upon him a gift of land.

Matilde López Serrano, whose study on the Alfonsine miniatures is well known, believes that another artist, a calligrapher named Juan González, was employed as a royal scribe for Manuscript b.I.2 of the Escorial Library.[11] The fact that in *Cantiga 384* we find mention of a "monk who wrote admirably letters in gold, blue and rose" is intriguing, but it cannot be demonstrated that he was a royal calligrapher in the service of Alfonso. Gonzalo Menéndez Pidal lists no less than six artists who illustrated Alfonsine manuscripts.[12]

Guerrero Lovillo believes he can identify the work of three different illuminators, or at least three whose contribution in the depiction of human figures, faces, and hands is sufficiently distinct to constitute a definitely individual style.[13] In the work of the first he sees a competent and careful craftsman who was especially attentive to details of facial expression and hand language. Though this illuminator painted somewhat chubby-cheeked faces with slightly pursed mouths, the eyes are animated and bright. Guerrero's second miniaturist produced figures with rather elongated faces tending toward either the rawboned or the very delicate. These visages when compared with those of the first artist do not, in Guerrero's opinion, reflect the calm of the first master but reveal instead a certain nervousness and rapidity of execution, and are poorly delineated. The third master is, he feels, frankly unskilled, quite lacking in that spirited and lively portrayal of faces and figures and devoid of the force and vitality so conspicuous in the other two.

Guerrero also suggests three locales in which the codices of the *Cantigas* may have been painted,[14] and we agree with him as far as he goes. Seville, Alfonso's favorite city and the most frequent site of his court, was also the only municipality that did not fail him during the successful uprising of his son, Sancho IV, and may well be one of the environments portrayed by the artists. In some of the miniatures one may perhaps see several of the particular Moorish walls still extant in La Macarena and the Callejón de Agua. One might also point out that the Almohadan gates, fashioned of bronze with interspaced designs, as seen in *Cantiga 32,* are certainly reminiscent of those which open into the Patio de los Naranjos. But why did the artists omit such well-known landmarks as the Giralda and the Torre de Don Fadrique?

Again, there is much in the *Cantigas* redolent of Toledo, a city steeped in Mudéjar art—tiles, architecture, carvings, and so forth. In many of the illuminations there appear elements of the art of the Moors who lived under Christian domination. Moreover, more than a few miracles take place in this staunch bastion of medieval Spanish culture. With regard to the third locale, Murcia, the whole region was undoubtedly a favorite of the Learned King, who governed it for a time even when he was a prince. Surely the palm groves are those of Elche in Murcia, as are the irrigation ditches so well illustrated in several of the miniatures. One further locale suggested by Victor Lampérez y Romea is Galicia,[15] a conjecture supported in *Cantiga 187* by the appearance of a Galician *hórreo* (Plate 9). We know that Galicia was the land of Alfonso's early childhood.

Quite probably Alfonso carried the *Cantigas* with him wherever he went, not only as a book dear to his heart and one he no doubt read or consulted frequently, but also as protection against danger and disease. For just as he carried Our Lady's image into battle or clothed the statue of her in his royal chapel in silk (woven, he believed, by silkworms to make good a promise by their owner), so too he was convinced that the volume of the *Cantigas* had curative powers. In *Cantiga 209* of the Florentine codex, which we reproduce in Plate 32, Alfonso may be seen clutching to his chest the volume we know today as that of the Escorial and being cured by it of a disease no physician could alleviate. Victoria was the city where he lay ill.[16]

The *Cantigas de Santa Maria* were volumes dear to the king. No more personal work endures from the Middle Ages, for in a surprising number of the miracles and hymns Alfonso himself appears depicted as a rather handsome man in his late twenties or early thirties, a most unusual occurrence in medieval Spanish works. His physical presence is constantly felt, for he frequently speaks in the first person as he narrates the stories and mentions his personal investigation of certain miracles. So great was his esteem for these volumes, so intense his reverence, that Alfonso X, dreamer and bibliophile, patron of the arts and sciences, specifically provided for their welfare and safekeeping in his last will and testament: "Likewise we order that all the books of the *Songs of Praise of Holy Mary* be in that church where our body shall be interred, and that they be sung on the feast days of Holy Mary. And if that one who inherits legally and by our will what is ours should wish to own these books of the *Songs of Holy Mary,* we order that he therefore make good restitution to the church from whence he removes them so that he may have grace without sin."

To this day the *Cantigas* are sung on certain feast days of the Virgin, when their clean, clear melodies reverberate through arch and apse, reechoing from vaulted nave and choir to the sarcophagus of Alfonso, as he had hoped they would. One wonders what compensation Philip II gave to Seville's cathedral when he had the *Cantigas* removed and placed in his library of the Escorial, where they have remained ever since.

These canticles have not only survived across the centuries but have today entered upon a new area of appreciation, interpreted by leading musicians, edited by distinguished musicologists, and enjoyed by a far larger public than Alfonso could ever have imagined.[17] It is their contribution to medieval art and all that this discipline offers in its detailed presentation of the medieval world, however, that now engages our attention. Fortunately, a facsimile edition of the miniatures in the Escorial codex has been published and is available in many libraries.[18]

Alfonso surely considered the *Cantigas* to be a pietistic undertaking, and yet he saw it too as a secular work. The portrayal of lay people, even of Moors and Jews, outnumbers representations of the clergy, though clerics quite naturally play an important role. Iconographic treatment here becomes a mingling of the secular and the clerical. The miniaturists employed by the king, both those of Spanish birth and training and artisans imported from France and other lands, were apparently quite familiar with the iconography of the Church, and indeed consciously utilized many of its most characteristic symbols in their work. Sacred art, then, is well represented, though secular overtones predominate, as we shall demonstrate. Sacred elements typically employed are the nimbus placed behind the head to indicate sanctity, and the hand emerging from the clouds, its thumb and two fingers raised in benediction. Missing is Jesus' cruciform nimbus of French sacred art, for example.

Even so, the artists who illuminated the miracles in King Alfonso's *Cantigas* did not utilize such symbols as frequently as we are accustomed to expect in medieval art. The *Cantigas,* though they relate celestial miracles in praise of the Queen of Heaven, are secular in the manner in which they detach themselves from purely pietistic tales and deal primarily with Everyman. The *Cantigas,* therefore, differ radically from Emile Mâle's description of thirteenth-century French art, which many mistakenly assume must hold true for Spanish art, as well. "Christian thought," he wrote, "is in effect what is permanent, as much in the fifteenth century as in the thirteenth, as the unique inspiration of our art. Medieval art seems entirely divorced from the vicissitudes of politics and indifferent to the defeats and victories of war; it recognizes no other effects than theological speculations and the abstractions of the mystics."[19]

Nothing could be more inconsistent with the facts in regard to the motives and artistic influence which inspired the *Cantigas de Santa Maria*. Far from ignoring the vicissitudes of the age, far from overlooking its civil strife and its secular sentiments and preoccupations, the *Cantigas* offers a survey of medieval secular attitudes and actions. Frequent battles between Moor and Christian and even between Christian hosts, attest to the fact that political motives lie at the heart of many conflicts. The speculations of theologians and the abstractions of mystics are noticeable only by their absence. In the *Cantigas* a straightforward simplicity abounds, coupled with a delightful ingenuousness, resulting in both artistic and literary realism. In the civil art of the *Cantigas,* as distinguished from its ecclesiastical representations, we find little of medieval symbolism and allegory. When we read of a dragon in *Cantiga 189* (Plate 8), the illuminations quite simply portray the creature in all its ugliness. Here we do not find the ordinary medieval dragon often associated with the devil or with the mouth of hell. This is a flesh and blood animal, not even called a dragon but a *bescha,* "a beast," which attacks a pilgrim on his way by night to the shrine of Our Lady of Salas. Though the traveler defends himself manfully, the creature spews its blood on him after he has wounded it in the neck, and the blood is so venomous and corrosive that in a few hours' time he has the appearance of a leper. The Blessed Virgin heals him when he reaches her shrine and seeks her compassion. This *cantiga* contains no subtle concepts which might be interpreted allegorically, but rather a tale of natural events satisfying to the mentality of the times. The *bescha* is no mythical monster, no fire-breathing Chimera, but rather a great doglike creature with the claws of a carnivore and the wings of a bat. It is a traditional figure of a dragon, whose origins may be found in ancient times. It does not eject its venom toward the pilgrim as a fictional dragon spits fire. The pilgrim must first shed its noxious blood, which then contaminates his body.

Both religious and secular medieval art everywhere leaned to the depiction of nature, often in very conventionalized forms. The *Cantigas de Santa Maria* felt this influence and incorporated it. Mâle believed, and we agree with him, that the simple love of nature attracts people more than the symbolism of scholars, and that the artists of the time carved and painted animals and flowers simply to express their delight in the aspects of nature which pleased them most. Probably, when they were not under the influence of an Honorius of Autun or the bestiaries, the animals and plants of Gothic churches—and of Gothic miniatures—had no more symbolism than the flora and fauna of Renaissance art, in which the meaning of many symbols had been lost.

Medieval people lived close to nature, for even in their cramped walled cities natural limits encroached upon them. Birds flocked into urban areas to pick at garbage thrown onto the streets below, while storks built their great ungainly nests on the steeples of churches where clouds of pigeons fluttered and were preyed upon in turn by hawks and eagles. Beyond the city walls nature ruled supreme, and in her realm all travelers—pilgrims, merchants, saints, and soldiers—bowed before her influence. The aristocracy owned hunting lodges or country homes, and Alfonso himself owned severeal pied-a-terres. Moreover, as a child he was reared in rural Galicia, still largely unspoiled today, where he learned to love the great outdoors. His miniaturists would have found in him a

patron able to appreciate whatever elements of nature they injected into the *Cantigas.* Indeed, as he edited and assessed their work in progress, he may have insisted upon the inclusion here and there of flowers, birds, and trees, even as he guided the redaction of the texts in prose, inserting words and phrases to improve them.

We are again tempted to use the word encyclopedic when referring to Alfonso's representation of nature, for in the *Cantigas* live many of the animals both wild and domestic known to medieval man. *Cantiga 29,* for example, discloses a remarkable scene in one of its panels, in which we can observe how the artist, with near-photographic realism, has portrayed a group of exotic animals. There can be no question that these beasts were painted from live models (Plate 3). The miracle as verbalized declares that even savage brutes ought to adore Our Lady, and there in proof are painted a giraffe, a zebra, a dromedary, an elephant, what resembles a hippopotamus, and many rare species of birds and fish. A passage in the *Chronicles of the Kings of Castile* explains the presence of these animals in Spain.[20] The King of Ethopia sent them to Alfonso to commemorate the anniversary of the death of King Ferdinand, Alfonso's father.

The encyclopedic quality of landscape art, and to a lesser extent seascapes, is also noteworthy, for in the *Cantigas* a sure sense of both exists. The seascape in Plate 4 is typical of the detail accorded such scenes. Within the landscapes a plethora of minute details comes to light: a group of brilliant magpies against a white sky (Plate 5); the biologically correct depiction of silkworms (Plate 36); in many miniatures trees with a suggestion of myriad leaves, and flowers with their petals, anthers, and stamens; geese, a cock, a hen and chicks, a sow with piglets (Plate 6), and vultures and other carrion birds (Plate 7). Much more, no doubt, is there to see for one who searches with a practiced eye. Even a nighttime landscape may be studied, as in the *cantiga* which narrates the encounter between a dragon and a pilgrim (Plate 8). Local color is stressed in *Cantiga 186* (Plate 9), which depicts a Galician *hórreo,* or storehouse.

Johan Huizinga, in his oft quoted *The Waning of the Middle Ages,* describes medieval art as wrapped in life and with the function of filling with beauty the forms assumed by life.[21] Art was to be enjoyed as an element of life itself and as an expression of life's significance. It was neither an escape from life's vicissitudes nor an entry into a world of contemplation, nor was it conceived as mere beauty; it was an "applied art," with a practical rather than an esthetic value. The illuminations of the *Cantigas* are certainly wrapped in life, expressing reciprocally both its mood and its significance, and King Alfonso must have been acutely aware of this vibrant aspect of his book.

But we see in the miniatures of the *Cantigas de Santa Maria* much more than Huizinga observed in that waning light of late and dying medieval art. We may recall that each tenth *cantiga,* and a large group of *cantigas* toward the end of the work, are songs of praise designed to lead to contemplation of Our Lady's importance in everyday life.[22] Indeed, there are scenes here quite conducive to extended contemplation of many of the miracles themselves. Contemplation of nature in the *cantigas* interacts in perfect harmony with the medieval love of the *locus amoenus,* in medieval England called "the pleasance," in which elements of the natural world provoke and stimulate an idyllic, dreamy nostalgia for an earthly paradise both past and future. The advantage of the miniatures in depicting the pleasance lay obviously in their visual appeal. A contemporary poet like Gonzalo de Berceo could describe a *locus amoenus* in his *Miracles of Our Lady* and evoke a simple, pristine beauty which to this day may be enjoyed as one reads his primitive allegory of a lovely landscape. But the craftsmen who toiled for King Alfonso's favorite book could carry the mind many steps further through their artful visualizations. Either the king's unswerving devotion to Our Lady inspired these artisans or they were themselves imbued with similar sentiments. The unparalleled aesthetic achievements of the miniatures, created at tremendous expense and over a period of many years, indicate to us an art transcending the mere utilitarian. The illuminations of the *Cantigas de Santa Maria* may not yet have reached that lofty sphere of art for art's sake, but they are far more attractive and significant than the kind of art Huizinga has described for us.

The world of the supernatural permeates both the miniatures and stories they reflect, a world as real to many medieval persons as earth itself. Life did indeed revolve around the Church, which had long since substituted its own heroes and heroines, its saints and Virgin, for earlier primitive and pagan figures. The devil, of course, survived, as indeed he had to in the Christian order of things, together with the hosts of hell—demons, imps, succubi, incubi, and revenants who forever tempted or attacked humanity. Medieval literature, secular as well as clerical, teemed with the demonic and the spectral. Most medieval people through legends, folktales, and iconography, knew the world of darkness and feared it. Many had seen or talked with people possessed, and if anyone began to doubt, he had Scripture and its visualizations to remind him of Satan and his minions and of their power to enter and occupy the souls of their unwilling victims.

The Evil One and his cohorts are central themes in the *Cantigas,* and though occasionally Satan is mocked and derided as the ridiculous monstrosity he later became in farcical drama, he is also depicted as a terrible and elemental horror, as in *Cantiga 3,* harking back to devils of previous centuries (Plate 10). He or his representatives are pandemic, and the realism and detail with which they are invested in the illuminations are moving even to the modern eye. Demonic hosts are all but fearless and go so far at times as to confront and berate the Blessed Virgin herself, although in every case she soundly defeats their efforts and puts them all to flight. The devil can enter a corpse and invest it with unholy life, causing it to act and appear to be a normal human being. He can send his imps to purloin human souls. In fact, he is all but invincible until he faces Our Lady, who inevitably deprives him of his prey. Thus the miniaturists have given us through the devils of the *Cantigas* a wonderful and macabre glimpse into the mind of medieval man.

Satan and his infernal fellows seem to have held a particular fascination for Alfonso's artist who apparently took delight in exploring the pictorial limits of satanic horror. *Cantiga 74* (Plate 26) provides us with an interesting example: an artist who has dared to portray the devil in less than flattering detail is confronted by a resentful Satan bent on revenge. The unsuspecting painter in these scenes—perhaps the best documentary evidence we have of the actual working environment of a medieval artist—is perched aloft on scaffolding to execute a fresco picture of the Madonna, the Christ Child, and a bestial, lurking demon. Interestingly enough, the words of the *cantigas* never mention the devil and his minions in detail, but the artists made up for this lack of descriptive verse in portrayals that would do justice to Dante's famous illustrator, Gustave Doré. Loathsome indeed are the cloven hooves, feet formed like the talons of birds of prey, scaly horns of goats and sheep, or the leathery, sculpted wings of a bat. The devil can, at will, assume other forms—a fierce lion, a ferocious bull, a wild man straight from the folklore of the age—to torment and harass a drunken monk (Plate 33), or perhaps to animate the corpse of a young gentleman (Plate 29). In the latter the body appears just as the man looked in life, but the artists have marked him for the viewer by painting a malevolent visage of the devil on the back of his head, an interesting and highly effective iconographical device. Devils are often found in their natural environment, for in some *cantigas* the Virgin must descend to the realms of darkness to rescue penitent souls.

Angels, single and amid the heavenly host, grace the miniatures of the *Cantigas,* for they are, after all, Our Lady's stalwarts who must wage continual war against the infernal foe (Plate 11). They appear as handsome, most often blond, young men, dressed in robes predominantly of brilliant white, though other hues are also present. As Our Lady's assistants they are quite naturally garbed in the colorful vestments worn by deacons to assist the celebrant at Mass. Their celestial or terrestrial strategies occur within a rosy cumulus or sparkling sunburst. Our Lady, the inspiration of them all, moves or stands or sits with a divine and sometimes also very human and familiar grace. She can at once appear as Queen of Heaven on her celestial throne, or momentarily catch the hem of her robe and use it as a banner to hold a fierce bull at bay (Plate 33), or she can resurrect a peasant's child (Plate 12). Very much a woman, she can react to broken vows in high dudgeon, entering a nuptial chamber to grasp the wrist of a recalcitrant groom, formerly pledged to her service, and lead him from his sleeping bride (Plate 2). As a warrior she stands forth in battle, the mysterious champion who substitutes for a pious knight who has stayed too long at Mass (Plate 15). Her lovely gowns are usually bedecked with gold, her blue robe draped gracefully over a white undergarment, her pure white wimple lined with scarlet. She is bedecked with rings and often holds the celestial Orb. The Infant Jesus frequently appears seated on her knee and is a handsome child depicted in a variety of poses.

Other supernatural beings are common in the *Cantigas,* including representations of both souls and ghosts. In *Cantiga 26,* a soul, after leaving the body, reappears as an infant, the universal medieval depiction of the soul. In Plate 13 the soul can be seen in a tug-of-war between Jesus and the devil to possess it. In *Cantiga 72* a ghost in a winding sheet, just as it might appear in art today, manifests to a man that his son is dead and in the other world (Plate 14).

From time to time the *Cantigas* contains illuminations which are less cleverly or skillfully executed, revealing inconsistencies in artistic ability. On the whole, however, a remarkable excellence prevails.[23] One is led to wonder whether the king himself may have painted these poorer pictures, with a subsequent and understandable reluctance to discard them on the part of his loyal craftsmen.

Medieval art has often been attacked for its lack of perspective. While we hesitate to state that true perspective exists, we hasten to add that what appears to be perspective, or at the very least a sense of space and depth, can indeed be found. In *Cantiga 34* a truly

noteworthy attempt at perspective is achieved. The viewer, especially as he examines the first panel (Plate 16), sees a city wall running from front to back: churches, houses, and buildings within the walls are painted to give a distinct impression of foreground and background. Or consider Plate 2, panel 2, in which a young man is about to bat a ball. It is true that he stands little more than a yard from the pitcher and that the men in the outfield are clearly crowded too closely together. Yet medieval people saw nothing awkward or lacking in verisimilitude in such an illustration, for they realized that if the artists had attempted to present a ball field to scale and had placed the various players in proper perspective, they could not have given the delightful details of apparel, gesture, and features. If perspective in this panel is missing, it is compensated for by a consciousness of space that is acceptable and even effective. The vigor and very ingenuousness or naiveté, the elegance of the action of this game in progress, with one ball about to leave the pitcher's hand while another, struck earlier, is still in the air, possesses considerable charm, for here too we have an example of "chronological perspective."

Perhaps the truest example of depth perception will be found in panel 6 of *Cantiga 144* (Plate 17), in which the viewer gazes through an arch set high in a wall and sees beyond the arch a trail of fleecy clouds. This is a truly remarkable miniature. The cloud seen through the arch may be a "first" in the opinion of some art historians.

The human body, clothed and nude, plays a prominent part in the illuminations.[24] Most figures appear to be rather short, but exceptions do exist. The artists always seem to have reproduced their subjects in strict adherence to anatomical accuracy. Christ on the Cross, for instance, is frequently portrayed not as the gaunt and haggard figure so often found in High Gothic art, but as the well proportioned and muscular individual we see in *Cantiga 59* who, wrenching one of his hands away from a bar of the cross, smites a runaway nun in the face (Plate 18). It has been pointed out that Adam and Eve in *Cantiga 60* (Plate 19) are not as realistically portrayed as some nudes, but we believe there is a reason. We have not seen in earlier or later Spanish medieval art a picture of Mother Eve endowed with large breasts. In these particular miniatures she is nevertheless depicted as a substantially graceful and well-built woman. Adam, though lacking the refinement we view in other nude representations, is still a robust figure with strongly defined pectorals, biceps, thighs, and calves. There is nothing awkward about his physique. Both figures are completely naked and unashamed as they eat from the Tree of Knowledge; even their genitals are visible in panel 2. In other scenes, a naked penitent reveals his genitalia and pubic hair in *Cantiga 46* (Plate 20). In *Cantiga 22* a very handsome and well-formed young peasant stands before his persecutors in *bragas* and skin-tight undershirt (Plate 21). His neck, arms, and torso are shapely, his bare thighs and calves revealing the play of muscle. In *Cantiga 76* we find gamblers with muscular limbs and well-defined pectoral muscles (Plate 23).

Thus the two manuscripts of the *Cantigas de Santa Maria,* illuminated with full-page illustrations, contain a vast presentation of thirteenth-century art. The richer Escorial T.I.j., numbering nearly two hundred illuminated pages, offers the viewer some 1,274 miniatures, since each page contains six separate panels. The other illuminated manuscript, *Banco Rari* in the Library of Florence (formerly MS II.I.213), contains eighty-odd pages and therefore some 540 miniatures, some of which are unfinished. Together, these two codices offer more than 1,814 separate pictures. It is no wonder, then, that these works contain such a vast array of artistic technique.

*Cantiga* manuscript T.I.j. begins with two introductory pages in which King Alfonso is seen as he reads or dictates a *cantiga* to his assistants. The second page (Plate 1) is the more detailed and merits interpretation. Here a long oblong miniature running the full width of the page and occupying approximately one-fourth of the entire area reveals under five arches what is obviously the practicing or presentation of a *cantiga.* Under the central cusped arch sits the monarch holding open a book which rests on a lectern, while with his right forefinger he points to its content. At the left under two triangular arches can be seen musicians tuning up to play, and a clerical scribe jotting down what the king reads. At the right can be seen, under two matching triangular cusped arches, musicians who sing from a book held by one of their number, while a secular scribe sets down what the king is reading. Beneath the miniature appears at the left a column of calligraphy which lists the various parts of Alfonso's kingdom, at the right are single lines of text interspersed by musical notations. In this remarkable introductory page the king's personal involvement in the *Cantigas* is very evident.

This rich manuscript, actually termed "el manuscrito rico," measures 485 by 334 millimeters (19.09 by 13.14 inches), but the full-page illustrations, including the friezes or frames which encompass the six panels of miniatures, measure 326 by 230 mm (12.83

inches high by 9.05 inches wide). The individual panels measure 109 by 100 mm (4.29 inches high by 3.93 wide). Each page of six miniatures faces a companion page of verse with musical notation, unless the verbalization runs to more than one page. The six-panel arrangement prevails throughout the *Cantigas,* save for the one-miniature presentation of the two introductory pages, and *Cantiga 1,* which contains eight separate panels or divisions.[25]

One is inevitably reminded of our contemporary comic book format, with its appropriate divisions and legends. Appearing above each panel is a single-line caption setting forth the content in the briefest terms possible. The scribes made free use of medieval abbreviation whenever the explanation was too intricate to fit the space allowed for the caption. As a glance at the color plates will clearly reveal, the six panels are themselves enclosed in a common frame, a cruciform design in red and blue running down the center of the page and separating three perpendicular panels on the left from three on the right. The frames and their designs are thought to be copies of ceramic designs or perhaps painted sculpture and ivories of this period, and some closely resemble several carved ivory triptychs found in France.[26]

For illustrative purposes, we have chosen *Cantiga 42* (Plate 2) because of the interest it always seems to arouse in contemporary viewers, and because its art work of excellent quality, with fine colors and well-defined actions, renders it a true representative of the best of the illustrations. It does not, of course, contain all the narrative techniques found in the whole codex, but it does contain sufficient nuances to offer a fairly comprehensive example. If the reader will refer frequently to color Plate 2, a much greater understanding will result. But before studying the illuminations it would be well to read the translation of the canticle itself and to understand the events of the story as they are verbalized.[27]

## CANTIGA 42

*This is how the postulant placed the ring on the finger of the statue of Holy Mary and the statue curved its finger around it.*

The most glorious Virgin, Spiritual Queen, is solicitous of those she loves, for she does not want them to do wrong.

Concerning this, I shall tell you a beautiful miracle, agreeable to hear, which the Virgin Mother of Our Lord performed to save from great error a fickle admirer who often changed his fancies.

It happened in the land of Germany that some people wished to renovate their church. Therefore, they removed the statue of Holy Mary, which was on the altar, and put it at the entrance to the town square under the portico.

In that square there was a lush green park where the local folk went to take their ease and there they played ball, which is the favorite game of all young men.

There chanced to come there once a great troup of young men to play ball, and among them was a youth who was in love. He wore a ring which his beloved, a native of that town, had given him.

This youth, for fear that he would twist the ring when he hit the ball, looked for a place to put it. He saw the beautiful statue and went to place the ring on its finger, saying: "From this day forth

that lady whom I loved means nothing to me, for I swear to God that these eyes of mine have never seen anything so beautiful. Hence from now on I shall be one of your servants and I give you this beautiful ring as pledge."

Kneeling before the statue in reverence and saying "Ave Maria," he promised Her then and there that from that moment on he would never love another woman and would be faithful to Her.

When he had made his promise, the youth arose and the statue closed its finger around the ring. The young man, when he saw this, was taken with such great fright that he began to shout: "Oh, Holy Mary, protect me!"

The people, when they heard this, came running up to where the youth was shouting and he told them what we have just recounted to you. They advised him to enter the order of the monks of Claraval at once.

They all believed that he had done so, but on the advice of the devil he did otherwise, for what he had promised to the Virgin of great worth melted from his thoughts as water melts salt.

He never more gave thought to the Glorious Virgin, but fell in love again with his first lady love. To please his relatives, he married her soon after and left the joys of the other world for earthly pleasures.

After the nuptials were over and day was done, the bridegroom lay down and went quickly to sleep. While sleeping, he saw Holy Mary in his dreams and She called to him angrily: "Oh, my faithless liar!

Why did you forsake me and take a wife? You forgot the ring you gave me. Therefore, you must leave your wife and go with me wherever I so will. Otherwise, from now on, you will suffer mortal anguish."

The bridegroom awoke, but he did not wish to depart. The Glorious Virgin made him go to sleep again and he saw Her lying between his bride and himself to separate them. She called to him angrily: "Wicked, false, unfaithful one,

do you understand? Why did you leave me and have no shame of it? If you wish my love, you will arise from here and come at once with me before daybreak. Get up in a hurry and leave this house! Go!"

Then the bridegroom awakened and was so frightened by this that he got up and went on his way without calling even two or three men to go with him. He wandered through the wilderness for more than a month and took up lodging in a hermitage beside a pine grove.

Thenceforth, as I found written, he served Holy Mary, Mother of the King Most High, who then took him with Her, as I believe and know to be true, from this world to Paradise, the heavenly realm.

The title of the *cantiga* appears as the heading of the poem, not above the page of illuminations, which carries only the roman numeral XLII.

The caption above each panel fairly well describes the illustration itself, and the six captions together succinctly narrate the main events of the miracle. The panels are to be viewed from left to right, beginning at the top. The upper left-hand panel is headed by scarlet rubrics, while the panel at its right is headed with deep but brilliant blue letters. In the second band, the color of the rubrics is reversed, the blue appearing at the left and the red at the right. The same rule of opposites is preserved in the lower band, so that one sees captions in red-blue, blue-red, red-blue.

At each corner of each panel there appears one of the two symbols of Alfonso's kingdom, the three-towered castle of Castile and the rampant lion of León. The rule of opposites again obtains here: the viewer now sees in order castle-lion-castle, lion-castle-lion, castle-lion-castle, and lion-castle-lion. This symmetrical reversal of symbols, like that of the captions, contributes charmingly to an esthetic whole.

Through the action in the six panels one can actively visualize and participate in the entire miracle. Panel 1, according to its caption, tells the viewer that workmen were repairing a church in Germany and had meanwhile set the image of the Madonna and Child in a portal, no doubt to shield it from possible damage. The viewer can clearly see the details of the work in progress, and the value of this miniature to anyone interested in the construction or repair of medieval buildings is obvious. One workman, his head covered by a type of leather cap still worn in Spain by masons today, mixes mortar, while another man, wearing a protective hat of a different shape, fills buckets which are in turn pulled up by a third workman with a type of kerchief wound around his head. A fourth mason, just to the left of the third, lays blocks of stone. This last worker also wears a leather hat to shield his head, but under its brim we can see a tiny patch of white and realize that he is also wearing a kerchief. This item of apparel appears constantly in the illuminations, and its appearance here emphasizes the degree of detail insisted upon by the artists.

Panel 2, captioned "How young men played ball in a meadow," reveals a game of bat-ball in full progress. The players visible are the batter, the pitcher, and four men in the outfield. There were no bases in this game, it is believed, and the object may have been to hit the ball without its being caught. If indeed the players ran to bases before being touched, it is not evident. The young men are painted in detail. All six wear the characteristic kerchief to confine their neck-length hair, and sport open-work shoes through which the colors of their long hose may be seen. All are clothed in belted, knee-length tunics and have long sleeves fastened at the cuff by what appear to be large buttons. They stand in a field of flowers, signifying that they are in the meadow mentioned in the text.

No one viewing this panel could fail to grasp its content. The words closely parallel the action, mentioning the meadow and stating that young men came there to play ball. The modern word *pelota* is used. The balls seem to be fashioned of cloth or perhaps leather, artistically decorated with stitching, and stuffed in all probability with wool or cloth.

Not one of the six players, we believe, is the protagonist, for we do not see him until panel 3. According to the poem and the caption, he does not play the game but, fearful of damaging the ring given him by his sweetheart, puts it on the finger of the Virgin's image. The caption of the third panel reads: "How the image of Holy Mary closed its finger around the ring which the young man gave her in token of love." The action unfolds graphically. The finger of the image holds the ring. The youth's hands indicate clearly the amazement and terror he feels, his face frozen in fear as he cries out in anguish: "Alas, Holy Mary, help me!"

In panel 4 we see the wedding feast, the young man having returned to his earthly sweetheart. Servants bearing covered dishes of food or gifts stand at the right of the table as we face it. The various eating utensils are clearly in evidence except for forks, which would appear much later in Spain. There is a tall wine pitcher on the floor in front of the table and to the left. We can see the feet of the diners, since the white tablecloth does not quite reach the floor. The groom sits at the left and beside him the bride resplendent in a robe of gold, crowned with a diadem of the same metal. The caption reads: "How the young man married the woman and left Holy Mary."

Panel 5, whose rubric reads "How Holy Mary made the young man arise from beside his bride and took him away," reveals the nuptial chamber. We see here a carved and canopied four-poster. In the bed lie the bride and groom, naked but concealed from the waist down by a blanket, while the Virgin hovers near attended by an angel in a white dalmatic and framed by beautiful pinions of cobalt and palest blue. Their heads are outlined by a rosy nimbus. The groom lies flat on his back, his eyes open. The Virgin grasps one of his wrists. The young man's free hand is outstretched in a gesture of resistance, for he does not wish to heed Our Lady's words. The groom, still averse, falls asleep again at Our Lady's command. Then (and this unfortunately is not revealed in the miniature) she lies down between him and his bride so as to separate them, urging him to arise and go with her. Though we cannot see him do so, arise he does and, terrified, goes his way without summoning any of his followers.

In the last panel, number 6, we see him in the hermitage, bearded and hoary with age and care, dressed in a monk's habit and reading. There he serves Holy Mary until she takes him with her at last to the celestial kingdom. Pines in profusion render this sylvan scene in detail, while wild shrubs and flowers impart a definite rural setting.

Colors are both vivid and pastel, and all six panels please the eye. Garments are tasteful in their shading, drape, and flow, while the people who wear them are stationed with considerable attention to balance and composition. Skin tones are natural, and every person depicted in the illumination is blond, no doubt because the miracle is supposed to have taken place in Germany.

Our Lady's robes are luxuriant and lavish, her white wimple lined with scarlet. Both her halo and the Christ Child's in panel 1 are of brilliant hue, hers sky blue, his coral. The young protagonist's tunic in panel 3 is dark blue and lined with red. In panel 5 even the deep blue counterpane has a figured border and a red lining, as can be seen wherever its folds reveal it. The gray or white beard of the groom in the last panel is quite effective, for it indicates his long years of service, penitence, and devotion to the Virgin.

This illuminated page contains many representative elements of Alfonsine miniatures, and through its subject matter, its milieu, its characters, and its constant repetition of the castle and lion emblems, the viewer readily senses a certain degree of secularity. Secular, too, may be still another element and one which the king was perhaps aware of, as were possibly others who took part in the creation of this *cantiga*. The plot of the story is flagrantly pagan. As far back as the twelfth century in France, a tale in Latin existed about a ball player who placed his ring on the finger of the goddess Venus, and when he had plighted his troth to her, she came to carry him off. We venture to suspect that this story of Venus was adapted to the Virgin either in France or elsewhere and welcomed in the Iberian Peninsula as a miracle. Would the pious Alfonso have deliberately adapted a pagan tale, altering it to fit the scheme of Marian legends?[28] If so, it is a remarkable example of the process of alteration and adaptation St. Augustine recommended to his disciples when he urged them to turn the best of pagan lore into Christian belief.

There can be no doubt that King Alfonso's illuminators were eminently successful in their appointed task of visualizing the stories which their learned patron had collected. But in viewing the illuminations we may well ask how successful the artists were at incorporating into the miniatures those nine classical elements most often found in brief narratives, and even in longer novelesque sequences: plot, conflict, setting, characterization, theme, style, effect, point of view, and mood or tone. Medieval raconteurs, of course, never achieved the narrative skills of a Poe, a Bécquer, a Maupassant, or a Heine, but even so, to a varying degree they managed to assimilate and incorporate all or most of these nine components of the classic framework.

We cannot point to a manual of style which a medieval Spanish writer like Don Juan Manuel might have used in structuring his tales, nor can we prove that raconteurs, whether popular or erudite, actually took into account the elements of the classic design as essential factors in their narration. But we believe there were manuals, or at least models to be followed, in the form of stories told in the past and written down for medieval people to read. Gonzalo de Berceo and Alfonso X, who were contemporaries, had at hand some of the miracles they retold in their Marian works in the form of Latin miracles, usually written in prose. And the Latin authors had had earlier models. As far back as Aesop and Homer, the nine elements seem to have affected the writing of fiction. Probably no medieval author deliberately concentrated upon these elements to the extent that a twentieth-century writer may. Setting in medieval Spanish written tales and novelesque pieces is often barely taken into account, although in the hands of a writer like Berceo setting is manifest, either obviously and straightforwardly or in subtle ways. In the visualization of all stories, setting assumes a powerful role and may even become the prime element.

The use of the classic narrative design seems to be logical and correct, since as far back as the earliest recorded stories, and indeed today in the most primitive of folktales, authors have used all or most of the nine elements. Some use them consciously, as a modern writer would as he plans and writes his story, while others insert some or all of the elements unconsciously, for without them storytelling becomes all but impossible. The Spanish Middle Ages was a period of great activity in the production of stories both short

and novelesque, and of the translation of all manner of tales from the Arabic and Latin. Both of these foreign cultures depended upon the most ancient traditions of narrative art, and authors like Alfonso X and his son Sancho IV had the materials and the models needed for what they produced in the area of fiction. If these men and others who wrote fiction in the fourteenth and fifteenth centuries did not follow manuals of style which listed the nine elements of the classic design, they nevertheless followed an age-old literary tradition which had stood the test of time and served them well as they composed.

Were the artists of the brush who painted narrative miniatures for the *Cantigas de Santa Maria* able, even roughly, to parallel or approximate what their literary colleagues had already accomplished in the area of narrative skills? Our research leads us to believe they were. One clear example of this transference may be found in *Cantiga 42,* which exhibits a great deal of the classic design. Let us consider the following step-by-step analysis.

Plot surely is carefully handled in the illuminations, for the story hangs together, has a good beginning and ending, and narrates with clarity the incidents contributing to the story's development. Even without the captions which serve as a link between the verbal and the visual, the viewer can easily comprehend most of what is taking place.

The artists have likewise instilled a consciousness of conflict with considerable skill, just as the poets did from the very first line. In the first panel conflict quickly materializes, maintaining a sense of urgency which never fades. The verbal plot had well withstood the test of time and had been polished and refurbished across the ages. Its version here is a tightly-knit and even somewhat laconic report whose animated visualization generates a great deal of emotional clash as the eye passes from panel to panel.

Setting is most obviously well-defined, for setting in any picture contributes substantially to visual art. Where there are few or no words to describe the setting, an artist must perforce fashion a visually convincing background. The settings of all six panels in *Cantiga 42* are vividly clear and comprehensible and succeed remarkably well in conveying not only action but the serial movement of action through space and time.

One element of setting quite characteristic of these illuminations is the golden arch or set of arches utilized as a primary contrivance in most *cantiga* miniatures.[29] The narrative device of the arch is found in most European clerical art and to some extent also in secular scenes. Here each arch or series of arches serves to produce the effect of a spotlight which pinpoints a stationary moment of action. Since each panel is contained within a colorfully designed frame, each arch within such a frame thereby provides a species of frame-within-a-frame and often delineates a separate action. Arches do more than this, however, for they in a sense become parts of the action itself by contributing to the flow of events while offering a means of spatial transition from one separate point in time to another. Seeing a picture within a picture refines, contracts, and intensifies both the overall action in the frame and the encapsulated action within the arch. The "dramatic arch," common in many ecclesiastical miniatures, was adapted to the illuminations of the *Cantigas de Santa Maria* and made to impart, at the same time, a certain religious significance. Possibly the *cantigas* artists believed that this subtle implication of sacred association could excuse, or at least modify, the quality of patently scurrilous, scabrous, or even vulgar stories. The golden arches, then, could reduce the impact of stories of rapine, incest, fornication, drunkenness, and other unsavory deeds while providing a proper ambience for the Virgin's presence and a frame for her involvement in the action.

The dramatic quality imparted through the use of the arch has been much discussed. Quite simply, a scene within an arch takes on the characteristics of a *tableau vivant,* concentrating the viewer's attention so as to lead him to feel that he is actually observing a dramatic event or even taking part in it. In this same dramatic context, it may be recalled that arches were used to frame theatrical tableaux or scenes in medieval staging. Therefore the device of the arches may possibly be regarded as an adaptation of stagecraft to the art of miniatures. If viewers of these miniatures were actually conscious of such an adaptation (and we believe they were) they probably saw and savored various typological elements we moderns have not heretofore looked for. If we assume that miniatures are essentially static representations of equally inert prose narratives whose dynamism in both instances depends upon the intrinsic properties of these art forms to stimulate the viewer's or reader's imaginations, we may more readily comprehend how and to what degree the creators of the *Cantigas* were eager to enhance the vitality and animation of these illuminations through the conscious application of dramatic strategems or theatrical techniques. In this way, several subliminal stimulants would act simultaneously upon the imagination of the viewer, serving to break up and eliminate the inherent stasis of the minature.

The arches in panels 4 and 5 of *Cantiga 42,* though perhaps not so dramatic as some arches to be seen subsequently, are nonetheless representative. Panel 4 depicts the wedding feast, which unfolds beneath three golden cusped arches. The largest arch, to the left, encloses the most important characters in the scene, the bride and groom, though two other guests are also present. The center arch, much smaller, reveals two additional guests. The third small arch reveals servants bearing gifts or covered dishes of food. To the medieval viewer this sectioned panel may have indicated three separate and serial moments in space and time, and if so would considerably broaden the canvas of events. Surely the eye focuses on the first arch, studies what it contains, and then moves to the other arches. This mere focusing in and of itself provides sufficient pause to allow three separate actions to be seen and comprehended. In panel 5, we see two arches. The smaller one at the left reveals the foot of the nuptial couch and the figure of the angel who accompanies the Virgin; but the large arch encapsulates the two protagonists, the Virgin and the groom, and the sleeping bride.

Elsewhere we have attempted to develop the connections between medieval drama and the *Cantigas de Santa Maria* and have pointed out that often the images of the Virgin and the Child, seated on their altar, assumed different attitudes in different panels, leading to the belief that living models were used by the illuminators and that these models, posing on different days, did not take the exact positions they had taken previously, or perhaps moved to new positions during a single sitting. We now go further, just as Mâle did in his work, and postulate that there may have been a true connection between the Renaissance of the pictorial and the plastic arts and the beginning of medieval theatre, since the two were indeed contemporary. Certainly the arch in the *Cantigas* possesses a dramatic function. Mâle, under fire from his critics, went so far as to water down his beliefs in the connections he had previously drawn between the two media. But he never rejected his views entirely and held that in a limited number of cases twelfth-century French iconography had been enriched by liturgical drama and that the dramatic enactments of the Gospel story served to free artistic imagination from the strictures of iconographic conventions, thus bringing artists face to face with life. He saw, and we see too, that the intrinsically static arched tableau could turn the entire picture toward the beholder, who might well have felt, as we have emphasized, that he was now being directly addressed by the artists.

Mâle saw something of this in Spain, as well as in his native France, for he believed that one of the sculptured reliefs in the cloisters of Silos was possibly among the earliest representatives of dramatic influence, an idea he derived from his observations of the similarity of costume in these reliefs, which he thought had been borrowed from the *peregrinus* play.[30] Mâle was very much aware that arches had been used much earlier to frame episodes and characters in the visualization of biblical and secular illustrations before there was any evidence of liturgical or secular drama, but we believe that this has nothing to do with the interaction between the plays of the thirteenth century and the miniatures of that same century, since both secular and ecclesiastical dramas were current in Alfonsine Spain.

Setting, then, is vital in the illuminations of the *Cantigas de Santa Maria,* and by setting we mean not only the forthright presentation of background but also the "dramatic setting" provided by the arches which enabled secular artists, who deliberately eschewed the tenets of timelessness found in ecclesiastical art, to stress a very temporal and varied chronological depiction of events.

Characterization in the Alfonsine miniatures deserves comment. Here let us return again to *Cantiga 42.* Did miniaturists actually portray facets of character? We believe they did, for the painters were able to fashion various emotions and character traits almost as successfully with the brush as did the poets in verse. The two protagonists, the ball-player and the Virgin Mary, live and move, gesticulate and assume postures which reveal much about them. In the poem the Virgin appears as a jealous woman and is human enough to feel and be swayed by hurt, anger, and the desire for vengeance. She reacts as would an angry sweetheart and speaks irately to her fickle devotee about the bride she considers to be her rival. She even goes to the recalcitrant lover, carrying him off by force and punishing him, obliging him to fulfill his vow to her.

Medieval man understood these womanly qualities and saw Our Lady as quite definitely human. We see her character in the *Cantigas* as clearcut, strong, simple, and uncomplicated, but above all very human and realistic. Medieval people liked to regard her as such and felt a vigorous empathy for her.

The young man's character too is finely drawn in a matter-of-fact fashion. He is deeply religious, or would seem to be from his attraction to Our Lady's beauty. Inspired, then, by piety and by the extreme fairness of the statue and by all that her pulchritude represented spiritually, he plights his troth to her. In the miniature, of course, we do not see him in the act of placing the ring, but certainly we view his consternation at the sight of the stone finger curling around it.

The poem continues to develop his character when it reveals that he forsakes his vow and marries his sweetheart, forgetful of the promise to love no other lady than the Virgin. The illumination, without the written word, save for the ever-helpful caption above the scene, nevertheless captures the exact moment when the bride and groom are seated at table with their guests, and surely no words could convey more accurately the mood and convivial ambience of this wedding party. It is a festive scene and in it one sees the groom gazing affectionately at his earthly bride, making it perfectly clear that his love for Our Lady was merely a passing fancy.

If we have neglected the importance of the captions, let us stress again that they sometimes coincide with the action painted, though more often they tend to portray the scene inchoately. For example, in the bedroom scene the caption reveals that Our Lady obliges the young man to arise from his bed, an act not yet begun in the picture. But the artists have managed to achieve a good visualization of the exact moment when he is being made to do so. Carrying their portrayal of his character beyond the fickle desertion of the Virgin, they place him naked in bed with his similarly naked bride, and what is more important in character development, they show his unwillingness to arise and follow her. He draws away as she takes his wrist and physically repudiates his vow, saying "no" in this visualized resistance. The carnality of earthly marriage is suggested in the couple's nudity, while the purity of heavenly marriage is connoted by Our Lady's presence. To characterize his ultimate repentence and rejection of worldly existence, the artists have depicted him in the final panel dressed in monastic robes sitting alone outside his hermitage. The lover has erred, repented, resolved his problem, and paid the price for his lack of devotion and inconstancy by abandoning his former life.

We believe that in nearly every *cantiga* the illuminations develop character to the extent that it can very often be deciphered without the aid of the captions. Sometimes this development lies in facial expression, as in the malignant, baleful face of the devil on the back of the dead man's head in panel 3 of *Cantiga 67* (Plate 29), or the wrath and despair of the Jewish father whose child is born with its head facing backward because the father has doubted the reality of the Immaculate Conception (Plate 39).

Theme is not neglected by the miniaturists, since each visualized narrative has a specific theme which coordinates with the dual nature of Mary: the ever-present, overall themes of the Virgin's grace and power and the love of all mankind for her, operating in consonance with the human and earthly theme in each *cantiga,* which underlies the unfolding of the plot. Both are obvious in *Cantiga 42,* where the human theme is directed toward the personal problem of the ball player, the course of whose life is threatened and eventually altered. Indeed, there may be a third allegorical theme with the peripheral implication that the young man's problem is also humanity's problem—the eternal conflict between this world and the next.

Style, whether in literature, in music, or in art, is not always easy to identify. One feels or senses style and finds it elusive when one attempts to pin it down or analyze it. Literary style is the manner of expression characteristic of a particular writer or school or writers or of a period, and even of an orator. Style in art, according to the tenets of art historians, is the manner of expression characteristic of a particular artist or artists or of a period. Style in literature may also be considered as composed of those features of composition which belong to form and expression rather than to the substance of the thought or matter expressed. We believe that style in art has similar composition.

In the *Cantigas de Santa Maria,* literary style is always evident in the poems, and it carries over into the pictorial area. Some *cantigas* are couched in long lines of verse, some in lines of no more than a few syllables. It may be that length itself, or brevity, should be regarded as a stylistic element. Terseness in some of the stories helps to intensify their message and bring out their power, while more lengthy and detailed stories naturally allow for other stylistic developments. We are conscious, too, that the melody to which each *cantiga* was set controlled the length of the lines and may quite possibly have obliged the artists to paint in a special way. If the events of a miracle are many, the artists were expected to concentrate them in order to encompass the compulsory elements of plot and scene. A very short miracle with few details of plot demanded imagination on the part of the illuminators, as well as restraint, if they were to produce a comprehensible illustration. Thus the illuminators' style was no more than visual presentation, and so art historians regard it. Usually artistic style must be more direct than its verbal counterpart. *Cantiga 42,* a story of medium length in verse, lent itself well to direct and simple handling by the miniaturists. Imagery, movement, and background had to be stylized skillfully with something like biblical simplicity so clear that no one could misinterpret what was seen. Without dialogue, which of course the verbalized account possessed, the miniaturists were driven perforce to body language, attitudes of stance, facial expression, and gesture, the last having quite precise and usually well

understood meaning—indeed, to any and all of the means employed by living people to express feelings or carry out actions, exclusive of speech. Movement, rapid or leisurely, had to be indicated and could be neatly portrayed by able artists. The merest angle of forward inclination with regard to the posture of the painted figure could tell much, and this is an element of pictorial style. In *Cantiga 42* the young man's hands, as he observes the stone finger close around the ring, speak with a silent eloquence and are the epitome of visualized style.

That effect is a constant desideratum, and a very real accomplishment can hardly be denied. Each viewer may perceive a different effect, since effect stimulates people in different ways. But the artists were cognizant of major, unmistakable effects such as awe, fear, devotion, zeal, nostalgia, and other easily depicted emotions. For example, in *Cantiga 42* we may see the effect wrought by the purposefulness of the Virgin, aimed at winning back the young lover, whose countenance is cast in resignation before a higher power.

Mood, or tone, is usually evoked from the first lines of each *cantiga,* for the initial lines and accompanying melody establish it. In *Cantiga 42* the mood is set by a refrain repeated before each stanza:

The most glorious Virgin, Spiritual Queen, is solicitous of those she loves, for she does not want them to do wrong.

From the outset, once the young man has made his vow to her, she never falters in her efforts to bring him to his senses and force him to keep his promise to her. The reader cannot forget this invocation of mood as he studies the text, nor can the viewer as he witnesses the evidence of the Virgin's love.

We believe the musicians were commissioned to discover melodies or to compose them so that the music might complement the subject matter of the various *cantigas,* linking sad melodies with sad *cantigas* or pairing lively *cantigas* with melodies that moved rapidly and could not be mistaken for melancholy pieces. Musicologists assert that both folk songs and those written either by seasoned minstrels or courtly troubadours provided the musical background for the *cantigas.* If a poem had to adapt itself to a particular preexisting melody, it follows that the visualization, which naturally sprang from the verbalization, must also feel the melody's influence, though indirectly. The melody of *Cantiga 42* is a case in point. It is quite suited to its subject matter, for it moves with the catchy lilt of what is probably a popular song and possesses the definite undertones of a triumphant paeon.

The point of view of each *cantiga* is omniscient, although frequently it is Alfonso himself who is cast in the role of narrator. In *Cantiga 42* he simply states that he will recount a beautiful miracle. Occasionally, however, a character in a *cantiga* speaks in such a way as to assume the omniscient narrator's role. To catch this in a visualization, the artists used various gestures, facial expressions, and body language. *Cantiga 209* is so much Alfonso's that he actually writes of his own experiences in the first person and is subsequently revealed by the artists as he undergoes the traumas he describes.

The classic design of the visualization of the *Cantigas de Santa Maria* parallels that of the verbalization to such an extent that the two media attain a nearly equal degree of success in their total impact.

One of the most curious and yet practical narrative techniques found in the *Cantigas* is the use of multiple action within a single panel. Obviously this serves to increase the number of visualized incidents in a miracle and to enlarge thereby the sphere of dramatic action. Apparently the *Cantigas* artists found that in some cases six panels were simply insufficient to convey the miracle adequately, and therefore availed themselves of an age-old device for expanding the narrative in their pictures. They had many models from earlier art. The sheer pressure of economy dictated the use of as little paper or parchment or other materials as possible, so Alfonso's artists crowded their work with figures, much as writers and scribes developed the science of abbreviation in order to extend the utility of a precious commodity. Sometimes both artist and amanuensis condensed so diligently that the result must have been incomprehensible to all except those professionals trained in a kind of verbal and visual shorthand.

Multiple or continuous action in a single illumination, whether planned and used as a narrative device, or the result of conflation, a concept generally accepted by art experts, was certainly not original to Spanish art, since it may be observed in the narrative art of many nations in the thirteenth century and even earlier. The twelfth-century life of St. Cuthbert, for example, utilizes this technique to a greater extent than the *Cantigas de Santa Maria,* for in the saint's life one customarily finds two modes of action in each of the two panels on every page.[31] Each episode in the English manuscript thus represents but one of the pair in each panel and serves to explain the other, forming an interlocking tie to express two moments in time.

Here, as in the *Cantigas,* where multiple or continuous action is often present, the knowledgeable viewer could certainly interpolate his own ancillary image between the two episodes, thus instilling an even broader concept of time and space into the entire framework. As we shall discuss later, numerous gestures within the two incapsulated moments further contributed to the scene by serving as a type of cross-reference to facilitate the comprehension of the visualized story.

The original source for this technique has not yet been discovered, though it is known that Italian artists were adept in its use, as several manuscripts at Monte Cassino (the lives of St. Benedict and St. Maur, for example) bear eloquent testimony. Indeed, in the life of St. Maur there appears an interesting device, also found in the *Cantigas,* by means of which the saint was able to cross over from one panel into the next.[32] In passing, it is worthwhile to note that the St. Maur text is arranged in pages of four and six panels, like the *Cantigas.* The same phenomenon can also be observed well before the Middle Ages in Byzantine and classic times, and it continued well beyond and into later centuries.[33] Spain felt these influences, particularly the Byzantine, and expressed them in the frescoes and miniatures of Catalonia, but Spaniards were also acquainted with the art of Italy, so that the actual degree of extrapeninsular influence is undefined. Artists often had to travel either to sell their services or to answer the invitations of foreign patrons such as Alfonso, whose cultural revolution and largesse in the employment of foreign legists, scientists, historians, and artists must have attracted many to his court.

The entire problem of foreign influence upon the *Cantigas* is still virtually unexplored. So far as we are aware, no one except Gonzalo Menéndez Pidal (see note 7) has yet suggested Islamic provenance in the miniatures, as has been the case in other areas, e.g., in the music of the *Cantigas,* in versification, in concepts of courtly love, and in the inclusion of Moorish architecture and other aspects of life in scenic backgrounds. Nevertheless, certain Islamic books did contain miniatures, in spite of the Prophet's prohibition against the depiction of living creatures, and occasionally other media transgressed Islamic law. Consider, for example, the animal figures in the Court of the Lions in the Alhambra. Is it not quite possible, even probable, that some of those fabulous books of Persian miniatures existed in enlightened Moorish Spain? Illuminated manuscripts of *Kalila wa-Dimna* existed in the East, and the presence of this ancient oriental work is attested in Spain even before a Castilian translation was made in the thirteenth century. Be that as it may, within the corpus of the over two hundred full-page illuminations of the *Cantigas* one comes upon miniatures from time to time which are suspiciously like several found in both earlier and contemporary Persian art. Definite eastern influence seems to us to be at work in all six panels of *Cantiga 181* (Plate 24). And even if Spanish artists had not seen Persian illuminations in Spain itself (though they may have) it is plausible that they were exposed to them in North Africa or in the Middle East. If a king of Ethiopia was on sufficiently good terms with Alfonso to send him a consignment of exotic animals to honor his father's memory, it seems reasonable to assume that other cultural interchanges may have taken place.[34] Islamic artistic influence is still another chapter to be researched.

A most worthy and striking prototype of double or continuous action in the miniatures of the *Cantigas* may be found in Spain in the famous Biblia Romanica of 1162, housed today in León's Colegiata de San Isidro. So outstanding is this early paradigm of a technique much used in the *Cantigas* that we offer it as Plate 22. In this single illuminated page we are witness, in the upper panel, to the battle between David and Goliath, while in the lower panel the battle's finale depicts the Hebrew forces riding full tilt after the Philistines. Multiple or continuous action is achieved in the upper sequence, where at the right we see the young David whirling his sling, while at the left he decapitates the giant. The action, moving from right to left, is unusual in that it departs from traditional manuscript progression as found in the *Cantigas,* for example, whose action always moves from left to right, as it would in modern illustrations. We can only speculate as to why, in the first scene, as the stone strikes the giant in the temple, Goliath wears a pinkish coat of mail and blue hose and carries a brilliant blue shield, while as he topples to earth and David decapitates him he is dressed in brown mail and pinkish hose and carries a scarlet shield. Byzantine prototypes in which such color changes appeared may explain the Spanish miniature of David and Goliath, although the alteration in colors may have been effected for artistic reasons cherished by the miniaturist. The possibility of color symbolism, however, should not be overlooked.

The miniature beneath the illustration of David and Goliath is separated from it by a portion of the biblical text and portrays the Hebrew army in hot pursuit of the Philistines, galloping furiously over the giant's head, spearing enemy soldiers, and toppling them from their mounts. David and Goliath in both

incidents are clearly though unnecessarily labeled in minium. The fall of Goliath is realistically developed: as David sinks his sword into the foe's neck, the giant's arms fly outward, his legs leaving the ground in a head-over-heels tumble, while gore from his severed head and battered temple matches the scarlet hue of David's hose and shoes.

Multiple action, then, did not originate with the *Cantigas*. It is a device used time and again across the centuries, from at least as early as the twelfth century Biblia Romanica to the great bronze door of the Baptistry in Florence, as well as in later medieval and Renaissance works of art.

Multiple action similar to that in the Biblia Romanica appears in many *cantigas*. In *Cantiga 9*, panel 4 (Plate 25), a cleric returning from a pilgrimage to the Holy Sepulchre rides his horse through the wilderness. The caption reads, "How the monk was liberated from the lion and the robbers by the image of Holy Mary." Without a previous understanding of the device of multiple or continuous action one might certainly believe that two monks were confronting two separate dangers. Actually we are viewing the same monk twice, first as he faces the lion, and later as he encounters the band of robbers. Only a hint of separation of the events is suggested in the form of a cliff's edge, darkened by a shadow to divide the two incidents. In the first the lion stretches out a menacing paw and the horse shies away, while the pious monk, undaunted yet posturing in prayer, passes unharmed. The robbers, armed with spears, knives, and long poles with hooks affixed for pulling down riders, gaze up in awe into the sky, where we see the Virgin outlined with a nimbus, the monk again assuming an attitude of pious supplication, offering no resistance.

In *Cantiga 65* (there are two so numbered, since those *cantigas* whose final number is 5 are illuminated by two full six-panel pages), we find what is perhaps the most startling example of multiple action: the caption of panel 2 (Plate 27) reads, "How the madman fell down before the altar and soon was raised up by the letter." Here we see the demented victim in both positions in a single panel—lying on the floor before the altar, his head resting on one of its steps, and again standing above his own prostrate form. There is nothing to indicate that the two visualizations of the madman are not those of two different people.

*Cantiga 74,* seen in toto in Plate 26, portrays two incidents, both adequately and logically separated. In panel 1 a column obviously divides the two events. In the first an artist seated on a scaffold within a church executes a fresco of the Madonna and Child; on the opposite side of the column he is seen again as he paints a hideous likeness of the devil. [35] In panel 2, with two arches, again divided by a column, the artist vigorously argues with the devil, and we can see in the frescoes that the beauty of the Virgin and the hideousness of the devil have been painted on the same wall, thus throwing a new light on the double action shown in panel 1.

Panel 4 of *Cantiga 64* (Plate 28) offers still another fine example of two clearly separate actions combined in one scene. This time the scene on the left takes place on the street in front of a house, while that on the right is inside another house. The division is clear and acceptable. At the left a young would-be seducer of a nobleman's wife conspires in the street with his go-between, while on the right, in the woman's home, the faithful intermediary persuades her to accept his proposition.

In Plate 15 we reproduce the full page of illuminations of *Cantiga 63,* where in panel 1 we see a knight mounted on his horse and dressed in a distinctive "zebra-like" armor to distinguish him from the other knights present.[36] He appears again in the same panel separated from the first scene by a column and framed in an arch as he petitions his general for permission to hear Mass before riding into battle. As we follow the flow of action from left to right, we find that this page of illumination offers one of the finest examples of the several techniques for presenting continuous action. (In addition, no scene in medieval miniatures offers a richer opportunity for the study of armor, shields, helmets, banners, lances and other accoutrements of war.) Panel 3 shows the Spanish army moving against the enemy. Of particular note are the hindquarters of the same horse, covered with the zebra-like design of its panoply, extending into panel 4, where appear the horse's forequarters and the rider bedecked in similar blazonry. This horse, charging, as it were, from panel 3 into panel 4, even crossing the perpendicular frame-design between the panels, is a vivid and striking representation of the unobstructed stream of visualization achieved by Alfonso's artists.

The action in panel 4 is simply extraordinary in the wealth of detail displayed in a few square inches of miniature. Here we may observe the serried ranks of Count García in full charge against the assembled host of the great Moorish caliph, Almanzor, among whose columns ride not only turbaned Moors and blacks, but also renegade Christian knights. One of the rebel Christian foes has been pierced by a faithful crusader's lance and is caught by the painter as he topples from his steed, clutching the spear with mailed and bloody hands. Gore flows from the wound as he makes heroic efforts to hold his seat. His horse strains every muscle to keep from falling, one foreleg thrust straight forward to gain traction, the other bent at the knee and pressing against the ground. Also in panel 4 we find an exceptional degree of facial expression, yet another facet of narrative technique, among the combatants: the grimly determined look on the visages of the Christian knights as they charge from the left and the stark consternation of the two turbaned Moors, or the fierce, unchecked anger of the black.

Panels 5 and 6 offer the dénouement of the miracle and do not contain elements of either double action or transition. At this point, it will be helpful to include the story of this very popular and strangely moving miracle, so that we can more profitably discuss other elements of narrative technique as well as the artists' visual adherence to the classic design of narration. It is a compelling tale and one well calculated to attract the interest of a populace reared on deeds of derring-do and chivalry. Its title contains a synopsis of the action, but only outlines it, for the poem and the illuminations are filled with remarkable detail.

## CANTIGA 63

*How Holy Mary saved from disgrace a knight who was to be in battle in San Esteban de Gormaz {in Soria}, but could not appear there because he heard three Masses. The story begins thus:*

He who serves well the Mother of Him who died for us never falls into disgrace.

Concerning this, I wish to tell you of a great miracle which Holy Mary performed, as God is my aid, for a knight whom She spared from a grievous disgrace which he thought had befallen him.

This knight, as I learned, was generous and valiant and was unequalled in arms in the place where he lived and all the country round.

He lived virtuously and would never give any quarter to the Moors. Hence when Almanzor was trying to take San Esteban de Gormaz,

he went there with Count don García, who held the place at that time, and who was a good man and of such great courage that he was greatly feared by the Moors.

This Count was Lord of Castile and waged fierce war with King Almanzor, who surrounded San Esteban on all sides, planning to capture it.

However, the Count defended his position well, for he was good and wise.

He did not give the Moors an inch, but began to attack them vigorously.

The knight of whom I told you performed so many feats of arms, as I learned, that there was no battle nor tournament where he did not prove his prowess.

One day he intended to go forth with the Count to attack the Moorish army, however, first he went to hear Mass, as he did every day.

When he had entered the church, he repented of his sins

and heard the Mass of Holy Mary, omitting nothing, and then two more that were said,

which were of the Spiritual Queen. However, a squire of his reproached him saying: "He who does not go forth in a contest like this should never show his face again."

The knight paid no heed to the urgings of his squire, but prayed to Holy Mary: "I am your servant, spare me this shame, for it is in your power to do so."

When the Masses were heard, he rode away and encountered the Count on the way, who threw his right arm around his neck saying, "It was a fortunate hour

when I met you, for if it were not for you, I swear to God that I and my troops would have been defeated, but you killed so many of King Almanzor's Moors that he surrendered.

You did so much to earn merit that no knight has ever done so much nor suffered at arms as you suffered just now to defeat the Moors.

But I beseech you, for it is urgent, to care for your wounds, my Lord. I have a physician, one of those from Montpellier, who can soon cure you of them."

The Count told him this and more than three others said the same thing to him. He was so embarrassed by them that he thought he would die of mortification.

However, when he saw his weapons and realized that they were battered, he knew that it had been a miracle, for he well knew that it could have happened in no other way.

When he understood this, he was sure that Holy Mary had saved him from falling into disgrace. He offered her money [maravedís] and other gifts.

The plot, obviously compact and decisively laid out, is presented visually in such a way that the viewer fully understands what is occurring. Scene, perhaps more than any other aspect of the miniatures—and much more than in the verbalization—takes the viewer from the street in front of the church in panel 1 into the shrine itself in panel 2, where we see the knight kneeling before Our Lady's altar while hearing Mass. Then in panels 3 and 4 we are thrust into the heat of battle, and finally, in panel 5, move to a post-conflict scene, and back again into the church in panel 6 to view the knight praying devoutly at the brilliantly tiled altar of the Blessed Virgin.

Arches play their part in this page of illumination. A large and much scalloped vaulting of bright gold nearly fills panel 1 and focuses our attention on the virtuous knight as he bends his knee in homage to Count García. The scene to the left, which portrays the knight before the audience with his liege lord, is archless, since the artists have used it for the sole purpose of illustrating the minor action of the knight's arrival at the church. The character of the knight is patently pious and Count García in full recognition of his virtue holds his mailed arm in a respectful pose.

In panel 2 the illuminators have altered the scene outside the church to reveal at the left of the building a tall and very leafy tree, together with the knight's squire, who holds his horse. The knight, kneeling to receive the blessed sacrament, which the priest prepares before the Virgin's altar, is enclosed most effectively within a gold arch. Here again a panel contains two incidents or two parts of the same one. The knight looks over his shoulder at the squire, who stands almost over him to berate him, saying, "he who does not go forth to a contest like this should never show his face again." The squire's face is grave, as he points with his right hand to the knight's helmet on the ground just beneath the black and white shield hanging from a convenient tree. Medieval man would have seen in the squire's attitude just what a devoted attendant might have said to his master whose reputation he feared would suffer irreparable damage. The lines of the poem here parallel quite closely the mood and ambience of the visualization.

The caption of Panel 5 reads, "How the count came from battle and found the knight who was just going out to battle." We see the count, together with his victorious knights, arriving from the left and the knight approaching from the right in what is clearly a head-on confrontation. The poem reveals how delighted the count is to greet the knight, because he exclaims, "You did so much to earn merit that no knight has ever done so much nor suffered at arms as you suffered just now to defeat the Moors." He even places an affectionate arm around the knight's shoulder.

Panel 6 once again uses arches, two narrow and one much wider. Though only one event is taking place beneath these arches, the viewer is struck, as usual, by images of three separate stages or at least of three separate portions of the same event. The eye is drawn to the arch at the far left, where most of the noble combatants kneel, facing the altar beneath the large right-hand arch. In the central arch other knights, including the protagonist of the miracle, kneel, while the head and mailed forearms of the hero project into the right-hand arch, in which the dénouement is effectuated at an altar surmounted by the image of the Madonna and Child. Like the final lines of the poem, panel 6 stresses the knight's devotion. His head is bowed and his hands are folded in prayer. The poem reveals that "he was sure that Holy Mary had saved him from falling into disgrace. He offered her money and other gifts." Perhaps of all the events in miracle lore or supernatural incidents which deal with the mysterious substitution of a celestial protector for a mortal being, none surpasses *Cantiga 63* in either artistic merit or literary presentation.

*Cantiga* 67 reveals one of the most remarkable of all the illuminated pages to be found in the Escorial codex. Scarcely any other rivals it in brilliance of color, intensity and multiplicity of action, psychological impact, sociological background, compelling plot, or suggestion of pure terror at the confrontation of man with the supernatural in the form of the Ancient Enemy. We reproduce it in Plate 29.

The story as related in the verbalization falls far short of what one encounters in the visualizations, for the artists have clearly allowed their imaginations to run riot in what may perhaps be the most outstanding example of this iconographic narrative phenomenon; and this is so even though the narrative account runs on longer than most other poems in the codex.

## CANTIGA 67

*How Holy Mary caused the good man to realize that he had the devil as his servant and how the devil would have killed him had it not been for the prayer he said.*

The Glorious Queen is of such great saintliness that with this power She defends us from the devil and his malice.

On such a theme as this, I wish to recount a beautiful, magnificent and wondrous miracle which Holy Mary performed. There has been none so marvelous since the times of Nero, who was emperor of the great city of Rome.

It happened that there was a powerful and handsome man who was wise and generous, and so good a Christian that he gave all he acquired to God, for above all things he loved charity.

And to better carry out this charity which he so fervently sought, he built a hospital outside the city where he lived in which the whole year round he offered bread, wine, meat, and fish, and beds in which to lie, to all who came.

And as one who is very eager to accomplish his goals, he sought capable young men of good comportment to serve the poor. But the devil, out of envy, entered the dead body of a very handsome man

and came to him with gentle manners and benign countenance and said: "My lord, take me for your servant, and I shall gladly do service for the poor, for I see that you are doing worthy things.

And I shall even donate my services to you." When the man heard this, he was very pleased, and furthermore, he saw him to be handsome, well-bred, and eloquent, and he judged him to be active in good faith.

In this way, the devil, malicious and crafty, did so much that the good man took him as his squire, and in all his needs he found him first to volunteer, saying to his master: "What do you wish, sir? Give me your commands."

So well did the devil know how to please his master that the latter believed everything he said, and furthermore, there was no one else who knew how to serve him so well in all matters according to his wishes.

Therefore, he persuaded his master to hunt often in the rugged mountains, and to fish in the sea, and he tried many artful ways to kill him so that he might have the soul and another the property.

In all this, the good man did not notice anything suspicious and so he went trustingly where the devil advised. However, every morning when he arose, he said a prayer of the Glorious Virgin, Queen of Mercy.

For this reason, that devil whom he had as a vassal had no power to kill him. Nonetheless, he did not desist from tempting him day and night, although it availed him nothing, just to show his cruelty.

In this way, the good man, who was filled with saintliness, lived a very long time, until a bishop came there who was to see into the devil's heart, as I shall now relate to you. In God's name, listen well.

Wherefore it chanced that one day the bishop and his host were dining and all the servants, except that one, were waiting on them. The good man asked them where this servant was. They said that he hadn't come to serve because of his ill health.

When the bishop heard this, he asked him what man was this, and his host told him everything—how the servant had come to him and how he always had performed faithful services for him. The bishop said: "Summon him at once, for I wish to see him."

Then that good man sent for him quickly. When the devil found out, he tried to make excuses, but finally he came before them, trembling, and when the bishop saw him, he perceived his falseness.

He said to the good man: "God loves you, be assured, for He saved you from the false devil and his treacheries. I shall show you now how this man in whom you trusted is the devil, without any doubt, but be silent for awhile."

He then said to the devil: "Tell me all you have done, so that this company may learn of your deeds. I beseech and command by the power of Jesus Christ who is God in Trinity, that you withhold nothing."

Then the devil began to relate how he had entered a dead man's body, by which means he thought to deceive his master, whom he would surely have killed if the man had not prayed to the Mother of Charity.

"When he said this prayer, I dared not do him any harm." And when he had finished speaking, he shed that body in which he was enclosed, and vanished into nothingness before their eyes.

The first panel of Plate 29 conveys a scene in the hospital in which three male nurses are feeding a number of bedridden patients. In panel 2 we see the benefactor employing several young men to tend the sick, and the brief caption relates this quite succinctly: "How the good man hired men at salary to serve the poor." This good Samaritan points apparently to the hospital, gesturing toward men who are would-be employees, whose hands appear to indicate, at least in one case, the act of bargaining, and, in the cases of the other two, doubt, uncertainty, or dissent.

Panel 3, whose caption reads, "How the devil put himself in the body of a dead man and entered service with the good man," relates how the devil, having entered the cadaver, approaches the unsuspecting philanthropist and declares that he would like to be his servant and to share in his good works. The benevolent fellow is delighted and hires him forthwith. Here the artists have created for the viewer, but not for the employer, a graphic indication that the resuscitated corpse is indeed the devil, for on the back of his head we see Satan's ugly and balefully glaring face.

So far the artists have not strayed from the poet's version, but in panel 4 visualizations take on great originality. The caption reads, "How the demon caused his master to go hunting and fishing in the sea in order to kill him." The poem tells little more, except that the devil hoped thereby to take possession of the good man's soul. This panel reveals startling and unexpected events, for the artists have concentrated on the double episodes of the hunting and fishing trips. In the upper part of the panel is a forest scene with trees and hills on the horizon. The good man, mounted and clutching a lance, defends himself from a large bear which apparently the demon has sent to attack him. The bear rears up on its hind legs as the hunter fends it off with his spear. The devil appears in all his hellish power, shaggy-thighed and satyr-like, knees and elbows bearing insets of glaring demonic visages, an evil finger pointing toward the bear as if to urge it on in its vicious assault upon the good man.[37] With his other hand, the fiendish false servant points to the scene in the lower half of the panel, where we view the fishing episode. There the good man, angling from a small boat, is set upon by a smaller demon with the wings of a hawk and the lower extremities of a goat, replete with tail and cloven hooves. No one observing the caption and the scene portrayed could possibly misinterpret the double action intended to show how far the devil goes to ensnare and slay his would-be victim. The action here, both real and implied by the devil's pointing hands, is executed so deftly that we can but marvel at this model of the plenitude of the Alfonsine miniaturists.

Colors in each panel are brilliant and attractive, but in panel 4 they run riot. The landscape, the trees, the sky, the shaggy, bleeding bear, and the hunter in bright tunic, flash forth with unaccustomed brilliance, while in the seascape the water is cerulean blue, contrasting with the colorful, fluttering wings of the diminutive, hawk-winged demon.

Panel 5's caption reads, "How a bishop, who was the guest of the good man, recognized the evil servant." The bishop is seen sitting at table with the good man, as servants bear before them plates of food and one a goblet of wine. The false majordomo kneels before the bishop, who, with his finger raised in admonition, speaks to him. In panel 5, the visualization runs parallel to the verbalization.

In panel 6, however, the artists have outdone themselves, providing a macabre and remarkable view of the way in which medieval man conceived of a corpse when the devil inhabiting it decided to leave or was exorcised, as is the case here. The caption reads, "How the bishop made the devil flee, and the corpse in which he had walked fell down before them." In the picture we glimpse a strange scene, indeed, for the bishop exorcises the demon while the good man makes a sign of blessing, and yet another gentleman folds his hands in prayer. Both the bishop's hands are raised. The servants, amazed, turn to stare as the corpse decomposes before their eyes, metamorphosizing into an emaciated, black, and ghastly cadaver, while the devil—wings, legs, and cloven hooves—emerges from its mouth.

The visualizations of this *cantiga* bring out clearly the nine elements of the classic design to a degree rarely found in illustrated narratives anywhere, and few of the *Cantigas de Santa Maria* can equal what the artists accomplished in this particular example.

*Cantiga 74*, discussed above briefly in its use of the device of double action, is a well-known miracle, popular in many countries of the medieval world, and mentioned by Mâle as one of the miracles depicted in stained glass windows in the Church of Le Mans.[38] The version in the *Cantigas* deserves careful reading for its literary quality and its unusual handling of a strange motif, and in order to see the character of the devil in one of his most petty moods.

## CANTIGA 74

*How Holy Mary saved the painter whom the devil tried to kill because he painted him ugly.*

The devil can do no harm to the one Holy Mary defends.

Concerning this, I wish to relate a miracle of how Holy Mary saved a painter of Hers who tried to paint Her as beautiful as he could.

He always painted the devil uglier than anything else. therefore, the devil said: "Why do you hold me in disdain and why do you make me look so bad to all who see me?"

The painter said: "I do this to you with reason, for you always do evil and will never have anything to do with good."

When the painter said this, the devil got angry and

threatened to kill the painter and sought a way to make him die quickly.

Therefore, one day he spied him there, as I learned, as he was painting the image of the Virgin. He tried to compose it very well, as I am told,

so that She would appear very beautiful. However, then the devil, in whom all evil lies, caused a great wind to blow, as when a thunderstorm draws near.

That wind entered the church and knocked down to the ground the platform on which the painter was standing. However, he called on the Virgin, Mother of God, to come to his rescue.

She came to his aid at once and made him hang on to the brush with which he was painting, and so he did not fall nor could the devil harm him in any way.

The people came at once at the loud crash the falling timbers made and they saw the devil blacker than pitch flee from the church where he met his defeat.

Then they saw how the painter was hanging by his brush, and they gave thanks for this to the Mother of Our Lord, who assists Her own in time of great trouble.

The artists have produced in panel 1 of Plate 26, under the first two arches a most interesting scene which faithfully documents the manner in which fresco painters pursued their trade. The protagonist is perched on a scaffolding with his pots of pigment and various mixing dishes beneath him. His hand wields a brush in a very lifelike fashion. The *tableau vivant* produced by the arch closely parallels the words of the caption, "How the painter painted the image of Holy Mary very beautiful and that of the devil very ugly." It is under the second arch that the painter has rendered the devil so hideous. A common column supports this arch and the one which precedes it, providing a line of demarcation between the two stages of the painter's work. A glance forward into panel 2 reveals that he has rendered both the Virgin and the devil on the same wall and only a few feet apart.

The panel 2 caption reads "How the demon appeared to the painter and threatened him sorely because he painted him ugly." Again, the miniaturists have utilized two arches, but this time the painter no longer sits on the scaffold, but stands under the left-hand arch. There is obviously no true double action here, for the two characters engage in a single confrontation. Even so, the arch containing the painter and the one framing the devil focus attention on the two simultaneous actions, and may have suggested to medieval viewers first the painter's salvo against his adversary and then the demon's ferocious reply.

Characterization here is effectively presented, for the painter shows great spirit and fearlessness as he shakes a finger at his fearsome and hideous enemy, who makes ready apparently to attack him physically.

The demon's vengeful character flares forth from his bestial face, twisted, it would seem, with fury and punctured vanity. One of his hands seems about to reach out and strike the painter, while the other points as though to refute his ugly likeness on the wall. His wings are terrible to behold, with veinings outlined against their black membranes, and their tips are pointed with hooks.

Panel 3, which reads, "How the painter painted an image of Holy Mary up in a vaulted arch," reveals another scaffolding, this one reaching much higher than the first, and on it the painter, again rendering *al fresco* the pictures of the Virgin and Child. Beneath him stand four clerics gazing upward, evidently to assess the progress of the work, or else filled with awe at his temerity. Their hands speak for them as they watch the painter's brush apply the finishing touches to the face of Our Lady. In these and all subsequent panels he wears a white kerchief to confine his hair, where as in the first two panels he worked bareheaded. A very large Gothic arch occupies most of the panel and projects into the space allotted to the caption in such a way as to interrupt the flow of calligraphy. This arch authoritatively spotlights the action, and appears in all subsequent panels of the illumination, causing the events to flow in an unmistakable continuum, never allowing the viewer to lose his awareness of the transition.

The caption over panel 4, "How the demon knocked down the painter's scaffold," heads one of the most successful renditions of utter confusion and disarray to be found in the *Cantigas*. High in the vault of the church the artist hangs in mid-air and, as the scaffolding crashes down, sees the devil literally shaking the structure to pieces with his hands and feet. The stool on which the painter has been sitting plummets to the floor, along with the beams, poles, and cross bracings of the scaffold. The devil's face is baleful indeed, and his every limb indicates the depth of his fury. In the demon the artists have most effectively made motion a primary aspect of their portrayal. The appearance of the devil in the flesh is their original contribution in this panel, as they have visualized something not actually in the poem, which only states that the devil caused a great storm to arise whose "wind entered the church and knocked to the ground the platform on which the painter was standing."

Panel 5, "How the people came at the noise and saw the devil fleeing and the painter hanging," matches the caption perfectly, for one can see the devil as he flies out of the space allotted to the arch and into that belonging to the caption. The scaffold, piled on the floor in a jumbled maze of lumber, separates the viewer from the curious onlookers, who gaze up in wonder, hands in the attitude of prayer, at the painter who still grasps the brush which clings to the painted face of Our Lady. The countenances of the spectators reflect a full range of emotions from dumbfounded awe to abject terror.

The last panel, "How all the people praised Holy Mary for this miracle," presents the images of the Virgin and Child on their altar. A lamp now hangs just below the recently completed fresco, and the faithful, both kneeling and standing, congregate in ardent adoration.

Arches frame the scene in every panel in this illumination, and their effect is remarkable. We have observed how in panel 1 two arches separated by a common column, which also supports them, highlight two separate phases of the painter's activity, and again in panel 2 how the two arches emphasize the painter's courageous stance against the demon and the latter's vicious response. The last four panels utilize larger arches with surprising results. As in panel 3, where the great arch projects into the caption itself, a similar phenomenon now occurs in panels 4, 5, and 6. In the apex of the arch in panel 4, the resolute and uncompromising determination of the painter, as he labors to finish the face of the Virgin, is accentuated in a most skillful representation. Staring directly at the brush he wields, completely absorbed in his craft, and resolute in his devotion to the Virgin, the artist labors in a scene whose strength and vigor lend an unmistakable realism and a sure degree of finesse and constancy to this particular panel. In this panel with its scaffolding midway through its dramatic collapse, the faithful painter holds tightly to the brush, which has adhered to the painting itself. A similar sensation is evoked in panel 5, for here the painter still hangs high in the arch, his face now turned toward the fresco, which he continues to paint, his gaze again intently fixed on his work. The great arch of panel 6 now focuses the eye on the fresco itself, which dominates and shares the frame with the image of the Virgin on its colorful altar.

Scene, plot, and conflict blend and harmonize in these panels to produce a notable example of visualization. Character is particularly well drawn. The painter is dauntless as he stands up to the threatening demon, whose visage is fierce enough to cow the bravest soul. His piety and determination under great stress as he finds himself suspended far above the floor are evident in his face, the tilt of his head, his industrious hands. Obviously he is a man of deep faith.

*Cantiga 142* is unusual in several ways: it depicts King Alfonso himself hawking, and develops his char-

acter as a devotee of great faith, while the iconography of this particular occasion (Plate 30) represents a peculiar break with events within the miracle's plot in such a way as to forestall what might have been a departure from artistic presentation and esthetics. [39]

## CANTIGA 142

*How Holy Mary saved from death one of the King's men who had entered a river to retrieve a heron.*

> In great affliction, the Virgin always comes to the aid of those who trust in Her goodness.

As once She rescued, in the presence of King don Alfonso, a man who would have died, I am sure, if it were not for Her who protects us, as I shall tell you now.

This happened on the river which is called Henares, where the King had gone to hunt. A falcon of his had boldly killed a heron there.

For although the heron flew very high, that falcon quickly overtook it and with a powerful blow, broke its wing. It fell into the water, and,

in spite of their efforts, the dogs could not reach it, for the river was running swiftly. Therefore, they gave the heron up for lost. However, the King shouted: "Who will it be?

Who will go in after the heron and bring it back to me here?" A man from Guadalajara answered thus: "My lord, I shall bring it

out of the river." At once he jumped in, wearing his boots, for he didn't stop to take them off, and swam to the heron and grasped it by the head.

He tried to swim back to shore, for he wanted very much to give the heron to the King, his lord, but the water swirled him around so that he lost his senses.

The force of the water seized him so powerfully that it submerged him two or three times, but he called on the royal Virgin who bore Jesus Christ in Bethlehem.

Everyone else also called on her, and the King said: "No harm will be done, for the Spiritual Mother who protects us and has us in Her power will not suffer it."

Although they all said "he is dead," the King kept saying: "He is not, by my faith, for the One who is always with God and does not abandon us would not so will."

And so it was, for soon, in all truth, the Virgin caused the man to come out of the river alive and well and approach the King with his heron, which he brought out with him.

He presented it forthwith to the King, who greatly blessed the Lady of Good Will for this wondrous miracle She performed, and all responded promptly: "Amen."

Panel 1, "How King Alfonso loosed a falcon at a heron," initiates this miracle so filled with local medieval color. The king, attired in pinkish robes, sits his mule and with a gloved hand casts the hawk into the air. On his cap in a square of white appears the black lion of León, an insignia included to leave no doubt in the viewer's mind as to whether this is indeed the sovereign. Behind him in blue and gray costumes his hunting companions, similarly mounted, watch their lord and master.

Panel 2, "How the falcon struck the heron and broke its wing and the heron fell into the river," represents a significant divergence from the scenic presentation of the first panel, for it concentrates upon the river itself. The stream in some turbulence flows straight at the viewer, so that he looks directly into it as though gazing into an aquarium, seeing the surface as well as the depths. High verdure-clad banks rise on either side. Three entire panels forming a single column on the right depict this scene, while to the left three panels in which the king and the hunters appear create a similar columnar unit, lending balance and a sense of symmetry to the entire folio. In panel 2 three simultaneous actions occur: while the heron flies above the river, we see this same heron falling with its broken wing, having been struck by the hawk, which flies out of the panel and into the caption, effectively imparting a three-dimensional illusion of space and freedom from the confines of the frame; the heron sitting helpless on the surface of the water provides the third element of action. One does not, then, see three different herons, but the same bird in three separate moments of its existence. Double action in a panel is common enough; triple action is a rarity.

Panel 3, "How he began to ask loudly who would enter the river after the heron," shows Alfonso speaking to his huntsmen. No one, as their attitudes suggest, is willing to venture into the river, and even the dogs at the feet of the king's mount refuse to enter the roiling flood. Panel 4, "How a man went into the water after the heron and went down a good three times," reveals that a man has at last answered the king's request. He struggles, holding the wounded bird, and sinks with it, as the viewer can clearly see in the frontal cross-section with its aquarium effect. Through the opaque turbulence indicated by coiling lines, the drowning man struggles, but nevertheless sinks.

At this juncture the poem makes it clear that all except the king give the man up for lost, crying "He is dead." But the devout Alfonso stoutly maintains, "He is not, by my faith, for the One who is always with God and does not abandon us would not so will." Panel 5, "How he gave it to the King and the King and the others praised Holy Mary," departs from the norm of verbalized action. Recall that in panel 4 the man entered the river and was immediately submerged. One would therefore expect panel 5 to reveal how he somehow managed to surface and come out of the water, whereas in fact it does not. Instead, panel 5

shows him offering the heron to Alfonso, while the caption over panel 6 reads, "How Holy Mary caused the man to come out of the river with the heron in his hand." Panel 5, then, is the actual visualized dénouement, as its caption states, and yet it precedes panel 6 in the illuminations. The reason for this apparent confusion is evident from the esthetic point of view, for the artists had previously planned to present three panels on the left in descending order with the king and his men, the horses, and the hunting dogs in a single artistic pattern, while the right-hand column was to offer three panels depicting those scenes taking place in the river.

This page of illuminations is one of many cases which required the Alfonsine artists to paint stories and locales for which they had no immediate models, obliging them to improvise and establish their own norms, to develop imaginative approaches and techniques. The entire codex of the *Cantigas de Santa Maria* stands as eloquent testimony to the originality of a nascent art form whose disciples were constantly challenged by their task, for time and again we are constrained to realize how and to what extent invention rises to the demands of unusual or novel narrative content. Spain was not the only land where artistic ingenuity was so tested. In other countries, most notably Germany and England, artists were equally compelled to contrive graphic procedures which would adequately portray the entire gamut of adventures transpiring in a myriad of biblical events, from apocryphal scriptures and pietistic tales to contemporary supernatural occurrences, which apparently proliferated in this period of time.

*Cantiga 94* sets forth Alfonso's version of a very well-known miracle, disclosing the secret of a nun who fell in love with a young gentleman and fled the convent to be with him, leaving the keys of her office at the foot of the Virgin's altar. She stayed away long enough to bear three children, but at length repented and returned. The *Cantigas de Santa Maria* contain five distinct versions concerning runaway nuns.[40]

## CANTIGA 94

*This is how Holy Mary served in place of the nun who left the convent.*

The Virgin Mary ever strives to protect us from shame and sin and error.

She protects us from sin and shields us even when we lapse into error. Then She makes us repent and atone for the sins we commit. Concerning this, the peerless Holy Queen who guides us performed a miracle in an abbey.

There was a lady there who, as I learned, was young and beautiful. Furthermore, she observed the rules of the Order so scrupulously that there was no one as diligent as she in turning everything to good account. Therefore, they made her treasurer.

However, the devil who was displeased by this, made her love a knight passionately and gave her no peace until he caused her to leave the convent. Before she departed, she left the keys she wore at her belt in front of the altar of the One in whom she believed.

"Oh, Mother of God," she then prayed, "I leave you this charge and commend myself to you with all my heart." Then she went away to do as she would with the man she loved more than herself. She lived a long time with him in sin.

After the knight took her off with him, he had sons and daughters by her. However, the benevolent Virgin, who never condones willfulness, performed a miracle and caused the girl to detest the life she was leading and to return to the cloister where she used to live.

Moreover, while the girl lived her wayward life, the Virgin took good care of everything she had left in Her charge, for She assumed her place and performed all her duties and was remiss in nothing, according to the opinion of all who saw Her.

As soon as the nun repented, she left the knight and neither ate nor slept until she saw the convent . She entered fearfully and began to inquire of those she knew about the conditions of the place, for she was very concerned.

They told her frankly: "We have a most excellent abbess, prioress, and treasurer who do us great service and have no faults." When she heard this, she began to cross herself, because she heard them speak of her this way.

In great alarm, trembling and pale, she went to the church. The Mother of the Lord showed her such great love—for which may She be blessed—that she found the keys where she had placed them and picked up the clothes she had formerly worn.

At once, without hesitation or shame, she joined the other nuns and told them the great favor which the One who has the world in Her command did for her. To prove to them all that she told them, she had her lover called in to tell it to them also.

The nuns of the convent thought it a very great miracle when they saw it to be a proven thing and swore by St. John that none so beautiful had ever been told to them before. They began to sing joyfully: "May God save you, Star of the Sea and Light of Day."

*Cantiga 94* is the best-known of these stories of nuns, and as such receives noteworthy treatment in the *Cantigas*. Panel 1 of Plate 31 is divided into three sections. In the one at the far left a belfry is seen. In the central arch the nun kneels before Our Lady's altar, shown in the right-hand arch. A handsome lectern stands behind the nun, and on it a book bound in red and silver. She is bidding the Virgin farewell and leaving the convent keys on the altar. Color abounds in the book, the arches of gold, the rooftops in blue and red, the brilliant tilework of the altar, the hue of

the Virgin's robe, and her crown and that of the Child. Each object stands out prominently against the white walls and the nun's white habit. Since tales of runaway nuns were fairly common, the viewer would have quickly recognized a familiar topic. The caption reads, "How the nun commended her keys and habit to Holy Mary."

Panel 2, "How the nun left the convent with the gentleman," reveals the renegade sister attired in secular garments, eloping with her lover. The artists attempted, and with some success, to render sensuality in the eyes of the young man as he gazes at his beloved. One of his hands is over her shoulder, the other on her arm. The walls of the convent in white, blue, and red, contrasted with ever brighter reds and blues in the skyline of the city, conjure up an indelible and suggestive scene.

Panel 3, "How Holy Mary served in place of the nun who had departed," presents interesting developments of double action. At the left, without a surmounting arch, we see the Virgin clothed in the nun's habit, her head framed by a cobalt nimbus, crowned in gold and rubies, and pulling a rope to toll the convent bells in demonstration of one of her many duties. In the center and under a golden arch, she leans on a lectern, reading from a lesson to the assembled nuns. At the far right under another arch, the images of Our Lady and the Christ Child sit upon their altar, resplendent with multicolored tiles. The viewer clearly understands that the Virgin is performing those tasks in the convent to which the nun had been assigned. In both pictures she wears the crown and nimbus, which the viewer can see but which, of course, are invisible to her companions.

Panel 4, "How the nun returned to the convent and went to inquire about the condition of the place," shows the return of the errant sister, her secular transformation manifested by her gown and hat. She speaks to two citizens and a nun, gesticulating as she questions them. The men, too, appear to use hand language. Everyone seems to be blond in this polychromatic scene, where the men's garments, the runaway nun's purplish ensemble, and the primary reds and blues of the roof tiles combine with the golden arch to produce a lively and animated view.

Panel 5, "How Holy Mary guarded the nun's keys and habit and gave them to her when she came," divides the action into three sections, an oblong space and two golden arches. No one appears in the space at the far left, but we are familiar with it, for it shows the same belfry as in panels 1 and 3, its ropes trailing down the wall. In the central arch, which spotlights the primary action of the panel, we see the nun kneeling, still in temporal garb. The same lectern rises behind her and the gold lamp hangs above her head. One hand touches a cross which Our Lady extends to her, the other grasps the habit she will soon resume. The Virgin stands now clothed in celestial raiment and looks sweetly at the kneeling sinner, while in the arch at the far right the altar with the images of the Madonna and Child is aglow with the colors of their robes, crowns, and haloes accentuated by the tilework.

The last panel, "How the nun had her children and her lover come before the convent, and he told what happened," is framed with entirely different arches, whose mundane and true-to-life composition stands in stark contrast to the usual golden, celestial frames. Here there are two arches, both of a creamy masonry whose individual stones are perfectly distinguishable, as are the truly beautiful carved capitals of the convent's columns. The arch to the right is Gothic and not as large as the expansive romanesque arch at the left curving over the five nuns who sit judge-like. Under the Gothic arch stand the repentant nun, now in her habit, her lover, and their three children, while the nuns stare as though transfixed at the tableau they provide. The reformed nun points with one hand to the man and with the other to the children. The blue and red robes of the children and colorful garb of the father offer sharp contrast to the subdued black and white habits of the sisterhood and the pale white arches and walls.

This is an unusually perceptive presentation of narrative, and one in which the artists captured all the elements of the classic design, just as the poet did in the verbalization.

*Cantiga 209,* "How King Alfonso of Castile fell ill in Victoria and had such severe pain that he thought he would die of it. They laid the *Book of the Canticles of Holy Mary* upon him and he was cured" (Plate 32), is narrated succinctly, even in this title.[41] This is the most personal of all the *Cantigas de Santa Maria.* It appears in the Florentine Codex on folio 119v. Not only is it a truly delightful miracle in verse, but it contains some of the most brilliant illumination to be found in either of the narrative codices of the *Cantigas.*

Because the story revolves entirely around the monarch himself, the artists seem to have lavished more color and gold here than on any other folio of miniatures. The page literally blazes with this precious metal—in arches, columns, Alfonso's crown, even his great four-poster bed, and in the motif of the castle and the lion which forms the border of his counterpane. Even the frame or frieze glows with exceptionally rich hues and intricacy of design. It is truly a royal

illumination, sparing nothing in its conspicuous attempt to be unique among the *cantigas.* The interesting aspects of this miraculous event lie in the iconography and in the revelation of the monarch's most intimate feelings as he expresses them in the first person. Nowhere have we encountered a similar account by a king of how he felt in the midst of an illness and how he prayed in the depths of his despair. He call the Virgin *his* Divine Mother, and relates that "I cried out, 'Holy Mother, help me, and with your power dispel this malady.' "

## CANTIGA 209

*How King Alfonso of Castile fell ill in Victoria and had such severe pain that he thought he would die of it. They laid the Book of the Canticles of Holy Mary upon him and he was cured.*

He who denies God and His blessings commits a great error and is grievously in the wrong.

However, I shall never fall into this error by failing to tell of the benefit I have received from Him through His Virgin Mother, whom I have always loved and whom it pleases me more than any other thing to praise.

And how should I not take great delight in praising the works of this Lady who assists me in trouble and takes away sorrow and grants me many other blessings?

Therefore, I shall tell you what happened to me while I lay in Victoria, so ill that all believed I should die there and did not expect me to recover.

For such a pain afflicted me that I believed it to be mortal and cried out: "Holy Mary, help me, and with your power dispel this malady!"

The doctors ordered hot cloths placed on me, but I did not wish it and ordered Her Book to be brought. They placed it on me and at once I lay in peace.

I neither cried out nor felt anything of the pain, but at once felt very well. I gave thanks to Her for it, for I know full well She was dismayed at my affliction.

When this happened, many were in the place who expressed great sorrow at my suffering, and began to weep, standing before me in a line.

When they saw the mercy which this Holy Virgin, Lady of Great Worth, showed me, they all praised Her, each one pressing his face to the earth.

In panel 1 of Plate 32, the king lies supine in his great four-poster with the pink counterpane drawn up around his body, leaving one arm languidly exposed. His head is propped up on a pillow striped in gold and blue, and since he is king, he wears his golden crown even in bed, for he must be easily recognized by the viewer. The gleaming golden arches, one large romanesque at the left, the center and far right Gothic, frame the action. The first and largest arch focuses attention on the monarch. At the king's left and just behind the head of the bed stands a servant wielding a fan of peacock plumes. At his right, physicians consult. Alfonso's face reveals pain, insofar as the artists were able to capture and depict it (probably the result of the tumor in his jaw recently revealed by a forensic examination of the king's dessicated corpse). Alfonso has grown worse in panel 2, "How the physicians ordered hot cloths placed on him but he refused." He turns his face away from them as they proffer the cloths, and waves them back with his hand. Behind the doctors stand courtiers or members of the royal family who cover their heads and weep.

In panel 3, "How the king ordered the Canticles of Holy Mary brought," Alfonso is still lying in bed, but he reaches for the treasured volume, bound in scarlet and silver, which a tonsured priest presents ceremoniously. Doctors and courtiers stand behind the cleric, and the servant with the fan has not deserted his post. Panel 4 shows Alfonso still supine but seemingly relaxed, with the book's open face resting on his chest. "They put it on me," he wrote in the poem, "and immediately I lay at peace." His body certainly seems at rest. Several people in expectation of the miraculous, or out of respect for the Virgin and her wondrous book, have gone to their knees, while others stand and stare in pious awe. The king's hand now lies flat across the book.

In panel 5, "How the King was instantly cured, felt no pain, and praised Holy Mary," he sits up in bed, wearing a bright blue bed-robe over his samite gown. He raises the volume in both hands and kisses it devoutly, while all kneel except the fan-bearer, who appears, just as earlier, to be part of the panoply of kingship rather than inserted for esthetic reasons, as might be supposed. "I neither cried out," wrote Alfonso, "nor felt anything of the pain, but at once felt very well." His face wears an expression of devotion. The striped pillow, now that this head is no longer on it, reveals a square white doily where it had rested, calling attention once more to artistic insistence upon the inclusion of the smallest detail. Panel 6 depicts the king still sitting up in bed, the volume now face down on his lap. All kneel, save the fan-bearer, as Alfonso raises both his hands in prayerful devotion. The caption reads, "How the King and the others who were there praised Holy Mary." Indeed, the kneeling, weeping men lower their faces all the way to the floor and press them against it, just as the verses recall.

Gesture and facial expression play a strong role in this *cantiga*'s illumination: the king's hand in panel 1, listless on his chest, his face strained; the royal head turned peevishly from the two physicians (recognizable by their typical hats), and from the two mourners with their robes pulled over their faces in grief, in panel 2; his face relieved in panel 3 as he receives from

a priest the volume of the *Cantigas* he has requested, while the doctors and others watch; a look of repose as he places the book face up on his chest and holds it open with his hands in panel 4, while some of his attendants kneel; his expression ecstatic in panel 5 as he sits, wearing a blue bed robe, holding the precious volume at face level and kissing it; and in panel 6 his expression joyful as he remains sitting up in bed, his hands now clasped in prayer, as he gives thanks to the Blessed Virgin, with the book open on his lap but face down, all kneeling except the fan-bearer.

In this *cantiga,* perhaps more expressively than in any other, can be found the nine components of brief narrative in briefest verbal form as well as in detailed and lavish pictorial representation. The simple, unadulterated plot and its conflict never falter and are constantly manifest; scene certainly is gorgeous, explicit in detail, and laid effectively against the oyster-white walls of the royal bedchamber; characterization is primarily Alfonso's, for the others are mere minor supporting actors in the scenes. In the king definite character emerges: his disdain for worldly cures; his confidence in the divine; his belief in Our Lady's power and willingness to heal him; and his pious respect for the wondrous book he has caused to be written and illuminated in her honor; even his deep love for his patroness is apparent as he lifts the volume in his hands and kisses it.

Iconography in these miniatures, as well as style in the poem, is so direct, clear, and unencumbered, despite the lavish details of the scene, that without captions the viewer can unravel most of the action with little effort. Theme is obviously faith and devotion and their rewards; effect is powerful and perhaps more complex than meets the eye at first.

Viewers may well have been so thrilled at the series of scenes in the intimacy of the royal bedchamber amid so much luxury and pomp, that other effects may have been diffused. Point of view is most unusually personal and like no other found in either verbal or visual form, since King Alfonso allows the reader to hear him speak, and through the visualizations and their captions, to see that he is speaking. The king has actually versified a vignette straight from his own personal experience, from a mortal illness he himself suffered. Mood or tone is one of deep religiosity. Of all the *cantigas* in which Alfonso appears, none is more intimate.

*Cantiga 47,* surely intended to convey elements of humor, even as it portrays awful and inspiring events, differs markedly from others, for the viewer sees a drunken monk and the terrible results of his addiction to the cup. Medieval man may have taken the story either as a bad case of delirium tremens or as a factual account in which an inebriated ecclesiastic faces terrifying apparitions. The plot is simple to the extreme, and both poet and artists present it in the triple-incident technique found in many folktales, even paralleling such popular tales by offering a series of three ever-worsening perils until the protagonist is relieved in a climactic incident.

## CANTIGA 47

*This is how Holy Mary saved the monk whom the devil tried to frighten in order to seize his soul.*

Holy Virgin Mary, protect us if You will from the wiliness of the devil.

For night and day the devil tries to lead us into error so that we will lose God, your Son, who suffered torment and death on the cross, so that we might have peace.

Concerning this, friends of mine, I wish to tell you now a beautiful miracle on which I composed my song. It tells of how Holy Mary protected a monk from the temptation of the devil who despises goodness.

This monk was ordained, as I heard it, and dutifully observed the rules of his order, so I learned. However, the cunning devil led him astray and made him overindulge in wine in the cellar.

Although he was very drunk, the monk attempted to go straight to the church, but the devil came out to meet him in the form of a bull to gore him with its lowered horns, as bulls attack.

When the monk saw this, he was badly frightened and called loudly for Holy Mary, who appeared at once and threatened the bull, saying, "Go away, you are disgusting!"

Then the devil appeared to him again in the form of a tall, thin man, all shaggy and black as pitch. Again the matchless Virgin chased him away, saying, "Get out of here, evil one, worse than a thief!"

When the monk entered the church, the devil again appeared to him in the shape of a fierce lion, but the Holy Virgin hit him with a stick, saying, "Scat, infamous creature, disappear right now!"

After Holy Mary rescued the monk, as I have told you, and quieted his fears caused by the devil and the wine which had addled him, She told him: "Be careful from now on and don't misbehave."

In panel 1 of Plate 33, whose caption reads, "How the devil made a monk drink so much wine that he got drunk," the oft-used arch device spotlights the occurrences and sets the scene. Two arches frame the hogsheads of wine, which are large and made of brown wood with hoops clearly delineated. In the right arch sits the monk guzzling from a large goblet and apparently enjoying himself hugely. Since his habit is white, as is the wall which forms the background, color

must be supplied from outside the actual scene—in the golden arches, the blue and pink tiles of the roof, and the colorful band of designs which frames the panels.

In Panel 2, "How Holy Mary liberated the monk from the devil who appeared to him in the figure of a bull," one can see the monk swaying precariously in his drunkenness, his hand outstretched as though to balance himself. The center arch reveals Our Lady in a robe of deep blue and a puce cape. Her left hand gathers its folds while her right holds a stick with which she fends off the bull as it lowers its head as though to toss her or the monk. Her raiment and the brown and beige of the animal afford the only color in the panel, but above the action runs a rooftop of blue and pink tiles arranged in such a way as to contrast with the arrangement of tiles in later panels. The bull is ferocious enough, but he is a shade less terrible than the apparition in the next encounter.

The caption of Panel 3 almost minimizes the creature, for it says, "How Holy Mary saved the monk from the devil who appeared to him in the figure of a very ugly man." This antagonist is described in the verses as "a tall, thin man, all shaggy and black as pitch." We believe he is one of the many wild men populating medieval folklore and fiction, and therefore terrible enough to the poor monk.[42]

A beard covers his face and his hair is shaggy. The skin of a bear or of some other wild beast falls from his waist to just above his knobby knees as he moves toward the Virgin and cowering monk behind. The artists portray the wild man just as he is stopped in his career toward the Virgin, and his hand seems to try to repulse her as she extends an admonitory palm in his direction. The monk, more tipsy than before, has gotten a staff to hold him up. He leans very drunkenly toward his protectress as he tries to escape. One hand dangles limply, as a drunken person's might. Color again is provided by the tiles, the deep brown of the animal skin the devil wears in his guise as a wild man, and indeed in his utter blackness. In the central arch, since it contains the Virgin, color is in her bright robes.

Panel 4 represents the monk's final adventure with the Evil One. It reads, "How Holy Mary saved the monk from the devil who appeared to him in the form of a very fierce lion." This panel has the same three arches, but in the one at the right can be seen an altar of the Virgin without the images generally present, and this is very unusual in *cantiga* miniatures. She occupies the lefthand arch with the monk, who has sobered up enough not to stagger. The Virgin extends her hand toward the lion, which scratches at her with one of its paws and apparently roars, for its mouth is wide open with its long red tongue protruding. It is a lifelike king of beasts, and one can be certain that the artists had seen a lion, or a very good picture of one. Probably Alfonso owned a lion or two, as did many medieval monarchs—Charlemagne, Richard the Lionhearted, and Frederick of Sicily, to name but three.

Panel 5, "How Holy Mary berated the monk after she had delivered him from the devil and the wine," depicts her standing above him as he kneels, his hands upraised in prayer. To drive home her sermon she uses her right hand in a gesture familiar to everyone. She now stands just to the left of the empty altar. The last panel, "How he told it to the monks and they all greatly praised Holy Mary," reveals the altar no longer bereft of the images. Under the right-hand arch the image of the Virgin now stands on the altar wearing the exact costume she wore when she protected the monk from his adversaries. The only difference is that she now holds the Christ Child in the crook of her arm and faces the viewer. A standing image of Our Lady is rare in the *Cantigas,* and the artists may intend the viewer to see the image just as it has returned to the altar and before it has had an opportunity to seat itself. The verses make no mention of the image's leaving its place on the altar. The brotherhood in habits, some with cowls pulled up, kneel in adoration.

This simple and folkloristic plot keeps scene to a minimum, but fills out the story with sustained action and with excellent depictions of the adversaries, the staggering steps of the monk, and the remarkable activities of Our Lady. Drunkenness was familiar to all medieval people, the clergy not exempted, and the presentation of the monk, from his eager look as he swills wine in the monastery cellars through his swaying walk, his vacuous expression, and his dangling hand, until he falls on his knees in repentance, would have delighted the popular mind. Criticism of the clergy, frequent in the *Cantigas de Santa Maria,* and a much-employed theme in the literature of the times, would have made this miracle most acceptable.

To savor the essence of humor in this story, one must read the epithets hurled by Our Lady at the devil in his confrontation with her. To the bull she says, "Go away, you are disgusting!" To the wild man she cries, "Get out of here, evil one, worse than a thief!" But her words to the devil in the form of the lion surpass the others in true humor, for she says "Scat, infamous creature, disappear right now!"

*Cantiga 157* is concerned with a miracle which takes place on a pilgrimage,[43] a miracle about petty crime, not some heinous sin caused by the devil.

## CANTIGA 157

*How some pilgrims were on the way to Rocamadour and took lodging in a town and the landlady stole some of the meal they were carrying.*

God, for His Mother's sake, at times punishes severely the one who does wrong, and very quickly, at Her behest, makes him well again.

Concerning this, He performed a great miracle for some pilgrims who served His Mother who were going to Rocamadour. They took lodging in a village, as I learned, my friends. However, their landlady did a very mean thing to them.

Whereas they bought fairly from her all that she sold them, she began to covet the meal they carried with them from which they made fritters. One of them put good fresh cheese on them, for it was summertime.

In her desire for this, she stole some meal from them and when they had gone away, she set about at once to make fritters just as they did. However, the devil thwarted her, for when she tried to taste one of them, the result was very bad.

When she stuck a knife in the fritter to try how it would taste, she thrust the knife through her mouth all the way up to the hilt and could not pull it out, for it pierced her jaws more than a palm's length.

Many doctors came there, but they could not draw the knife out of her by any of their skill or wisdom. She, when she saw this, went off to Rocamadour to pray to Holy Mary where every good Christian man or

woman who asks her sincerely for mercy finds it. Therefore, this woman went there, weeping sorely. After she made her confession, a priest, not a surgeon, drew the knife out of her.

Quickly they learned of this miracle in all the land around, and all gave thanks and praise to the Glorious Virgin, Mother of Our Lord. All of you heed the miracle, which happened not so very long ago.

A great deal of color is found on this page of illumination (Plate 34). The frieze is vivid, the rooftops are bright with blue and pink tiles, and the costumes worn by the people who move through the panels are colorful. Panel 1 develops action under three arches. Under the left arch stands the woman just as she is helping herself to the meal belonging to the pilgrims. She looks guiltily over her shoulder at them as they kneel or stand around a tripod on which rests a large skillet under which a fire burns redly. It is a remarkable depiction of a kitchen in an inn with its cooking utensils—the tripod, the skillet, and a large iron cauldron which hangs from the ceiling and can be lowered by a chain to the fire when the skillet is not in use. One of the pilgrims wears the characteristic robe and broad-brimmed hat, and stands gazing intently into the skillet, where fritters are frying. Another man, bald and robed in brown, sits beside the tripod; and the third, a young man in a purple cloak with a white kerchief over his head, kneels. The caption reads: "How a woman stole the flour from the pilgrims which they put in her house."

In panel 2, "How she made fritters of the flour and wanted to taste one on the knife and it wounded her in the mouth," she can be seen seated on a stool before the fire under the central of the cluster of three golden arches. Her brilliant blue robe contrasts with the black cauldron and skillet and the ruby glow of the fire. She has just popped a fritter into her mouth, and the knife has run through her jaw and projects from behind her ear. The penetration must be in the process of occurring, for she has not even had time to remove her hand from the handle of the skillet, in which the fritters can clearly be seen frying. The left arch reveals only a tall, half-open door, while the arch to the right frames the tripod, skillet, and hanging cauldron.

Panel 3, "How the physicians came to pull out the knife and could not," shows the poor woman lying in bed as two doctors in characteristic robes and flat caps work over her fruitlessly, one pushing the blade from behind her head, the other pulling it from in front. Ladies watch, while in a very realistic touch the youthful pilgrim in the kerchief assists by holding the sinner's hands. Two arches spotlight these actions. Panel 4, "How she went to Rocamadour to beg Holy Mary to make the knife come out,"[44] transpires under four arches. Beneath the two narrow arches at the left the pilgrim youth stands with a tonsured cleric. The central arch reveals the woman, still transfixed by the knife, kneeling. A golden lamp burns above her head, for she is now in the shrine of Our Lady of Rocamadour. She lifts her hands and beseeches the image on its altar under the right-hand arch. The image and the altar tiles are brilliant.

Panel 5, "How the woman made her confession and a priest drew out the knife," reveals action under all four arches. In the two to the left the pilgrim youth is about to kneel and the priest still stands, staring at the central arch under which the woman, still kneeling, sees the blade coming out of her mouth in the hands of the priest. The right-hand arch still reveals the altar and the Madonna's image. Panel 6, "How they all lauded Holy Mary for this and for other miracles," provides a very colorful scene with little action. The people are on their knees in their brilliant robes under the left and central arches, while beneath the right-hand arch the image on its altar offers the usual dénouement.

Plot and conflict are executed well enough to make clear and cogent what is taking place. Scene is carefully laid and filled with local color, while the artists deal

exceptionally well with the woman's character. She is dishonest, as her stance and face prove when she steals the pilgrims' supplies. Her crime would have seemed worse to medieval people than to us, since the pilgrims trusted her. When she is punished cruelly she first lets the physicians treat her, as most people would, but when they can do nothing she repents and travels to the shrine to beg forgiveness and assistance. She is a typical middle-class woman, with the usual human frailties and pettiness, but she has an inner faith in Our Lady. The theme is obvious, and certainly effect and mood or tone are present and dutifully portrayed.

Among the most winsome of miracles in the *Cantigas* is *Cantiga 8,* which shows how Our Lady rewards a musician who always sings his lays to her. One day he comes to sing a lay to her in Her great shrine at Rocamadour and to play his fiddle. The iconography presents the story as well as the verbalization does, and much more colorfully, for the illumination is particularly brilliant.

## CANTIGA 8

*This is how in Rocamadour Holy Mary caused a candle to descend to the fiddle of a minstrel who sang before Her.*

We who hope for the blessings of Holy Mary should all praise Her with songs and joyfulness.

Concerning this, I shall tell you a miracle performed by the Holy Virgin Mary, Mother of Our Lord, in Rocamadour, which will please you when you hear it. Listen now to the story and we shall relate it to you.

There was a minstrel whose name was Pedro of Germany who could sing very well and play the viola even better. In all the churches of the Peerless Virgin he always sang of lay of Hers, according to what I learned.

The lay which he sang before Her statue, with tears in his eyes, was about the Mother of God. Then he said: "Oh, Glorious One, if you are pleased by these songs of mine, give us a candle so that we may dine."

Holy Mary was pleased at how the minstrel sang, and made a candle descend on his fiddle. However, the monk who was treasurer snatched it out of his hand, saying: "You are an enchanter and we shall not let you have it!"

But the minstrel, whose heart was dedicated to the Virgin, would not stop singing, and the candle once more came to rest on his fiddle. The irate friar snatched it away again, quicker than it takes to tell it.

When the monk had taken the candle away from the fiddle of the minstrel, he put it right back where it was before and fastened it down tight. He said: "Sir minstrel, if you take it from there, we shall consider you a sorcerer."

The minstrel paid no attention to all this, but played his fiddle as before, and the candle again came to rest on it. The monk tried to snatch it, but the people said: "We shall not permit you to do this."

When the obstinate monk saw this miracle, he realized

that he had greatly erred and repented at once. He prostrated himself on the ground before the minstrel and asked his pardon in the name of Holy Mary, in whom we one and all believe.

After the Glorious Virgin performed this miracle which rewarded the minstrel and converted the unenlightened monk, each year the minstrel of whom we have spoken brought to Her church a tall wax candle.

Panel 1 of Plate 35 is set under three cusped arches. Above the action, colorful rooftops, with towers and turrets, continue throughout the panels. The left-hand arch in panel 1 frames a number of richly robed worshippers, some kneeling, others standing to watch the musician as he performs. In the second arch, the fiddler kneels, while two men stand behind him. Above his head is a shelf on which four candles burn. The right-hand arch reveals the usual altar with the Madonna and the Child, but the tilework is exceptionally intricate and colorful. The caption reads, "How the minstrel was playing before the altar of Holy Mary and he asked her for a candle."

In panel 2, the miracle begins, for down from its shelf one candle has descended and come to rest on the end of the fiddle. The central arch spotlights this. People sit on the floor at the minstrel's feet, and a monk stands and seizes the candle. The caption reads, "How the candle descended to the fiddle and the monk seized it." The cleric is furious and grasps the candle in one hand while with the other he points to the vacant spot where it was moments before. The hands and faces of the listeners indicate confusion.

Panel 3, whose caption reads, "How the monk returned the candle to its place and tied it," shows in the first arch the minstrel still standing and playing, while in the second arch the monk, still surrounded by sitting people, is engaged in tying the candle to the candlestick. His fingers seem to move very realistically. The artists are particularly apt in this depiction. In panel 4, "How the candle descended to him again and the monk wanted to seize it," we see under the central arch people now standing around the monk and arguing with him. One man actually reaches for the candle which the monk holds, and various fingers are shaken in his face.

Panel 5, "How the monk begged the minstrel to pardon him," is a moving illumination. In the first arch, bareheaded men and women with hats, kneeling in colorful robes, complement the minstrel's pink; the second arch frames the minstrel, vigorously playing, with the monk prostrate at his feet; and the right-hand arch depicts again Our Lady's image on its altar of brilliant tiles. The faces of all present—the minstrel's, the monk's, the people's—are serious. In the last

panel, the caption runs, "How the minstrel brought every year a candle to Holy Mary." Kneeling worshippers, both men and women, fill the left-hand arch; the middle arch frames the minstrel, still in his pink cape and blue robe, but with a white kerchief holding his hair in place as he kneels to set a candle "the height of a man" in a lovely silver candlestick at the foot of the altar.

All the elements of brief narrative are well depicted, particularly action, scene, and characterization. The minstrel is a model of pious devotion, while the monk's cantankerousness is most evident. Stubborn to a fault, he clings to his resolve to prevent the candle from alighting on the fiddle. It is only when the people say, "We will not permit you to do this," that he is driven to realize his error.

In *Cantiga 18,* of most unusual content, dumb animals respect the Blessed Virgin and do her will. The miracle has definite literary quality and should be read *in toto* before studying the iconography.

## CANTIGA 18

*This is how Holy Mary made the silkworms spin two wimples, because the lady who kept them had promised Her one and had not given it to Her.*

It pleases Holy Mary to perform Her beautiful miracles each day in order to free us from doubt.

To prove Her worth to us, She performed a great miracle in Extremadura, in the city of Segovia, where dwelt a lady who produced much silk in her home.

The lady lost some of her silkworms and had little silk. Therefore she promised to give a length of silk for a wimple to honor the statue of the Peerless Virgin, in whom she fervently believed, which was on the altar.

As soon as she made the promise, the silkworms thrived and did not die. But the lady became negligent about her promise and kept forgetting to give the silk for the wimple.

Then it happened that on the great feast in August, she came to pray before the statue at midday. While she knelt in prayer, she remembered the silk cloth she owed. Weeping in repentance, she ran home and saw the silkworms working diligently to make the cloth. Then she began to weep with happiness.

When she stopped weeping, she examined the cloth. Then she called in many people so that they could come to see how the Mother of God could weave with miraculous skill. The people, when they saw it, praised the Mother of God with great joy and went out into the streets shouting: "Come see the great miracle which She who is our guide has performed!"

One by one and two by two they came quickly to the place and saw. Meanwhile, the silkworms made another wimple, so that there might be a pair, and if someone wished to take one of them, there would be another left.

Therefore, King Don Alfonso, as I learned, brought the

more beautiful of them to his chapel. On holy days, he has it brought out to eradicate heresy in those who foolishly doubt the Virgin.

Panel 1 of Plate 36, "How the woman begged Holy Mary to cure the silkworms and that she would give Her a wimple in return," sets the stage.[45] So brief in incident is this miracle that it reminds one of a short dramatic piece, since each arch in each panel spotlights action. The large cusped arches in panels 3 and 4 are especially interesting in that behind them, and therefore some distance deeper into the picture than the arches themselves, rises a column supporting another arch which fans outward and upward to support a vaulted ceiling not visible. Panel 1 is interesting also because it contains iconographical devices not often seen in the illuminations of the *Cantigas:* the caption runs beyond the space allotted it and ends within the panel itself on the white wall against which the action is set. We see here an unusual linkage between verbalization and visualization, since the former is literally painted into the latter. The eye quickly passes over the small arch to the left, in which the images of the Madonna and Child appear on a brilliantly tiled altar. These figures should be examined closely, for later in the illuminations they change their position and postures. In panel 1, the Child stands on the arm of the Virgin's throne, places his arms around her neck, and snuggles his face close to hers, while her face, turned toward his, seems about to bestow a kiss. In panels 5 and 6 the Virgin faces the viewer, and the Infant Jesus sits on her lap and faces in the same direction. The reasons for these differences provide food for thought. Were models used, models who have tired as painting proceeded, or who forgot how they had posed on different days? Or did the artists sketch religious dramatic productions in action, depicting actors in different postures.

Panel 1 under its large right-hand arch reveals a woman kneeling before the altar of the Virgin and holding toward the image a large, shallow dish filled with sick silkworms. Now, silkworms are small, no larger than one's little finger, and if painted to scale would not have been identifiable. The artists therefore painted them as large as good-sized sausages, but they have not deviated otherwise from the correct physiological depiction of silkworms. The woman, as the caption indicates, asks for the Virgin's help and promises the wimple. She holds the tray in one hand and with the other beseeches Our Lady. The dish of worms is held with its opening toward the viewer, with the rim of the dish perpendicular to the floor so as to reveal its contents. If it were held in the normal posi-

tion, the worms would not be visible. This device in secular iconography is also common in Alfonso's *Book of Chess, Dice and Backgammon,* in which the boards are presented on their edges and made to reveal the various aspects of these games. It is a normal medieval arrangement for showing an object in its most characteristic aspect.

In panel 2 the caption again runs into the illumination, and states, "How, being before Her altar, she remembered the wimple she had promised Holy Mary and was troubled because of it." The verbalization states that much later she again visited the church and remembered her promise. We see her homeward bound. Folds in her long robe and a slight indication of limbs in motion make it plain that she is walking rapidly. The images of the Virgin and Her Son under their arch have not altered their positions.

Panel 3, whose entire action unfolds beneath a large cusped arch, depicts the miracle in progress. The caption is, "How the woman went home and saw the worms were making a wimple." She kneels before the long trays or shelves on which the worms live and feed on bright green mulberry leaves, whose outlines are clearly delineated, even to the veins. The trays seem to stand on end to reveal their contents, and again we have an example of the artistic device of showing that part of an object that is most characteristic of it. The artists must certainly have visited a silkworm establishment to gather their information and to sketch from living models, but one more example of the thoroughness required by the king as he directed the preparation of the illuminations. Since the trays are turned to the viewer, we can see a group of fourteen worms busily weaving a wimple. Beneath, some dozen other worms lie entangled, waiting to begin similar work, since we are to see a second wimple under construction in the next panel. The unoccupied worms foreshadow the action, then, of the following panel. Even their legs and pseudopods can be seen perfectly clearly.

Panel 4 relies on the device of double action. In the small arch to the left appears the woman, identifiable by a peak on the back of her headgear, hands gesticulating, as she tells people in the street about the miracle. And under the large cusped arch, a group of kneeling men stares in fascination at the trays where the original team of worms has finished its wimple and the second team is hard at work. The caption, part of which is on the wall here, as in panels 1 and 2, reads, "How she ran into the street to call the people, and the worms commenced to make another wimple."

In panel 5, whose caption reads, "How the woman

gave to the friars the wimples made," three arches contain the scene. On the left are the Madonna and Child, their images now in different poses. Two priests stand under an arch to receive the wimples, while in the third arch the woman extends one to them, and another woman stands behind her. Panel 6 is of special interest, for in it appears King Alfonso himself. The caption reads, "How King Alfonso took one to hang in his chapel." He stands holding one side of this wimple, while with his left hand he seems to trace a design he sees on it. Indeed, on this wimple, obviously the finer, one can dimly make out figures human or divine, a matter never pointed out before, which reveals that the artists went far beyond the statement that the king chose the more beautiful for his chapel. He chose, according to the miniature, the one worked in miraculous figures by the worms, or perhaps illuminated by Our Lady herself. Actually this in itself is a miracle, so *Cantiga 18* may be unique in that there is a miracle within a miracle in its illuminations. Alfonso's face is lifted to view the cloth as he holds it up, and there is expression here as well as on the faces of the two priests and the bystanders.

Color in this page lies in the scarlet and blue roseates of the frieze, in the bright tiles of the altar, and in the colorful garments of the people, especially Alfonso's, and in the gold of his crown and of the arches. In the lower margin across the full width of the illumination run lines of Castilian prose rather than the usual Galician, which summarize the poetic rendition of the miracle. The same is true of the illuminated pages for miracles 2 through 25. These lines have been transcribed and are available for study.[46]

There is little need to dwell upon the nine components of the classic design as these are reflected in the panels of *Cantiga 18,* for by now they must be obvious to the careful viewer. All nine are represented.

The illuminations of *Cantiga 144* may be the first depiction of a Spanish bullfight, or at least of a bull baiting. Stories of animals in the *Cantigas* seem especially, even remarkably, able to evoke emotions of tenderness in the viewer. This story contains considerable suspense.

## CANTIGA 144

*How Holy Mary saved a good man in Plasencia from death by a bull which came at him to kill him.*

It is only right that the beasts have great fear of the Mother of that Lord who has power over all things.

Concerning this, Holy Mary, the Peerless Virgin, performed a great miracle in Plasencia, as I heard it told by good and reliable men.

They recount this miracle thus: a good man lived there who loved this Lady above all things, as I learned.

Whenever anyone would come to him to ask something for Her sake he at once granted it to him without fail, with no delay or deceit, for he would not for anything go back on his word.

He fasted faithfully on the eve of all Her holy days and never failed to hear Her holy hours, for his only thought was of how to please Her.

Then a knight from that city was married and he had bulls brought for his wedding. He selected the fiercest of them and set it running

in a large park which is there in front of the house of the aforementioned good man, but the latter didn't choose to go over there to see it.

However, this man had a companion who was a priest, Matthew by name, who sent for him, as I learned, because he wished to discuss some things with him.

So the man went out to go there and the bull lunged at him to wound him treacherously by thrusting his horns through his back.

The priest, when he saw this from a window, asked mercy of Holy Mary, and She did not fail him, for She came to his aid at once.

She aided him in such a way that the bull fell down on the ground and stretched out all four legs, as though he was about to die.

He lay in this manner until the man was at the entrance of his friend's house. His friend received him warmly and took him into the house.

The bull got up and from then on never did he harm anyone, because of the power of the Matchless Lady, who will not let Her servants come to grief.

Few *cantigas* offer more of local color and daily life, more action, and a better presentation of the nine components of short story. In Plate 37, the caption of panel 1 reads, "How a man trusted greatly in Holy Mary and always praised her." Three golden arches frame the incidents. The left-hand one contains nothing save a door, but the center arch reveals the devoted gentleman who "never failed to hear Her holy hours" as he kneels and prays, his hands raised and his eyes fixed on the images of the Madonna and Child in the right-hand arch. Above him rises a beautiful line of rooftops, which achieves depth with great success, and a strange blue column, or perhaps a very narrow tower, figured in swirling white arabesques, rising between the left-hand arch and the central arch. The man is fashionably and elegantly dressed in a deep blue cape with a red gown beneath it, sports a fine red cap, and wears a black beard neatly trimmed to follow the line of his jaw.

Panel 2, whose caption reads, "How he gave his money to anyone who asked him for it out of love for

Holy Mary," is unusual in that the artists omitted certain elements of scenic background. The pilgrim is outlined starkly against empty space as he receives money from the hand of the devotee, who stands in a doorway formed by two black columns supporting a Roman arch arranged with alternating blue and red tiles or bricks set in white mortar. He has apparently just drawn the money from a golden purse with a long fringe and is handing it to the pilgrim, who receives it gratefully.

Panel 3, "How they fought a bull at the wedding celebration which a knight was holding," depicts possibly the earliest rendition of a Spanish bullfight.[47] No one is bold enough to face the bull in the plaza where the baiting is held, but instead the people remain on the safety of the rooftop and hurl over the carved balustrade either darts or spears attached to ropes which may be pulled out of the bull's hide and cast at him again. One dart seems about to bury itself between the animal's horns, which sprout from a growth of dense curls. This is a noble bull, powerfully muscled, and made ferocious and grim by the torture inflicted upon it. Panel 4, "How the bull charged at the good man in order to wound him and Holy Mary came to his aid," is filled with action par excellence, for the bull is indeed in full charge with lowered horns. People throw more spears as the man flees toward the door of the house of his friend, a cleric, who can be seen in an archway above, praying to Holy Mary to save him.

In panel 5, "How the bull fell to the earth, stretched out as though dead," the artists manage most skillfully to portray a bull lying prone, its muzzle on the ground, a posture no bull ever assumed. People on the roof gaze in wonder, and no one continues to molest the poor animal. The face of the priest is no longer in the arch above. Panel 6, "How the bull got up and never afterwards tried to do any harm to anyone," reveals him on his feet, his muzzle actually touching one man's hand, while the fellow pats his head and another man his back. The legs of the bystanders, who have left the rooftop vacant, form an interesting and artistic pattern of black and white. The archway above, in which the cleric had prayed, is now empty, and the artists have depicted with delightful clarity a trail of fleecy clouds framed by the arch, creating a true sense of depth and perspective. A white cloud as a symbol of the Blessed Virgin was well known in the Middle Ages.[48]

*Cantiga 107* may be historical, since the niche of the protagonist can be seen today in Spain. This is also one of the best of the miracles which deal with the Jews of Alfonso's realm.

## CANTIGA 107

*How Holy Mary saved from death in Segovia the Jewess who was thrown over a cliff. Because she commended herself to Holy Mary, she did not suffer harm.*

The Holy Virgin will aid those in distress if they believe in Her.

Concerning this, the Mother of Mercy performed a miracle, in all truth in that city of Segovia, as this song will relate.

It was for a Jewess who was caught in a crime and arrested and taken to be hurled from a high and rugged cliff in that place.

She said: "Oh, woe is me, how can anyone who falls from here remain alive unless it is by God's will?

But you, Queen Mary, in whom Christians believe, if it is true, as I have heard,

that you succor the unfortunate women who are commended to you among all the other guilty women, come to my aid, for I have great need.

If I remain alive and well, I shall, without fail, become a Christian before another day dawns."

The Jews who led her, dressed only in her chemise, let go of her and pushed her over the cliff, shouting, "There she goes!"

But when she fell from there, the Virgin came to her aid. Therefore she did not perish, but fell clear of the rocks

right at the foot of a fig tree. She sprang nimbly up and went on her way, saying:

"May the Glorious One, precious Mother of God, who was so merciful to me, be ever praised. Who will not serve her?"

She arrived at the church of Her who should always be blessed, where she saw a great crowd of people, and she said:

"Come at once and baptize me, then you shall hear of a miracle which will astound all who hear it!"

Those people baptized her without delay and she was henceforth always a devoted believer in Her who prays

to Her glorious Son for us, that He have mercy on us on the fearful day when He comes to judge us.

The long title virtually tells the story of the Jewess who later in legend would be called Mari Saltos. Her crypt with a lead placque over it can be seen today in the wall of the cloister of Segovia's cathedral and above it a fresco of the miracle in progress, though it differs from the illuminations of the *Cantigas* and is of later vintage.[49]

Panel 1 of Plate 38, "How they arrested a Jewess of Segovia who was caught in a crime," shows the woman surrounded by citizens, at least one of whom is a Jew, to judge by the artists' characteristic caricature of his nose. A mounted officer of the law suggests the idea of her arrest for whatever unspecified crime she has committed. A distant arch is seen behind the woman. Above the heads of the people extends a series of tile roofs and towers depicting realistically the irregular and haphazard topography of medieval Segovia.

Panel 2, "How they led her to be cast down from a high cliff which was there," shows her on the way but certainly not at the site of execution, for we see in the background, in order to make it quite clear that the city is indeed Segovia, the great Roman aqueduct of the city (though one cannot but wonder how the artists could have painted it with key-hole arches rather than with the Roman ones it ought to have). The woman is now in the hands of Jews, as the verbalization states and as the faces of her captors, with greatly exaggerated noses, make quite plain. Some push her roughly along as she resists. In the left background the corner of the city's wall retreats into the distance, another attempt at diagonal perspective. The colorful robes of the men provide interesting contrast with the Jewess's white gown.

Panel 3, "How they cast her down and no harm was done because she called out 'Holy Mary,' " depicts her falling headlong, against the dark background of the stony cliff, brightened here and there by brilliant blossoms. A very tall fig tree enables the artists to impart the conception of great height. Even in midair she steeples her hands in adoration. The six Jews who have thrown her from the clifftop stand gleefully and watch her fall. One points with his hand as they cry, "There she goes!"

Panel 4, "How she got up unhurt, praising Holy Mary for it," shows the Jewess standing near the fig tree, her hands together devoutly in prayer and raised high toward the Virgin, who can be seen giving her benediction from the clouds. The Jews on the cliff point or throw their hands up in amazement. The dark cliff, the green tree, the blue sky, the many-hued blossoms, and the white chemise of the Jewess produce one of the most colorful scenes in the *Cantigas* and some of its most lively action.

Panel 5, "How she entered the church of Holy Mary and told the people about the miracle," reveals the woman under a large cusped arch, one hand pointing toward the image of the Virgin on its altar, the other, index finger upward, explaining what has occurred. The Christians have fallen to their knees under a smaller arch. The Jewess's face is keen, the people's rapt. At the right is the image of the Virgin on a bright tiled altar. Panel 6 reads, "How the Jewess turned Christian." Under a large golden arch at the left, the Jewess sits in a font whose rim covers her lower extremities. She folds her hands in prayer as a priest pours baptismal water over her from a large pitcher. Three Christian ladies are her sponsors in baptism, and they stand opposite the priest.

*Cantiga 108* tells a terrible story to demonstrate how Holy Mary punishes those who oppose her. The story is set in Scotland and concerns a Jew named Cayphas and Merlin, the son of Satan.[50]

## CANTIGA 108

*How Holy Mary caused the son of the Jew to be born with his head on backwards, as Merlin had asked of Her.*

It is befitting that he who opposes Holy Mary should suffer grave consequences.

Concerning this, I heard tell that Merlin chanced to be discoursing with a Jewish sage who, as I was told, had no equal in learning in all of Scotland.

That treacherous Jew began to speak of the Virgin and to swear by the name of the Creator that Our Lord did not choose to become incarnate in Her nor could it be so.

Merlin was sorely troubled when he heard him say this, and he said: "God help me, but indeed it could be, for He who created land and sea by His great power could certainly do it!"

The Jew began to argue and said: "God could never enter into such a place, it stands to reason, for how could He who contains so many things be contained?"

Merlin began to get angry and then and there got down on his knees and said: "Oh, Mother of Him who came to save us, this man is saying things about you that he should not.

Therefore, as I know for certain that He truly was your Son, I pray to you to reveal what I ask of you now to this false believer who persists in his madness.

He has gotten his wife with child, so I beg you to cause the son who will be born to him to have his countenance not facing forward, as others have, but looking backward, and that he always be that way."

The time came for the Jewess to give birth. Well might anyone who saw that child of hers cross himself in fear, for God caused him to be born as Merlin in his ire had prayed of Him.

God made the child's face to turn backward, as Satan's son had asked of Him, in order to shame the child's father, Cayphas, who did not believe what he told him.

Therefore, the father tried to kill the baby as soon as he was born. But Merlin saved him, for he well knew how it had come about. When the child grew older, Merlin used him to convert the Jews in order to lead them from their erroneous belief.

Panel 1 of Plate 39, "How Merlin argues with a Jewish sage concerning Holy Mary," depicts an archless scene with an open door at the far left and a tile roof above the entire scene. Merlin argues vehemently with the Jew, behind whom are two arched sets of shelves inset into the wall displaying vials and jars, for the Jew is a scientist also. The table is covered with a fringed cloth worked in arabesques. The Jew, with a most exaggerated nose, shakes a long finger at Merlin, who replies also by gesturing. His face is irate, for he scowls darkly. In panel 2, "How Merlin prayed to Holy Mary that the son of the Jew be born with his head on backwards," reveals the same scene as in panel 1, but now Merlin is on his knees, his back to the Jew, making his awful request to Our Lady, while the Jew gesticulates.

Panel 3, "How the son of the Jew was born with his head on backward just as Merlin said," shows a terrible scene. In it appears the Jewish mother who has just been delivered of a baby deformed as Merlin has prayed it would be. Clearly visible is the little head looking backward over the child's shoulders with its arms, legs, and torso pointed in a normal way. The mother's hands speak eloquently of her horror and grief, as do those of the midwives in attendance. Curtains on rods and pulls form a beige background to the bed, with its red and blue counterpane and mattress. In panel 4, "How the Jew tried to kill that son of his and Merlin took the child from him," portrays the Jew, his hands outstretched in rage, his great beak of a nose silhouetted massively against the background, his face a mask of hatred and fury as he confronts Merlin, who angrily grasps the collar of the Jew's cloak. A Jewess, no doubt the mother of the unfortunate infant, stands behind the father, her hands raised to her cheeks in grief or consternation. The baby's face stares toward the viewer over his bare buttocks in mute testimony to his deformity.

Panel 5, "How Merlin converted the Jews with the little Jewish boy," is divided into three arches in a Christian church with many golden lamps. Under the left-hand arch stands a rabbi shaking his finger in the direction of Merlin, who is beneath the arch at the right. In the central arch, sitting on the floor, are many Jews watching Merlin as he uses his right hand to emphasize what he is saying, while his left rests on the head of the malformed Jewish boy, who has now reached adolescence. Like other Jews he is depicted as having an exaggerated nose, in this case one that is large and bulbous. In panel 6, "How they baptized the Jews whom Merlin converted with the little Jewish boy," two golden arches, both cusped, contain the action. In the left stands a large font with a naked Jewess sitting in it as the priest pours water over her head from a ewer. Christian ladies stand as sponsors in baptism. In the right-hand arch appears the usual altar of the Virgin, and there another Christian watches.

The few illuminations we offer are, of course, but a fraction of the many in the *Cantigas de Santa Maria*. The illuminated volumes which illustrate the miracles contain a vast world of untouched and barely studied materials and offer opportunities for research in many areas.[51]

Plate 1. Alfonso X with his scribes and musicians. From the Prologue to the *Cantigas de Santa Maria,* ms. T.I.j (Escorial). Authorized by the Patrimonio Nacional, Madrid; reproduced from the facsimile edition of EDILAN.

Plate 2. *Cantiga 42*, "How the postulant placed the ring on the finger of the statue of Holy Mary and the statue curved its finger around it." Authorized by the Patrimonio Nacional, Madrid; reproduced from the facsimile edition of EDILAN.

Plate 3. *Cantiga 29*, panel 5.

Plate 4. *Cantiga 33*, panel 2.

Plate 5. *Cantiga 175*, panel 4.

Plate 6. *Cantiga 148*, panel 5.

Plate 7. *Cantiga 124*, panel 6.

Plate 8. *Cantiga 189*, panel 1.

Plate 9. *Cantiga 186*, panel 2.

Plate 10. *Cantiga 3*, panel 2.

Plate 11. *Cantiga 175*, panel 2 (of second page).

Plate 12. *Cantiga 167*, panel 5.

Plate 13. *Cantiga 26*, panel 4.

Plate 14. *Cantiga 72*, panel 4.

Plate 15. *Cantiga 63,* "How Holy Mary saved from disgrace a knight who was to be in battle in San Esteban de Gormaz." Authorized by the Patrimonio Nacional, Madrid; reproduced from the facsimile edition of EDILAN.

Plate 16. *Cantiga 34*, panel 1.

Plate 17. *Cantiga 144*, panel 6.

Plate 18. *Cantiga 59*, panel 3.

Plate 19. *Cantiga 60*, panel 2.

Plate 20. *Cantiga 46*, panel 6.

Plate 21. *Cantiga 22*, panel 4.

Plate 23. *Cantiga 76*, panel 1.

Plate 24. *Cantiga 181*, panel 1.

Plate 22. David and Goliath, from the Biblia Romanica
(Colegiata de San Isidro, Leon).

Plate 25. *Cantiga 9*, panel 4.

Plates 23-25. Authorized by the Patrimonio Nacional, Madrid;
reproduced from the facsimile edition of EDILAN.

Plate 26. *Cantiga 74,* "How Holy Mary saved the painter whom the devil tried to kill because he painted him ugly."

Plate 27. *Cantiga 65,* panel 2 (of second page).

Plate 28. *Cantiga 64,* panel 4.

Authorized by the Patrimonio Nacional, Madrid; reproduced from the facsimile edition of EDILAN.

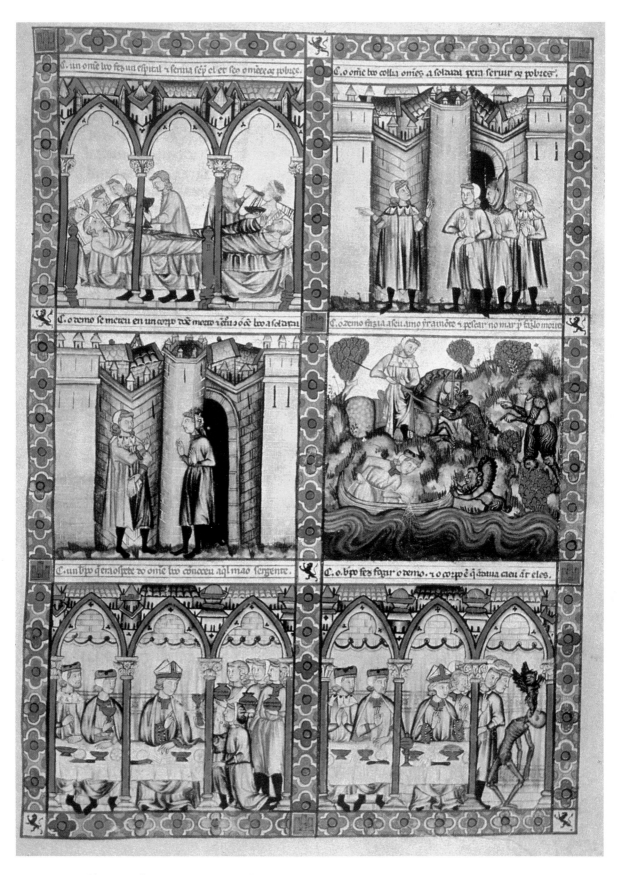

Plate 29. *Cantiga 67*, "How Holy Mary caused the good man to realize that he had the devil as his servant." Authorized by the Patrimonio Nacional, Madrid; reproduced from the facsimile edition of EDILAN.

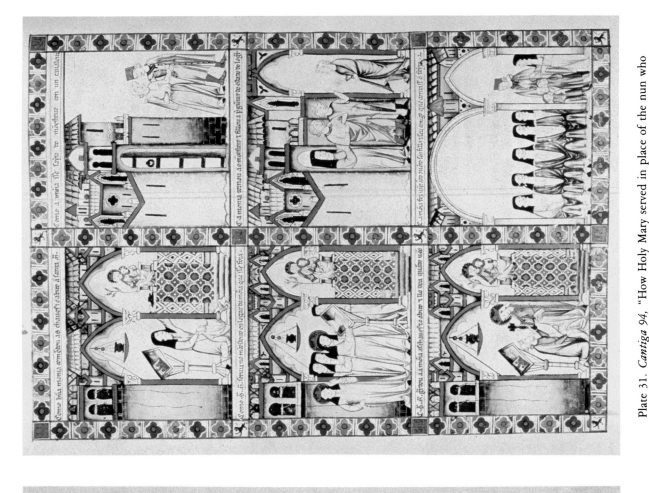

Plate 31. *Cantiga 94*, "How Holy Mary served in place of the nun who left the convent." Authorized by the Patrimonio Nacional, Madrid; reproduced from the facsimile edition of EDILAN.

Plate 30. *Cantiga 142*, "How Holy Mary saved from death one of the King's men who had entered a river to retrieve a heron." Authorized by the Patrimonio Nacional, Madrid; reproduced from the facsimile edition of EDILAN.

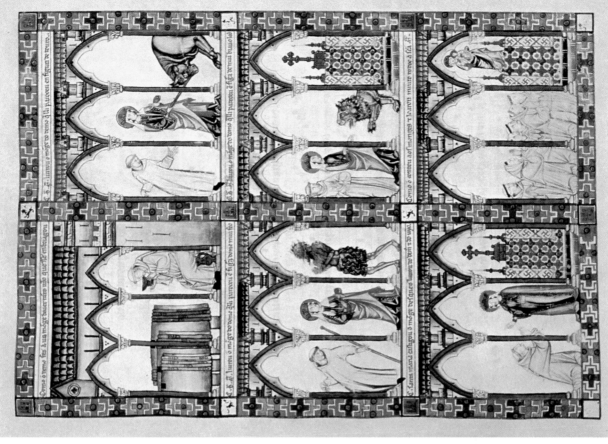

Plate 33. *Cantiga 47*, "How Holy Mary saved the monk whom the devil tried to frighten in order to seize his soul." Authorized by the Patrimonio Nacional, Madrid; reproduced from the facsimile edition of EDILAN.

Plate 32. *Cantiga 209*, "How King Alfonso of Castile fell ill in Victoria. . . . They laid the Book of the Canticles of Holy Mary upon him and he was cured." From Banco Rari ms., courtesy of the Biblioteca Nazionale, Florence.

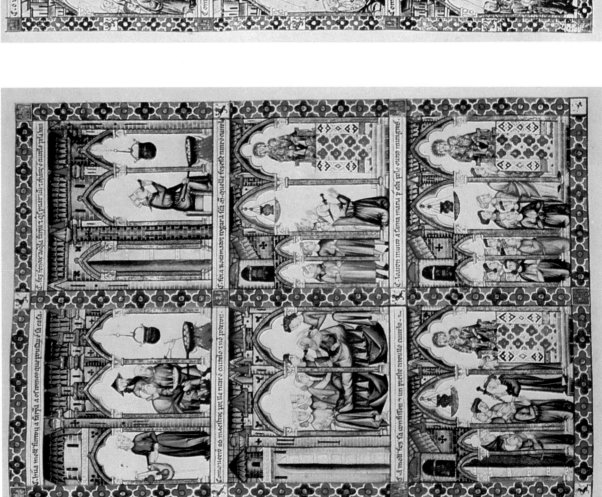

Plate 34. *Cantiga 157*, "How some pilgrims . . . took lodging in a town and the landlady stole some of the meal they were carrying." Authorized by the Patrimonio Nacional, Madrid; reproduced from the facsimile edition of EDILAN.

Plate 35. *Cantiga 8*, "How Holy Mary caused a candle to descend to the fiddle of a minstrel who sang before Her." Authorized by the Patrimonio Nacional, Madrid; reproduced from the facsimile edition of EDILAN.

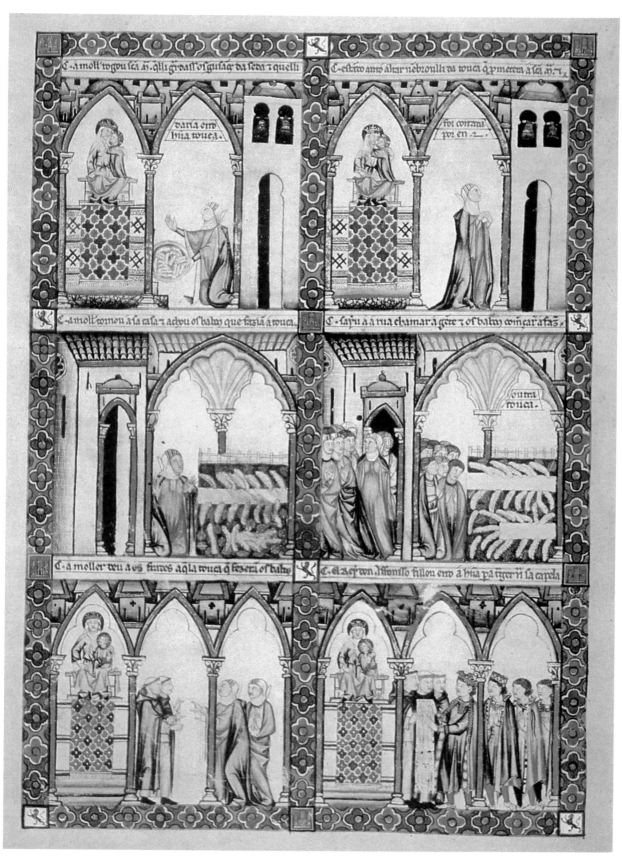

Plate 36. *Cantiga 18*, "How Holy Mary made the silkworms spin two wimples."
Authorized by the Patrimonio Nacional, Madrid; reproduced from the facsimile edition of EDILAN.

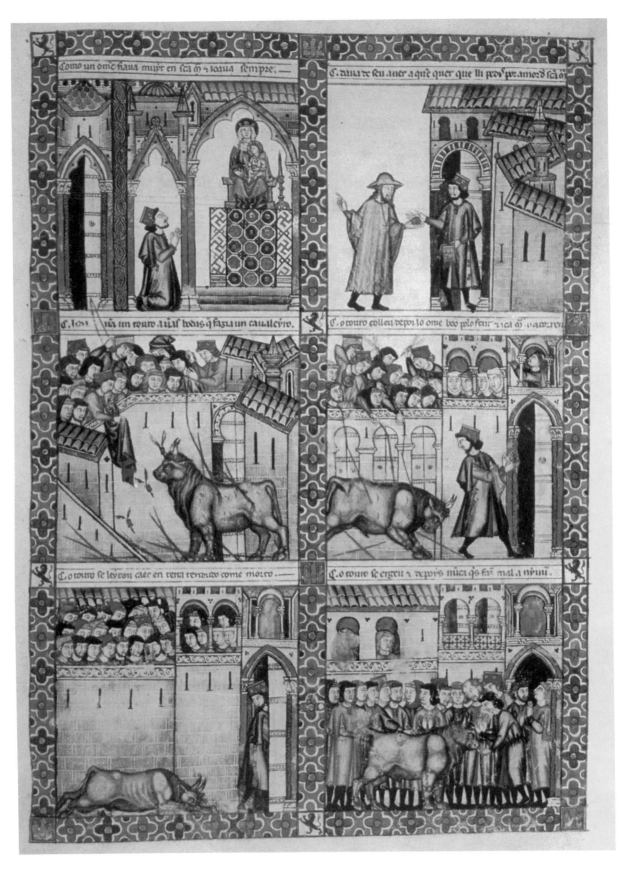

Plate 37. *Cantiga 144,* "How Holy Mary saved a good man in Plasencia from death by a bull which came at him to kill him." Authorized by the Patrimonio Nacional, Madrid; reproduced from the facsimile edition of EDILAN.

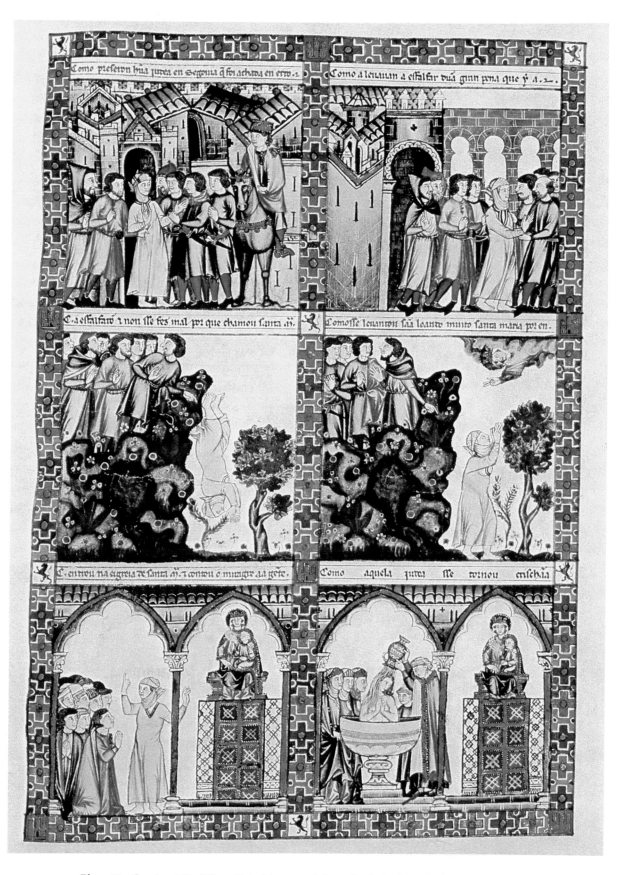

Plate 38. *Cantiga 107*, "How Holy Mary saved from death in Segovia the Jewess who was thrown over a cliff." Authorized by the Patrimonio Nacional, Madrid; reproduced from the facsimile edition of EDILAN.

Plate 39. *Cantiga 108*, "How Holy Mary caused the son of the Jew to be born with his head on backwards, as Merlin had asked of her." Authorized by the Patrimonio Nacional, Madrid; reproduced from the facsimile edition of EDILAN.

# El libro de Calila e Digna

n the year 1261, if we may believe the *explicit* in one of the extant manuscripts, a famous collection of eastern tales was translated into Castilian at the behest of Alfonso X, the Learned. In all probability the translation was carried out in 1251, since Alfonso is referred to therein as prince, not king. He was crowned in 1252. The ten-year error is probably attributable to scribal carelessness in a later transcription. Be that as it may, Alfonso caused the corpus of eastern stories known in Arabic as *Kalila wa-Dimna* to be translated into Castilian. The peculiar title is derived from the names of two jackals, who are the protagonists of about a third of the episodes in the book, which is divided into several lengthy novelesque sequences.

The thirteenth century was an age in which Arabic works were in great vogue and enjoyed many translations, since the West understood the value of eastern science, history, philosophy, and fiction. A year after the translation of *Kalilah wa-Dimna*, known in Spanish as *Calila e Digna*, Alfonso's colorful and treacherous brother, Fadrique, caused another eastern collection of tales to be rendered into Spanish, the *Book of Sindibad*, translated as the *Libro de los engaños e assayamientos de las mugeres*, or *The Book of the Wiles of Women*.[1] In the next century, Alfonso's nephew, the Infante Don Juan Manuel, would recast many Arabic stories, surely some from *Calila e Digna,* and include them in his famous collection of moral tales and aphorisms, *El Conde Lucanor.*[2] Still another member of the royal family, Alfonso's son and successor, Sancho IV, sponsored a dial of princes into which he inserted a number of exemplary tales in a composition he called

*Castigos e documentos para bien vivir*, a book to serve as a guide to his son, whose title we translate as *Teachings and Treatises for Good Living.*[3] It was the style in the thirteenth century to translate and in the fourteenth to recast stories from the East, and certainly in Castile it was almost a royal custom for two generations.

The story of the migration of the collection of narratives that was to become *Calila e Digna* in Castilian is too long to be related here in detail. Suffice it to say that in India around the middle of the third century of our era a miscellany of fables and short stories was assembled and entitled the *Panchatantra.* Many of these tales came from Buddhist fable lore and from the folklore of the Indian people. Sometime around the year 550 the entire *Panchatantra* was translated into Pahlevi, or Old Persian. Before two centuries had passed, many additional stories had gravitated to this famous collection, and the resulting work, also in Persian, came to be known by the names of the two jackals. It was translated into Arabic probably around 750 and, given the dominance of the Arabic language and culture at that time, found its way fairly early into Greek and Latin and thence, at least from Latin, into most of the languages of the western world.

Since Spain fell under Moorish domination in 711, we believe that the Arabic translation, *Kalilah wa-Dimna*, reached Spain not long after the Conquest. In Spain its stories were enjoyed just as they had been in the Middle East and for the same reasons. It was a wisdom book, but at the same time a work written for the pleasure of reading and, like the famous *Don Quixote*, held some attraction for everyone from sage to simpleton. Proof of this, at least insofar as the

*Panchatantra* is concerned, may be found in the literatures of virtually every nation in the East, from Syria and Egypt to Siam and the Philippines. Without the *Panchatantra* and its subsequent recastings in other languages and cultures, there could have been no *Thousand Nights and a Night*, no *Decameron*, no *Pentameron*, no *Disciplina Clericalis*,[4] in the form in which we read them today, and many other books would be the poorer—*The Canterbury Tales*, the *Quixote*, Grimm's *Fairy Tales,* those of Hans Christian Anderson, La Fontaine, Timoneda, and Samaniego and Iriarte, as well as the folktales of many nations, even our own in Appalachia.[5] Though Alfonso could not have known this, he was aware of the importance of *Kalila wa-Dimna* in the eastern world, which he respected, and it is not surprising that he caused it to be translated. Later reworkings came into Spanish from Latin, but the first complete edition was Alfonso's and it stemmed directly from the Arabic. Indeed, today Arabic scholars use the Spanish translation to fill in lacunae found in some Arabic versions.[6]

The two complete extant copies in Castilian are written in hands which betray a later date than the thirteenth century. One of these, a fourteenth-century codex known as MS h.iii.9 of the Biblioteca Nacional, attributes the book to Prince Alfonso and contains some seventy-eight miniatures in the form of line drawings together with 16 drawings of geometrical designs. This manuscript measures 278 by 193 millimeters, or 10.94 inches high by 7.59 inches wide. Individual line drawings vary in size, but none occupies more than a small part of the page. The other copy unfortunately has no illustrations. It is a pity that the famous *Libro de los engaños*, sponsored by King Alfonso's brother, Prince Fadrique, likewise lacks them.

The Spanish versions, albeit translations, offer all the various eastern narrative techniques of story telling, especially the so-called "Chinese box" presentation of a tale within a tale. *Calila e Digna*, like its eastern ancestors in Sanskrit, Persian, and Arabic, is an interrelated series of novelesque stories containing many shorter interpolated tales which serve to illustrate moral points or lessons of a more practical variety made in the primary narrative. The modern reader can easily lose track of which character belongs to which tale, but apparently in the East this difficulty did not arise, nor indeed did it seem to deter readers in medieval Spain.

Though we may be criticized for lack of scholarly modesty, we have perforce followed the transcription of John E. Keller and Robert W. Linker, since it is the only edition which both reproduces all the miniatures

and offers the running text of the two extant manuscripts. Therefore, when we refer to the number of a story or illustration, we refer to this critical edition, at once the most recent and most easily available.

In order to follow the line drawings, some understanding of the content of *Calila e Digna* is necessary. Therefore, as we discuss narrative techniques in visualization, we shall also offer a brief summation of the stories themselves. The Spanish version, following its Arabic source, opens with an allegorical introduction and two chapters describing the journey of a Persian doctor, who at the behest of his king travels to India and brings back the book we know as the *Panchatantra*.[7] All the interpolated tales in this section are from non-Indian sources, and they contain no visualized narratives, only two drawings—both of the king and the doctor. The other illustrations first appear in Chapter III and are quite numerous.

Chapters III and IV, which we shall summarize here, contain the framework narrative from which the title of the work is derived: There live in a thick forest a lion and his menage, two of whom, both jackals, Calila and Digna, are hangers-on, ever interested in bettering themselves and rising to power by advising and flattering the lion. When some merchants leave a wounded bull named Senceba in the forest, he recovers and, rejoicing in his newfound strength, bellows so loudly that the lion and his court are alarmed. The jackal Digna manages to bring the bull to the lion's court, where he allays the monarch's fear and unwittingly allows the bull to become the lion's favorite. Jealous of the bull who has displaced them in the King's favor, the two jackals, led by Digna, succeed in turning their monarch against the new favorite by a clever strategem. The lion slays the bull but soon discovers the deceit. Digna is tried and executed, while Calila dies of grief and shame. No doubt a satire on the courts of eastern kings and the villainy of ambitious courtiers, it is a tale which would nonetheless have been appropriate in any society where monarchs ruled. Apparently its universal appeal derives as much from its interesting utilization of animals with human foibles as from its obvious moralization and consequent exaltation of good over evil.

In the course of their dialogue with each other, these talking animals resort to moral examples and sententious narrative in order to emphasize their point or convince their opponents in carefully argued speech. Truth to tell, the interpolated stories, perhaps more than the novelesque sequences which contain them, possess an attractiveness and literary quality which is in many ways superior to the framework narratives, and the fact that these short tales exercised in time a greater influence upon literature than did the longer narratives is undisputed.

We may now turn to the line drawings, small enough certainly to be termed miniatures, which illustrate the most interesting of the two texts. Early Indian versions were probably illustrated, just as many modern versions of the *Panchatantra* are today. Most modern Persian and Arabic versions also contain pictures, but it is doubtful the Arabic texts from which *Calila e Digna* is derived had illustrations. In any case, the Koran forbade pictorial representations of both men and beasts, and Spanish Islam was perhaps more conservative than the somewhat liberal Persian and mideastern areas. The drawings in *Calila e Digna* are, of course, all the work of western, probably Spanish, artists, who apparently had no eastern drawings to emulate. Therefore the illustrations reveal western man's concept of eastern animals, while the human characters, of which there are many, wear the clothing of fourteenth-century Spaniards. (The number following each figure number indicates the number of the picture in the Keller and Linker edition.)

Seventy-eight drawings grace the manuscript, and all possess a kind of winsome elegance. Some simply represent single characters or incidents, (indeed, most are of this variety), but others appear in sequence so that the viewer can see a series of events from an individual story. The interpolated stories are also reflected in the visualized narrative. In a few cases one may even see the teller of the tale and the story he relates.

An example of the most basic and unadorned presentation of characters may be seen in Figure 1, in which appear the lionking and the two jackals before him, while to the right stands Senceba, the bull. Here the animals are enclosed in a simple oblong frame whose interior is bordered by a sober scallop motif. Most drawings, however, have no frame. All the animals here are realistically portrayed and resemble their living counterparts. It even seems that the artists have successfully endowed their subjects with convincing and subtle facial expressions. To us, the lion's visage reveals a benevolent interest, while of the two jackals, the one nearer the viewer, which we believe to be the gentler Calila, manifests interest tempered with respect; the other countenance, that of Digna, belies the animal's open duplicity, as disclosed by a cunning glimpse of his teeth and an eye filled with a definite slyness.

The matter of the species of Calila and Digna has aroused some controversy. In Figure 1 they are ob-

Figure 1 [3]

Figure 2 [10]

viously canine in appearance, but have well defined dorsal spots, which jackals do not. The text here calls them *lobos cervales*, a rather confusing term in both medieval and modern Spanish, since *cerval* can mean lynx, wildcat, or wolf, and may even refer to certain plants. In medieval French the word, or one much like it, also meant lynx, and this we believe may have been responsible for the spots in Figure 1. Because the two beasts were jackals in the eastern versions, we believe they were probably jackals in the Spanish rendition, too, even though in Figure 2 they are portrayed with the heads of cats minus the tufted ears of the lynx. Even here the long, doglike tail is present, and all lynxes, of course, are bobtailed.

One of the stories told by Digna to Calila is that of some trout and a crab, who live peacefully together in a pool and have no care until one day a crane, too old to catch fish successfully, tells them he has overheard several fishermen remark that they plan to seine the pool. The crane offers to carry them individually to a safer body of water, and they agree. Each day he takes a trout or two and flies off toward the other lake, but he always stops on some rocks to eat the fish, leaving only their bones. At last comes the turn of the crab, and the crane flies with him to the same rocks. But when the crab sees the heap of fishbones, he quickly understands the crane's treachery and strangles the bird with his sharp claws. Figures 3 and 4 show two incidents of this story. Each drawing is framed in the usual way when frames are used, but here the bottom frame is formed by water, indicated in a series of wavy lines. The action in Figure 3 is clear: the crane with a trout in its beak is about to take wing while the crab watches. In Figure 4 we see the dénouement, as the crab kills his treacherous enemy.

Figure 3   [12]

Figure 4   [13]

Figure 5   [20]

Figure 6   [21]

Figure 7   [22]

A longer sequence of action appears in the story about the lion king whose friends are a wolf, a jackal, and a raven. When a trusting camel asks to become a member of the menage, the lion accepts him and gives him a guarantee of safety. Unfortunately for the camel, the lion is wounded in a fight with an elephant and can no longer hunt and feed his followers. Therefore the others look about for a strategem to free the lion from his promise of safety to the camel. They hit upon the plan of offering themselves, one by one, to feed their king. Of course, he magnanimously refuses each offer, until it is the camel's turn. When he offers himself, the animals leap upon him and eat him.

Six separate line drawings illustrate this story. In Figure 5 appears Senceba, the bull, in the frame story as he relates to Digna the tale of the lion and his cohorts who trick the innocent camel. Here, then, appears the teller of the tale, who plays no real part in it. Figure 6 reveals the lion and the camel at parley. Obviously the artist had seen a lion and a camel or else a faithful representation of these animals. The lion appears to be speaking, for his mouth seems partially open, and the camel listens attentively, his expression quite as serious as the occasion of the treaty would warrant. Figure 7 depicts a battle between the lion and the elephant. The artist had certainly never seen an elephant, for he drew it here in the fashion of most bestiaries—like a wild boar with an elongated snout, tiny tusks, long tufted tail, and cloven hooves. The two are set against each other pawing the ground as each warily eyes his adversary.

Figure 8 reveals the lion with his vassals, a spotted jackal, a wolf (identical to the jackal in every way save the spots), and a rather diminutive bear. In this miniature the raven is conspicuously absent. The animals are conferring, and it is in this scene that they convince the none-too-willing lion to betray the hapless camel into offering himself as a sacrifice. In Figure 9 we see four animals evidently stating that they will offer themselves to the lion, while the camel, standing to one side, listens. Again the raven is missing.

Figure 10 offers a scene of intense action as the lion leaps upon the prostrate camel, fangs buried deep in his hump. The raven tears at the camel's neck, while the wolf and the jackal eagerly rush upon him. The raven is portrayed in vast disproportion to his true size, for had the artist drawn him to scale he could not have been made to assume the important role he plays. The camel's expression is glum, to say the least, while the raven is avid, the lion eager, the wolf determined, and the jackal apparently satisfied. Viewed in detail, the drawing displays a remarkable degree of agitation on the part of all five animals, heightened by the angle inserted in the upper border, which effectively pushes the animals toward the right-hand side, directing our attention and their action toward the luckless camel. Additional emphasis is provided by the tufts of grass interspersed between the predators and their victim, leaving no doubt in our minds that they have felled their prey, who grovels in an oval-shaped heap, tail tucked under and hooves curled, while his erstwhile friends are fully stretched out, tails flying, eager jaws rapaciously tearing at the camel's flesh.

Figure 8  [23]

Not all the characters in *Calila e Digna*, however, are animals. Two incidents from a bawdy tale serve to illustrate this point. We read that a certain rich merchant has a very beautiful wife who dallies with her neighbor, a painter. One day she tells her friend, "If you could devise something by which I could recognize you when you come into the garden by night, I would come out without your having to call me, and in this way no one would suspect us."

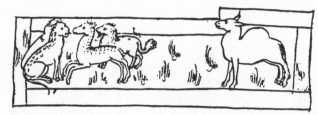

Figure 9  [24]

"I'll make a sheet as bright as the light of the moon and I'll paint on it pictures," he tells her, "and when you see it, you'll come out to me and this will be our sign."

And what he tells her pleases her. But a manservant of hers hears of this arrangement, takes note, and keeps it in his heart. When her paramour is summoned by the king to paint some houses, the lady's vassal goes to a maidservant of the painter who has charge of the sheet, for he is her confidant, and asks her for the sheet, and she lets him have it. Then the servant goes to his mistress at night. When she sees him with the sheet over his head she believes it is her lover and goes out to him, and he lies with her. Then the servant takes the sheet back to the painter's maidservant.

Figure 10  [25]

Later that night the painter comes home from the king's palace, covers himself with the sheet, and goes to his lady. At this she asks, "Why is it that tonight you have come back so quickly, one time right after the other, having already had your pleasure?" The painter understands that he has been duped, and returning to his house he beats his maidservant soundly. Then he takes the sheet and throws it into the fire, and it is consumed forthwith.

Figure 11  [44]

In Figure 11 we find the treacherous wife talking to her lover. She wears fourteenth-century dress, not thirteenth, as we may see from her coiffure. Her swain, too, is dressed in post-thirteenth-century garb. They are conversing intently and touching hands as lovers might. Figure 12 reveals the lady hastening to her supposed paramour by night, as he, covered with a sheet, rushes to embrace her. His hands are raised as though to clasp her to him, and hers are outstretched to meet him. The two drawings alone tell little, but

Figure 12  [45]

Figure 13　[5]

Figure 14　[6]

Figure 15　[8]

Figure 16　[9]

with the written account they form a delightful and droll little tale of adultery and its consequences. Humor is here derived from simplicity itself, both story and illustrations uncomplicated, even laconic, in their straightforward description.

A more complex series appears in the adventure of a mendicant priest who stops to spend the night in the house of a carpenter and his wife. Four drawings portray this ancient rehearsal of the wiles of treacherous wives. The carpenter, suspecting his wife of adultery with a man seen outside their house, has tied her to a pillar inside and has left to get drunk. Her friend, the barber's wife, unties her so that she can go to meet her lover, while she takes her friend's place to confuse the husband should he come home at night, as indeed he does before his wife can resume her place tied to the pillar. The barber's wife, however, will not answer the carpenter when he speaks to her, and in a rage he seizes a knife and cuts off her nose. In Figure 13 we see the carpenter binding his wife to the post, and in Figure 14 he severs the nose from the face of the women he believes to be his wife. Both drawings are gracefully executed, for all the motions needed to tie or cut are naturally depicted. The frames of each incident are especially effective, each giving the impression of depth and space within a central room inside the house where the action occurs by depicting the chamber walls in simple but effective linear perspective.

When the carpenter's errant wife returns and finds her neighbor bleeding and noseless, she unties her and takes her place, her friend returning to her own house with her nose in her hand. The two women now deceive their husbands in different ways so as to explain the innocence of the carpenter's wife and the mutilation of the barber's. The former calls out in the dark and asks God to restore her nose if she is indeed innocent of adultery, and when her husband brings a light, of course her nose is still intact. The barber's wife, with somewhat greater difficulty, manages to lay the blame on her husband. When he calls for his tools, so that he can go to work, she hands him only one, and each time he asks for them, all he received is one. Finally, in anger, he flings a razor in her direction (Figure 15) and she screams that it has cut off her nose. Her relatives hail him into court.

Figure 15 presents another example of double action. The angry husband makes ready to fling the razor while the wife without her nose stands, hands uplifted, apparently crying out in pain, as the implement she alleges has severed her nose falls to the floor. The carpenter's movements and his expression are those of a man in the heat of rage. Figure 16 reveals the barber standing bound before a judge, and beside him the priest who has lodged in his house explains all that has transpired.

The section of *Calila e Digna* dealing with the two jackals ends with a humorous drawing of Digna in chains and with toes turned up in death (Figure 17). At this point an entirely new sequence is initiated, known in the *Panchatantra* as "The Winning of Friends." This ancient section is one of the longest and most entertaining, wherein the Persian, Arabic, and Castilian versions have preserved the original sense of the need for friendship in a cold, hard world. The Castilian translation has only three interpolated stories, few of which are illustrated, since the entire set of line drawings stresses events within the frame story of *Calila e Digna*. The tale of the four pure friends, the raven, the mouse, the tortoise, and the stag, however, is accompanied by eight illustrations and is certainly the most winsome of all the stories in the book; this may indeed account for the fact that it is also the most copiously illustrated.

A raven named Geba lives in a forest often frequented by fowlers and other hunters. One day he sees a man bait a trap and catch a net full of doves led by one named Collarada, who successfully exhorts her comrades, though enmeshed in the net, to combine their efforts and fly away with the net, much to the bewilderment of the fowler, who gives heated chase. As soon as they have landed, Collarada calls a mouse who is her friend and he gnaws the cords of the net, letting the doves fly free, again to the hunter's rage and astonishment. The clever raven then seeks the mouse's friendship, but to no avail since mice form part of the average raven's diet. Undaunted, the wily raven threatens to kill himself, thereby convincing the mouse, with whom he then makes friends for life. Figure 18 reveals the net with the doves recently freed and the mouse beside it. Of course, a mouse is not much larger than the head of a dove, but this particular rodent has to be seen by the viewer, and hence his disproportionate size. In Figure 19 we see the raven and the mouse discussing the matter of friendship. Again the mouse has been drawn out of proportion and the raven's beak is short and blunt, but the idea of the parley is adequately depicted.

The raven, fearing the mouse may be in danger, flies him to a safe place beside a pool in which lives a turtle who is the raven's good friend. In Figure 20 we see the three of them: the raven has just landed and still holds the mouse by his tail, while the turtle, in the water, greets them. A glance at the turtle reveals that he has six legs, as though he were an insect. One wonders why this is; he also has six legs in the next

Figure 17 [54]

Figure 18 [55]

Figure 19 [56]

Figure 20 [57]

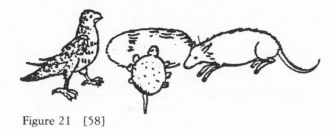

Figure 21   [58]

Figure 22   [59]

Figure 23   [60]

Figure 24   [61]

three illustrations, but the final drawings in this sequence show him with the normal four legs.

Figure 21 groups the three friends together in the happiness of pure friendship. Their life would be carefree except that a stag, recently escaped from hunters, has come to the pool to drink. His size frightens the small animals at first, but the raven, recognizing him, tells the others that the stag and he are the best of friends. He is invited to live with them in harmony, for the turtle assures them all that hunters never come near his pool.

But their idyllic existence abruptly ends when the deer falls into a snare and forlornly awaits the hunter he knows will come to kill him. His friends, noting his absence, set out to look for him. The raven flies about until he finds the deer, returning immediately to fetch the mouse to gnaw the ropes. By the time the mouse has freed the stag, the turtle has arrived to see what he can do to help. At this juncture, however, along comes the hunter, and since he cannot catch the raven, the deer, or the mouse, he picks up the turtle. Now, the alert hunter has witnessed the selfless collaboration of these animals to free their friend, and he is moved by their efforts, but he keeps the turtle nevertheless and prepares to go home. Figure 22 portrays the capture of our six-legged turtle: the raven is here, ready to fly to safety, and the man seems to creep cautiously up to the net, while the turtle, who looks as though he might be suspended in the air (due both to the artist's desire to maintain his size and to a lack of knowledge of foreshortening) is intended to be on the ground beyond the net.

The mouse, stag, and raven must now rescue the turtle. The raven concocts a plan whereby the stag will run in front of the hunter and stagger and fall, as though wounded. Each time the hunter approaches to catch him, he will rise and stumble along a littler farther, until he and the hunter are at a safe distance from the turtle, allowing the mouse to sever the cords of the net. All works out as planned, and the hunter, his net ruined, is constrained to remark, "This land, I believe, belongs to demons and God's enemies." Therefore he crosses himself and flees in terror from the forest, never to return. Figure 23 shows the hunter, hands raised in an attitude of astonishment, facing the open net and the four animal-friends. We may suppose the illustration is meant to reveal his understanding of the banding together of the animals, for all four are present in the illustration. Actually, in the story the animals do not return to sit on the net, as they are pictured, but the idea of their unity and the hunter's amazement are rendered perfectly clear. Here and in Figure 24 the turtle is shown with four legs.

In the last drawing in the sequence (Figure 24) the artists have most drolly and ingenuously visualized a happy ending to the story. The prose reads: "And afterwards the mouse, the raven, the stag, and the turtle were reunited, and all returned happy and content to the home where they used to take their pleasure." The iconography is particularly naive and indeed delightful, for the artists have actually created with a few simple strokes of the pen a perfect *locus amoenus*. The four pure friends stand, sit, or lie amid flowers, and the viewer cannot but feel the ambience of beauty, peace, and well-being. A modern cartoonist could hardly have accomplished more.

Chapter VI of *Calila e Digna* recounts the famous *Panchatantra* story of the war between the ravens and the owls. Almost nothing from this long sequence or frame-story is illustrated, however. Instead, several of the best short narratives of the book, those interpolated into the frame, are the subject of miniatures.

One of the ravens in the frame-story, in order to emphasize a point he wishes to make to his feathered fellows, tells how some rabbits outwit some elephants. It seems that during a drought a herd of elephants has found a lake and prepares to stay near it. Unfortunately they have also trampled upon the burrows of a community of rabbits, unwittingly killing many of them. A wise old rabbit goes to confer with the elephants; we see them speaking in Figure 25. These elephants, like that in Figure 7, above, are strange-looking beasts, indeed. Their depiction, like those of elephants in many other medieval manuscripts, indicates that the artist had never seen an elephant, unlike the illuminators of the *Cantigas*.

The rabbit tells the elephants that the lake belongs to the moon and that the moon is angry at the elephants for befouling it. Figure 26 shows the rabbit looking toward the sky and an elephant gazing into the water, where the moon is quite clearly reflected. The water ripples in the wind, convincing the elephant that the moon is indeed enraged, and he subsequently leads his herd to other parts, leaving the rabbits in peace. The two miniatures contain little action, but they most certainly illustrate the crucial elements of the tale.

Figure 27 portrays the story of the monk, the demon, and the robber, and illustrates an interesting scene in which the artist has inexplicably failed to depict the demon's face. This is all the more intriguing, for the *Cantigas* and many other manuscripts revel in portraits of demons and devils. Here in one figure we see two sequences of this story. At the left the monk is leading the cow given to him by a rich man. Along the way a demon and a robber see and

Figure 25    [62]

Figure 26    [63]

Figure 27    [68]

stalk him, the robber to steal the cow, the demon to kill the monk. The good friar arrives home, takes the cow into his house, has dinner, and goes to bed. He is soon awakened by a loud and furious altercation between the demon and the robber, who argue as to which should enter the house first. The thief fears the fiend will awaken the monk and prevent him from stealing the cow, while the demon contends that the thief will arouse the monk and foil his plans to kill him. Determined that the demon shall not profit at his expense, the robber cries out, "Wake up, for the devil is here to strangle you!" and the devil, replying in kind, yells, "Watch out, for the robber is here to steal your cow!" The brother, now well awake, crosses himself and raises a hue and cry, putting both demon and robber to flight.

The miniature shows the three characters in a confrontation which never occurs, for at no time in the story does the demon reach for the cow or the robber

Figure 28    [67]

Figure 29    [76]

rush at the monk with knife raised to strike. The reader will note the unusual absence of a face in the drawing of the demon. We see little besides an egg-shaped body and head, all fused together with no trace whatsoever of his visage. The usual cocklike feet and legs are clearly depicted, however.

Another interesting technique in visualization may be found in Figure 28, where we have the story of the monk, the stag, and the three knaves. The figures in the miniature are divided into two groups, those whose story is told and the story tellers. The crows and the king of the owls, are on the right, while the simple friar with his stag and the three wily villains occupy the left-hand side. The monk, who has bought a deer for sacrifice, starts home with it. Three artful dodgers are determined to fleece him, and to this end they plan that each shall meet him on the road and comment on the "dog" that he is leading. The first approaches him to ask, "What dog is this you're leading along with you? Are you going to hunt with this dog?" The second remarks, "Monks don't own dogs." And the last exclaims, "You want to sell that dog? I never saw one more beautiful."

Unaware of their larcenous intent, the credulous friar says to himself, "Perchance the man who sold me this stag put a hex on it and deceived me." So he looses the deer and the tricksters catch it and flay it. Clearly seen are the fraudulent trio and their victim, all striking poses appropriate to the roles they play in the

tale—the three rogues gesticulating in fulsome praise of the "dog," while the rueful monk, head bent, eyes downcast, with hands lifted in resignation, prepares to free the deer he believes to be a dog.

In the other half of the miniature, the raven points with one wing in the direction of the monk and his tormentors in a very interesting bit of visual narrative technique wherein we see the story teller outlining the events as they unfold. The clever combination of narration and description exemplifies the Chinese-box structure of the entire collection of tales, which tells a story within a story, whereby the reader loses his sense of direction—and fiction—as he penetrates deeper into the world of fable, which now assumes a solid feeling of reality.

As the narrative thread spins out toward the end of the manuscript, fewer and fewer miniatures appear. One of these, Figure 29, is another fine example of double action. Here again, two entirely different actions take place. On the left we see a pilgrim letting down a rope into a pit into which several animals and a man have fallen. The man is not visible but we can clearly see a badger—well-depicted—, a monkey, and a snake. The three animals and a man, we are told, have all fallen into a pit dug by hunters to catch wild beasts. The artist clearly portrayed the pit with one of its sides excised to allow the viewer to see the trapped animals.

The monkey, the snake, and the badger use the rope first, followed by the man, a goldsmith, whose occupation is crucial to the development of the story. It seems the goldsmith has promised to help his bene-factor if ever he is in need. As the pilgrim wanders about the land he chances again upon the grateful monkey, who brings him delicious fruit from high in the trees. Then the monkey calls the badger and asks him to help the pilgrim, and the badger brings him gold and jewels he has found underground. As it happens, the valuables came from the king's treasury and have been missed and sought after. At length the pilgrim goes to the city and seeks out the goldsmith, asking his help to dispose of his newfound treasure. But the ungrateful goldsmith, to ingratiate himself with the king, leads the police to the pilgrim, who is straightaway tried, convicted, and sentenced to the gallows. The snake now decides to repay its debt to the pilgrim. Going to the king's daughter he bites her badly but not enough to kill her, of course, her father thinks she will surely die. As she lies tended by physi-cians and magicians, she conveniently has a vision in which she learns that an innocent man has been sen-tenced to death and that only he can cure her. So the pilgrim is brought to her bedside. We see in Figure 29 the princess in bed, her father there with her, probably to show his concern for her, and the pilgrim blessing her. She is cured and justice done, for as soon as the king learns of what the grateful beasts have accomplished he takes note of it and resolves to admit to his court only loyal and grateful people. He gives the gold and jewels to the pilgrim. In one version of *Calila e Digna* he exiles the goldsmith, while in the other he has him tortured and then hanged at the city gate.

*Calila e Digna*, with its seventy-eight narrative illustrations, presents some of the best line drawings from the fourteenth century. It emphasizes as well the very real interest of the Learned King in wisdom books and his considered view of the lighter side of life. We are fortunate that this particular manuscript has survived when so many others have disappeared.

It is difficult and much less satisfactory to a attempt to adapt the classic narrative design to the miniatures in *Calila e Digna* than to the more detailed and far more carefully illustrated *Cantigas de Santa Maria*. However, the artists were able to incorporate some of the elements, for art can catch the reflections of literature.

Not many of the sequences of artistic presentation in *Calila e Digna* are illustrated sufficiently to reveal much in the way of plot. The few that are, however, are worth reviewing. Figures 5 through 9 definitely follow the events of the story: the beginning of the story as told by Senceba; the agreement as it is made between the lion and the camel; the battle between the lion and the elephant; the lion conversing with his vassals; the vassals plotting with their master while the camel waits to one side; and lastly, the murder of the camel by the lion and all his minions. Only a few words would be required to fill in possible gaps in visual understanding, since many knew the story.

Setting in the miniatures of *Calila e Digna* is minimal. In the story of the lion and camel there is actually none at all. In other tales, one drawing contains a little more. In the story of the heron, the crab, and the trout the only attempt at setting is the water indicated by wavy lines. In the story of the animal friends who save one another from the hunter (Figures 18 and 19) one sees the mouse with the doves in the net in the former and, in the latter, the crow conversing with the mouse. In Figure 22, in which the hunter captures the turtle, there is at least a tree to establish the fact that the events are taking place out of doors. The *locus amoenus* in Figure 24 is perhaps the most expressive of all the attempts at setting in the entire book of *Calila e Digna*.

In the story of the elephants and the rabbits whom they inadvertently trample, illustrated by Figures 25 and 26, the artist provides at least the barest minimum of setting in the depiction of the lake and the reflection of the moon in its water. The artist's only other bow to setting appears in the double action illustration in the story of the grateful animals who save the man who has rescued them from the pit. In Figure 29 the pit, with its side excised to offer a view of the imprisoned animals, offers at least a brief view of where the event is taking place; and as the princess lies ill, her bed is depicted with her in it. The settings of *Calila e Digna*, then, are a far cry from the elaborate and extremely detailed settings found in the miniatures of the *Cantigas de Santa Maria*.

Conflict in the majority of the line drawings is concisely but adequately handled. Considerable imagination was required to depict the attack of the lion and his court upon the pitiful camel (Figure 10). Here action and violence are apparent. The story of the carpenter and his treacherous wife also contains pictures fulfilling the element of conflict, which is sustained in all four miniatures (Figures 13–16). Even so, conflict is never represented as well as in the *Cantigas*.

Characterization in the line drawings is confined to expressions on the faces of the characters and to their movements, and is rather limited. Good examples of facial expression can be found in the faces of the murderous animals and the dying camel in Figure 10, and in the expressions of Calila and Digna in Figure 1. In Figure 15 the vengeful character of the barber is evident in his stance more than in his expression as he flings the razor at his wife, whose posture and uplifted hands indicate something of her emotions.

One further example should suffice to indicate characterization as visualized by the artists in their line drawings. In Figure 28, which illustrates the story of the tricksters who persuade the monk that the stag he is leading is a dog, gesture and stance, and to a lesser extent the expressions on the faces of the three rogues, reveal much of their character, while the simplicity and gullibility of the stupid monk are very evident in his face and the position of his hands.

Theme without the written word is hard to detect in these drawings. The style of the artist matches, we believe, that of the author, who injected humor, ranging from the mildest sort to incidents that are definitely funny. The droll quality of the written word seems to have been caught by the penman as he depicted what he read. The effect of most of the illustrations reflects that of the stories themselves. In point of view and mood or tone, as well, the artist strove to match the written account.

# Castigos e documentos para bien vivir

ing Alfonso's career as patron of arts and letters ended in 1284 when he died in the city of Seville, his power usurped by his son Sancho IV, dubbed by his subjects el Bravo, that is, "the fierce." Almost as he died, Alfonso dictated a bitter curse on Sancho, whose reign would not be happy. The literary monuments attributed to Sancho are the *Lucidarios,* a nonnarrative treatise, and the *Castigos e documentos para bien vivir,*[1] written in the style of the dial for princes and addressed to his own son, Fernando, who would rule as the fourth of that name.

We see no reason to deny Sancho's personal authorship of the *Castigos* for, as the first son of the Learned King, he would have had the necessary education. At any rate, throughout the book he alludes to himself, states that he "made this book," and addresses himself directly to Fernando, speaking to him as "Mio fijo." This does not mean that he actually penned the work, for there were scribes and calligraphers for such a task, but he may well have authored *Castigos e documentos,* just as his father actively participated in the composition of the *Cantigas.* That he states that he produced the book with "the assistance of learned scientists" need not lessen his claim to authorship. We dwell on this matter of the author's personal intervention because we would like to curb the tendency among scholars past and present, and some of quite notable repute, to deny authorship to great kings and other political and military figures. It is our opinion

that people who were industrious, intelligent, and well educated, even when saddled with the heaviest of official duties, could and often did take time to research, plan, and write good books. Don Juan Manuel, Sancho's first cousin and King Alfonso's nephew, composed some fifty-three finely narrated stories, perhaps the most literary of the Spanish Middle Ages, and one can hardly imagine a nobleman more actively engaged in war, intrigue, ruling, and study than this sagacious fellow. Indeed, he may have been quite as occupied in nonliterary pursuits as either of his close kinsmen, and yet no one doubts his authorship. Nor should one deny that of the Learned King and his rebellious son.[2]

No matter that *Castigos e documentos* was finished in 1293 when Prince Fernando was but six. He still may have been set to reading it and studying its adult content, for children were often introduced to learning at an early age, and even obliged to study Latin from the age of three if they were royal children. The copy we have used for studying the visual content of the work might have delighted Sancho himself, for it is a remarkably well wrought and handsomely illuminated volume, with all the sententious, measured prose earlier developed at Alfonso's court and present in all Alfonsine works. Unfortunately Sancho never saw this particular tome because it was penned and illuminated long after his death, which occurred in 1295. María Elena de Arizmendi, whose knowledge of medieval costume and hair styling is unimpeachable, dates the illuminated manuscript between 1420 and 1430, both illuminations and calligraphy. This dating is a considerable contribution and we are grateful to her for it.

Fortunately the formality of the literary presentation, with its underlying Semitic syntax and protracted sentences, could not carry over into the illuminations, which, though not presented in the six-panel format of the *Cantigas,* nonetheless illustrate artistically and esthetically some of the narratives. Testimony to its popularity lies in the fact that *Castigos,* years after its original composition, would be reproduced and illuminated.

A host of great works from the past served as sources for the *Castigos*—Holy Writ, ancient philosophers such as Aristotle and Plato, Roman writers like Seneca, Cicero, and Valerius Maximus, classic literature like the *Aeneid,* popular didactic-recreational books like the *Disciplina Clericalis,* Marian miracles like the *Cantigas de Santa Maria,* as well as miracles from other sources, and even stories about people of Sancho's own acquaintance. Primary and identifiable sources were the *Siete Partidas,* King Alfonso's great code of laws; the same king's *General Estoria, La historia troyana,* and *La gran conquista de Ultramar;* and the works of Peter Lombard, Gregory the Great, Boethius, and many others.[3] In its own way, King Sancho's guide for his young son is as encyclopedic as the volumes of the *Cantigas de Santa Maria.*

The copy known as MS Biblioteca Nacional 3995 (formerly MS 23) contains eighty three folios, which measure 370 by 265 mm (14.56 inches high by 10.43 wide). In all there are twenty miniatures, eleven of which we reproduce.

It is strange that this remarkable and valuable work has lain nearly forgotten for centuries and that even today little study has been made of it. The edition in Biblioteca de Autores Españoles, is faulty and more than a century old, while the only good critical edition is that of Manuscript C, transcribed by Agapito Rey of Indiana University and published in Bloomington in 1952. It is the early fifteenth century text that we are using, the only one of the *Castigos* manuscripts that has miniatures. If little has been written about the book as a piece of literature, virtually nothing has been said about its miniatures. Agapito Rey referred to them in a short note in his introduction as *toscas,* that is, "rough" or "crude," and felt that their greatest value lay in the light they might shed on studies of medieval dress. Both he and Amador de los Ríos, a nineteenth-century literary historian, published several of the miniatures in black and white, but by and large these

appealing pictures have simply been overlooked. Parenthetically, we might add that no one has yet, to our knowledge, translated *Castigos e documentos* into English, or probably into any other language, although a good translation is definitely a desideratum.

The miniatures are far from rough or uncouth, nor is there any reason why they should be, after all, someone important, perhaps even royal, commissioned them long after Sancho, perhaps for the guidance of his own princely son. They are the work of fine artists, not simply good ones, and the fact that they do not belong to the same school of art or possess the same style as the art of the *Cantigas de Santa Maria* in no way diminishes their quality or denies them the repute they ought to enjoy. Whereas the illuminations in the *Cantigas* occupy entire pages and never share space with the poems they illustrate or the accompanying musical notation, the miniatures in *Castigos* are surrounded, often entirely, by the very narratives they depict. Yet all of the miniatures, even the smallest, are of sufficient size and form to render in great detail what they illustrate. Each covers approximately as much space as a single panel in the *Cantigas,* that is, about 100 by 100 mm, although some are much larger and some much smaller. One observes in them, however, none of the great panoramic scenes of the *Cantigas,* none of the colorful frieze-like frames, none of the golden arches used to spotlight actions and endow them with a stage-like presentation. While the art of the illuminations of the *Cantigas* is crowded and at times even cluttered with detail and real complexity in its reflection of the elements of daily life and, indeed, of the entire panoply of medieval existence, the pictures in *Castigos* are frank, uncluttered, simple, and with a frequent sense of airiness we find delightful and far less formal than the earlier art. Since these miniatures were executed in the early fifteenth century, nearly 150 years separates them from those in the *Cantigas de Santa Maria.*

Colors are just as brilliant as in the *Cantigas,* for the same pigments were used, but there are subtle differences in shading and in the application of color. Human faces surpass those of the Alfonsine manuscripts, not only in detail and expression, including more authentic flesh tones, but also in the workmanship itself, for there is less stylization, probably because the artists had fewer details on which to concentrate and perforce treated what they could more graphically. These miniatures seldom present more than one moment of time in a story, with nothing but the prose account to connect the moment depicted with what has gone before and what is to follow. Their narrative technique injects surprising meaning and beauty into a very abbreviated sphere and militates against all that is irrelevant to the story per se. Some of these illuminations may have been meaningless to the uninitiated, that is, to people who did not know their story; but this would not hold, of course, for the depiction of universally familiar events, such as the expulsion from the Garden of Eden or perhaps the well-known story of the runaway nun. Lack of space for greater detail, then, offered fewer opportunities to employ the usual artistic devices, such as double action, and resulted in what can best be regarded as a more modern approach to narrative art, with subtler tones and novel techniques.

The element of dramatic parallel found so frequently in the *Cantigas* is all but absent in the *Castigos*. No one viewing the illuminations of King Sancho's book could feel he is looking into a *tableau vivant* to the extent that is possible in Alfonso's miracles. In the latter, the viewer is not always conscious of the fact that he is perusing the pages of a book, so far do the mind and the eye enter the panoramic panels, whereas in *Castigos* one can hardly do so, for the text itself, the written word that signifies that it is a book being viewed, touches each illumination and at times surrounds it, making words and pictures visually inseparable. And where the *Cantigas* illuminations fully narrate each story, those of *Castigos* narrate only a single episode of a story. This is not to belittle the later art, but only to point to a new kind of excellence and a remarkably talented and intelligent new approach to narrative.

Plate 40, from Folio 2r, depicts King Sancho seated, crowned, and resting his sword on his shoulder as he lectures to the kneeling Prince Fernando, who in the miniature appears to be more than the six years ascribed to him. At the same time it is a depiction of King Sancho speaking to his reader. Here is a pictorial depiction of point of view. The faces of the father and son are lifelike, with good flesh tones, and there are wrinkles in the king's forehead, while even the prince's fingernails can be clearly seen as his hands move, probably indicating that he is either asking questions or commenting upon the lesson. Recall that the introductory page of the *Cantigas* portrayed King Alfonso reading or dictating to musicians, singers, and scribes, and thereby depicted him as the person whose point of view is present in each *cantiga*. The only narrative element in the prologue of *Castigos e documentos*, then, is that of a lecture in progress, and the miniature faithfully portrays this.

One of the miracles in the *Castigos*, which we find in Chapter XIX, "How a Man Should Not Grieve God with Women with Whom He Ought Not Have To Do" (Plate 41), reveals on folio 74v a story somewhat parallel to number 59 of the *Cantigas de Santa Maria*, and some scholars state categorically that the story in the *Cantigas* is its source. This may be true, but there are differences between the two versions.

In *Cantiga 59* King Alfonso tells of a nun who plans to elope with a young man. As she takes leave of the image of Holy Mary, the image weeps, but the nun goes on until she passes the life-sized image of Christ on the Cross. The image wrenches one of his hands from the cross's bar and strikes her in the face, driving the nail in his hand through her cheek. She falls unconscious to the floor and there the nuns find her. Of course the errant sister repents. The king says that he went to that convent and verified the miracle, since the image's hand hung loose from the cross.

Sancho in *Castigos* relates the miracle somewhat differently. The nun is about to leave when the image of the Blessed Virgin cries out and asks the nun why she is deserting her and her son for the devil. At this, the image of the crucified Lord wrenches both hands and feet from the cross, leaps to the floor, pursues the fleeing nun, and smites her in the cheek, driving the nail in his hand into one of her cheeks and out the other. She lies unconscious until dawn, when the nuns find her. The image returns to the cross and fastens itself there, save for the one hand with which it struck the nun, for the nail has remained in her cheek. After the nail is removed, the nun repents.

These differences in the two verbalizations are reflected in the illuminations, not only with respect to the actual events but also with regard to the narrative devices used to portray them. The artists of the *Castigos* have contrived a much more violent and hostile scene. In the *Cantigas* (Plate 18) the figure of the Lord never leaves the cross, held by the nails through His left hand and feet, whereas in *Castigos* the entire figure of Christ has wrenched free from the cross and has pursued the nun down the aisle of the church to catch and strike her. Huge spikes project from his left hand and bleeding feet, and one can almost hear the clanking sound as the metal strikes the pavement. More graphic still, in the *Castigos* the effect of the blow is not concealed in the visualization, as it is in the *Cantigas*, for the viewer can see all too plainly the gaping wound in each of the nun's cheeks, and the spike transfixing them, no longer in the hand of the image. Much blood gushes from both wounds and pours down the nun's cheeks. In the *Cantigas* illumination the nail never leaves Christ's palm and even in the following panel (not shown), when the nun lies unconscious on the floor, we see no real evidence of what has occurred save for a patch of red, probably meant to represent blood, on the front of her habit.

Leaving nothing to the imagination, the artist or artists of the *Castigos* depicted the image of Christ carved artistically in wood or some other material in a most lifelike manner, revealing late medieval man's conception of a tortured and flagellated Jesus. His ribs stand out in stark relief, his fearfully enraged face is pinched with pain, and blood flows from the nail punctures. He is a Jesus unlike the less tortured renditions to be found in the *Cantigas*. The cross is also drawn in great detail, with the grain of the wood and a few swirls clearly indicating the knotholes. The nun's face, too, is faithfully delineated, even to brows and lashes, while her expressive hands are steepled in the attitude of prayer. In this scene she has not lost consciousness, as she does in the *Cantigas* immediately after the blow, but kneels perfectly aware of what has occurred. Her habit flows gracefully across the floor, pinned down by the bleeding feet of the image, which towers above her.

This miniature from the *Castigos* is filled with details and apparently depicts two separate incidents—the leap from the cross and the wounding of the sinner. A single scene captures the essence of the story with unusual vigor and a macabre touch. No frame, no arches, no spotlighting are required or employed, as was the case in most of the *Cantigas* panels. All that needed to be presented was set forth by the artists in a noteworthy and realistic piece of narrative art.

Rarely in *Castigos e documentos* did the artists illuminate two or more incidents of a story, as they frequently did in the *Cantigas*, apparently satisfied with a single representative illustration of the main event which could serve as a visual and thematic nucleus, leaving the rest to the active imagination of the reader. Perhaps the only true case of sequential action appears on folios 74v and 75r in Chapter XXXVII, "What a Good Thing Is Charity and Virginity."

Here we read that the devil, bent upon tempting a hermit whose chastity has endured for thirty years, pretends to be a poor, lost woman and presents him/herself at the door of the holy man's cave. Taking pity on her, the pious recluse offers her refuge within his dwelling for the night and feeds her what little he has of bread and water. To attract his attention and entice him, the devil keeps weeping, and the more the hermit looks at her, the hotter blazes a newfound lust. At last, the woman takes his hands and fondles them with loving caresses, kindling in him the hope that he may have his way with her. Just at this juncture, the devil sheds his feminine guise and assumes the shape of a goat, boasting that in one hour he has cost the hermit the chastity he has stored up in all those thirty years. He brags too, that he likes to tease men's passions right up to the last degree of lust, and then leave them unsatisfied. The hermit is desperate, but God takes pity on him, so that, confessing his transgressions to a fellow anchorite, he is absolved, and returning to his life of chastity, is at last taken up to heaven.

Folio 74v, in the first of the two sequential miniatures, depicts the devil in human form standing at the door of the cave (Plate 42). The artists apparently had their own distinct impressions of a temptress and did not clothe her in the rags of poverty we find mentioned in the text. Instead, they painted her in a very stylish costume. Her scarlet hat is shaped like an inverted saucer and expensively decorated with plumes. Her long, honey-colored hair falls in curls around her graceful neck. Her face, admittedly not truly beautiful, is nonetheless attractive, and indeed may have seemed beautiful to those who drew her. She wears a puce cloak trailing the earth, with a green collar or facing, and the neckline plunges past her cleavage all the way to her waist. The sleeves of the cloak give way at the elbow to long ruffles which match the color of her collar, sweeping down to the ground, while at the wrists we see the beige or white puffed sleeves of an undergarment. To touch off the woman's costume she wears a necklace of two strands, probably of gold, as several spots of reflected light would indicate. All this is a far cry from the feminine attire of wealthy women in the *Cantigas*. What was modern and stylish in Alfonso's or Sancho's day would have been passé in the times when the *Castigos* was illuminated.

The hermit is decently garbed in a long, thick, brown cloak whose folds fall gracefully, and he wears a black, close-fitting clerical cap. In his left hand he holds a volume bound in red whose pages, though it is closed, are skillfully indicated by lines.

There is more than passing attention to scene and background, for in this first miniature the hermit sits before his cell, a cave in a low, flat-topped hill crowned by two umbrella pines. Through the ascending greensward may be seen what is perhaps a path strewn with grass and flowers, indicated by most casual touches of the pen.

Verbalization in two columns of fine calligraphy covers the upper part of the page. Exactly which moment of time the artists have captured is uncertain, for no part of the verbalization precisely describes what is taking place. Since the anchorite's hand is close to the devil's, it may indeed be just that moment before the devil fondles it. The plot is developed and conflict ignited by the provocative stance of the woman as she inflames the hermit. "Hand language" is certainly in evidence, for her fingers move, apparently opening and closing, while his hand extends, palm upward, toward hers. Her gestures seem to explain her predicament, his to welcome her.

On the next folio the arrangement of text above with scene and action below is similar, though the left-hand column of the text now continues all the way to the bottom of the page, hemming in the two figures and effectively crowding them together in a reversal of roles, hinting at some collaboration between artist and scribe. In this second incident (Plate 43) we see the repentant hermit kneeling before another holy man, his own hands together in prayer, while the other, placing his left hand on the penitent's head, blesses him with his right, granting him absolution. Both faces are clear and expressive, with eyes, brows, mouths, and beards realistically depicted. Different viewers, then as now, might interpret their expressions in various ways. To us, the face of the hermit blessing his errant brother has assumed an expression of patience and tolerance, tempered with smug relief that he is not the sinner, while the sinner's face reflects true grief and repentance.

The second scene is similar to the first, for it is laid on a greensward on which the hermits either sit or kneel, their figures balanced and attractively offset by a grove of umbrella pines sprinkled with sienna-colored cones. Indeed, with considerable skill the artists contrived not only scene but conflict, visualizing in these two miniatures at least two phases of the rudimentary plot in such a way that the viewer can partially fill in those elements of the story transpiring between them. But they also imparted reflections of some of the other components of brief narrative, for characterization is clearly present in the costume of the devil in disguise, his facial appearance, hands, and stance, while the hermit surely looks the part of a man surrendering to seduction, just as he later appears to be quite grieved and remorseful. Effect is brought into sharp focus and the theme starkly revealed in a pictorial rendition which successfully parallels the verbal account.

Style in this story, as revealed in both verbal and visual forms, depends upon directness and simplicity. A more ornate hand in the miniatures might well have vitiated the effect. The artists apparently felt constrained to craft a precise image which would match the written words precisely, with the single exception of the stylish dress the devil wears. Point of view, as in all the miniatures in the *Castigos,* is that of King Sancho, who, ever the good story teller, does not refrain from putting words into the mouth of Satan. Theme, though directed as it ought to be toward one person's problem, is fraught with peripheral implications of universal import, for sin is committed and expiated, and heaven's clemency is bestowed on the hermit, just as it surely must be on all of us if we repent and seek absolution. God's forgiveness, the universally implied theme of both story and visualization, comes to the hermit as it will to all mankind when repentance is present and genuine. This unwaveringly pious mood or tone is evident from the very beginning, as we view the holy anchorite in his pastoral setting.

Perhaps one of the most striking portrayals in the *Castigos* occurs in a miracle Sancho claims he took from an historical incident and may indeed have heard from the mouth of the man whose experience it was and whose life it subsequently altered. As such, it stands in stark contrast to stories drawn from familiar sources in great books of the past. It belongs to the same chapter of the *Castigos* as the miracle of the runaway nun. On folio 49r (Plate 44) the illumination depicts a contemporary miracle which, like many related by Alfonso in the *Cantigas,* reveals the intensity of contemporary belief in the miraculous. Sancho relates that a Navarrese knight, Juan Corvalán, abducted a Cistercian nun named Marziella by force. Sometime later, in the midst of a battle with the Aragonese, the miracle took place. We are told that, as Corvalán retreated, Marziella suddenly appeared in front of him on his horse, seizing the reins and slowing him down. "Why are you doing this to me?" he cried, and she replied, "Take this as a reward for the evil you committed with me!" Nor did he escape, for she held him back a second time and his enemies overtook and captured him and held him prisoner until he paid a high ransom. For the rest of his life, the king goes on to say, Juan Corvalán never set foot inside a convent or any sisterhood whatsoever.

The verbal account in two columns covers approximately the top fourth of the folio. Beneath it the illumination fairly seethes with action. The moment captured by the artists shows Sister Marziella in her second attack upon Corvalán as she catches his reins and detains him. The horse seems to be about to rear. Marziella's face, in three-quarter view, is resolute, her mouth grimly set. Plainly we see her hand holding the reins while Juan Corvalán glares down at her in profile. Every detail of his armor is portrayed, as well as his scarlet leather saddle down to his knight's spurs with their circular, sawlike rowel. Beyond him knights sit their mounts with lances raised and a crimson pennant fluttering above their heads. The horse is well proportioned and seems to move in the fleeting moment the artists have frozen in time. It resembles one of the horses seen in panel 4 of *Cantiga* 67 (Plate 15), whose stance and coloration it parallels. Influence is possible, of course, but quite probably both the *cantiga* and the miniature in the *Castigos* drew from a common source which depicted horses according to a well known artistic pattern.

Conflict is obvious, so that viewers who did not know the story of Juan Corvalán, or who could not read it, would certainly understand what was taking place in the miniature. The setting is obviously a battlefield with knights in full armor prepared to attack. We can know nothing of their characters from the miniature, but much can be inferred about the two protagonists. The nun's bold stance, her free hand lifted in admonition while the other grasps the bridle, is a portrait captured at the very moment she answers Corvalán's question. How she shakes her finger at him! And how defiant Corvalán seems as he stares down at her before realizing that he is trapped!

The theme of vengeance is less well defined than in the verbalization, but perhaps medieval viewers could picture it in their own minds as they perused the page. The effect achieved is one of considerable emotional interest, and we are at once drawn into the picture and filled with wonder at the strangeness of the event, while our point of view as readers is omniscient, coming from the king and through the artists. The mood or tone is serious, pregnant with interest and implication. This entire miniature, though artistically quite different from the art of the *Cantigas,* possesses a special charm of its own.

Still another miracle occurs in Chapter VII, "About What a Noble Thing It Is to Give Alms, and How Many Virtues and Values It Carries With It." In the verbalization that accompanies Plate 45 King Sancho tells Prince Fernando that St. Edward of England, that is, King Edward the Confessor, rode one cold day after a stag. Soon he met a leper, naked and dying of cold, and when the man beseeched him to take him up on the horse and ride with him to some shelter, he generously agreed, even giving the man his own cloak. Then, as they made their way along toward a convent, the king had need to blow his nose and the leper urged him to do so. When he blew it, the miracle occurred, for he found in his hand a flawless ruby as large as a hen's egg; a ruby, King Sancho relates, which would become a part of the royal crown used in England for subsequent coronations. When, ruby in hand, King Edward turned to look at the leper, he had vanished.

The miniature found on folio 13v is completely surrounded by text, so to outline it the artists have drawn a thin, square frame in ink, providing a border between words and picture. Only the king's leg hangs from the frame into the space between the two columns of calligraphy. The crowned king rides on the cruppers of his steed, since he has placed the leper in the saddle. The royal cloak protects the back of the poor creature, whose face is gaunt and splotched with what looks like a reddish rash, while red splotches or lesions appear on his bare arms, legs, and torso. Edward, blond, and to us very English, has just blown his nose and is staring at the ruby in his fingers. The leper, who in the verbalization vanishes, has not yet disappeared in the miniature. Those with no previous knowledge of the event would have been confused, but those who knew the story must have been moved.

The king's hound capers proudly ahead of the horse, which is royally caparisoned with a fringed green saddle cloth. The saddle cannot be seen since it is hidden by the leper in the king's flowing cloak. The horse canters forward against a wooded scene with artistically arranged umbrella pines, utilized here in spite of the fact that they are not indigenous to the British Isles.

Good style demands that clarity be ever present, and this diminutive miniature certainly fulfills that vital function. It was consciously designed to achieve a striking visual effect, contrasting a foreground, ornate and rich in detail, with an eloquently simple background. Point of view, as always in the *Castigos,* is that of Sancho, who tells his son that he read the story in a history of the kings of England. The mood is pietistic with overtones that imply kindness and charity.

Not all the stories in the *Castigos* deal with the miraculous. Some stem from scripture, such as those illustrating Noah's ark or Daniel in the lions' den. The former manages to catch much of the ambience of the great Flood, as can be seen in Plate 46. In this unusual picture we have what may well be an example of multiple action depicting three parts of the Flood story. At the left appear men and women clothed in fine raiment. The three women stand in poses indicating fear and resignation, while each of the men carries a child on his shoulders. These represent the pagans who sought admittance to the ark. In mid-scene the Flood has arrived in all its fury. The ark floats on the crest of a huge muddy wave and through its arches we can see a sad-faced, shocked Noah peering out. His wife and one or more of their children, to the right, also stare at the awful scene in the heaving water. The naked dead float in large numbers, eyes closed, usually face upward, but some people struggle in the water and one man appears to be spewing up a stream of bubbles. Fish swim through the scattered bodies. The artists painted the ark in some detail, with a slab or shingle roof and artistically carved arches of ecclesiastical design separated by graceful columns. Under one arch, cattle stand out clearly. To the left are birds and beasts. Here we can identify a bear, wolves or dogs, and, in the arch enclosing the birds, an ibis and an ostrich. Careful scrutiny of the creatures seems to reveal the strokes of a pen, probably used because the detail required is too fine for a brush. We repeat that the illumination may depict three phases of the story or may simply be a three-faceted single scene, but we are inclined to the former supposition. The artists, as usual in the *Castigos,* managed to include most or all of the elements of brief narrative.

The expulsion of Adam and Eve (Plate 47) merits inclusion, for it reveals how successfully the artists captured a great deal of the event and again quite possibly painted with the technique of double or multiple action in mind. At the far left the face of God peers from the clouds, his head streaming thin rays of crimson light, while with a finger he urges on the avenging angel. This could well represent one facet of a picture containing several separate events in the story of the expulsion. To God's right we see the angel pursuing Adam and Eve as they flee before him. No *cantiga,* indeed few Renaissance angels in the canvasses of Giotto or Michelangelo, could scintillate more colorfully. His pinions blaze scarlet and purple, his nimbus glows a brilliant gold.

Adam, outdistancing his mate, runs from the angel, holding a large fig leaf over his genitals. He is bearded, a rare detail in Adam figures, and has long hair. His face reveals terror and his legs indicate rapid flight. Behind him Eve runs, her right hand holding a fig leaf over her private parts. In her left hand she holds a part of the apple, and some distance beyond her the serpent, as gold as the angel's halo, twines round a tree bearing red apples in its bright green foliage.

The overall effect of the miniature, coupled with its multiple action, produces a striking illumination. The story's plot and conflict, known to all Christians, are artfully executed. The scene, with its trees in the background, is attractive. It is indeed a beautiful garden, with flowers springing up around the boles of trees. The physiques of the first man and woman are more attractive than those found in many medieval illustrations. Their limbs are well proportioned and their faces expressive. Eve's face is even pretty. Her right foot projects into the margin between the two columns of calligraphy.

We reproduce the illumination of Daniel and the Lions in Plate 48. The artists offer one static incident.

Daniel, garbed handsomely and with a golden halo around his head, kneels in prayer, palms pressed together. Seven lions stand, sit, or crouch about him. They are true-to-life lions, save for their ears, which slightly resemble those of humans.

One miniature in the *Castigos* (Plate 49) is taken directly from pagan literature, though the immediate source of the story of Dido and Aeneas may well have been the version found in the *Gran e general estoria,* Alfonso's great history of the world. The first column of folio 78v is entirely text, but in the second a small miniature divides the verbalization. The story here, dealing primarily with Aeneas's betrayal of Dido and his departure from Carthage, ends with the queen's ascent to the top of a tower and her tearful speech as she plunges a sword into her breast just before she leaps to her death. The artists catch her as she begins to plummet earthward from the crenelated battlements. There is no sign of the sword or of a wound. The action is self-evident: her hair awry, but with the crown still clinging to her head, her long purple robes trailing behind, she falls headlong into the flames which lick at the foot of the tower below.

The last miniature which we select from *Castigos* stems from a well-known wisdom tale found in most eastern and western collections of *exempla.* Known for centuries in the East, it may have first entered western writing in the Latin *Disciplina Clericalis* of the twelfth-century Aragonese Jew, Moses Sephardi, baptized as Pedro Alfonso. It appears in Chapter XXXV of the *Castigos,* "How All Those Whom a Man Counts His Friends Are Not Equal." The source is uncertain, for Sancho could have drawn it from many books. Perhaps he used the version that is found in the thirteenth-century *Speculum Laicorum.* The miniature (Plate 50) appears on folio 68v. Briefly recounted, a young man boasts to his father of having one hundred friends, while the father says he himself has been fortunate enough to have only half a friend. To test the one hundred, the father has his son kill a calf, cut it up, place it in a sack, and go to all his friends, telling them he has killed a man and seeking their help in disposing of the "body" in the sack. All one hundred turn him away. At last his father's half-friend agrees to hide the body.

The single small illumination illustrates this very popular medieval story. The artists depicted the son of the good man with the sack on his back walking toward the door of one of his one hundred friends. His everyday, middle-class garb, like that of the friend he beseeches, is a purple doublet gathered at the waist by a belt. His scarlet hose and shoes contrast with the green hose and shoes of the friend, who also wears a green kerchief on his head. The face of the man carrying the sack is strained and the expression of the friend is bleak, rejecting as he does with an outstretched palm any thought of entrance into his home. The house itself is built of heavy masonry slabs on a foundation of brick with a roof of green tile, quite different from those found in the *Cantigas*.

Many of the illuminations of *Castigos e documentos* which we have presented contain art of good quality, as they should, considering their probable royal patronage. In its own way this art is as worthy as the art in King Alfonso's Marian miracles, although its artists painted in a definitely different style and used far fewer narrative devices and symbols. Surely the most striking differences may be found in the lack of panoramic scenes, multitudes of figures, and numerous details, and of course in the absence in *Castigos* of the six-panel arrangement.

Insofar as we have been able to determine, illuminations did not decline in quality after the thirteenth century, although there seem to have been far fewer book illustrations after Alfonso's reign and even though new styles of painting influenced the craft of miniature artwork. Surely they deserve deeper study, for they provide most valuable insights into the history of late medieval pictorial and narrative art.

While the Alfonsine miniatures are indeed the product of Gothic art and, as we have emphasized, representative of the very best of that particular genre, the skill with which the *Castigos* artists executed their scenes corresponds to the particular tastes of their era, whose pictorial needs, in conjunction with narrative style, were not as elaborate, in keeping with a more sober and pessimistic approach to life and its problems. We have moved from the encyclopedic emphasis of Alfonso to the synthetic, more compact and reserved period of Sancho and the fifteenth century, whose predominant mood was one of *fin de siècle*, the end of an epoch, the closing of the Middle Ages, and the careful, somber reconsideration of the preceding period.

# El libro del Cavallero Cifar

he *Libro del Cavallero Cifar, The Book of the Knight Cifar* (or *Zifar*),[1] is a most unusual piece of writing and a remarkable example of medieval Spanish illumination. Its style, content, and even character development may foreshadow some of Spain's greatest masterpieces, and it embodies most, possibly all, of the prose genres known up to its time. It could have been and probably was read and savored by both secular and ecclesiastical audiences. Surely such good stories as it contained may well have escaped from the world of books and back into the oral lore of the folk from which its author quite possibly obtained some of his ideas, for books were read aloud in those times to the illiterate. And yet this work, whose importance in the development of Spanish prose fiction and in the art of illumination can hardly be underestimated, has actually fared rather badly in terms of contemporary popularity. Only two rigorously critical editions, one some fifty years old, have appeared, though more recent editions in modernized form are certainly available.[2]

Since our contribution to *Cifar* will be an investigation of those artistic techniques employed to visualize events in the novel itself and its interpolated brief narratives, we cannot deviate too far from this aim. Even so, we will in passing make reference to other scholars who are at present researching this great and regrettably neglected masterpiece, for many of our readers will not have heard of the *Cifar,* and nothing of note has yet been written about the illuminations.

It is conceivable that the novel was more significant in its own time than has been hitherto suspected. A fourteenth-century manuscript and an illuminated manuscript of the fifteenth century have survived, and two references to the work in the latter century have been discovered.[3] Moreover, there were two printings in the sixteenth century, a period when novels of chivalry were much esteemed. Both were published in Seville by the famous Jacob Cromberger, one in 1512, the other in 1529. We do not know how many additional printings there may have been or how many copies of the two extant editions appeared. But whether or not there were more, either of the known printings may well have been available to Miguel de Cervantes while he was composing *Don Quixote.* Reputable scholars deny any traceable influence from *Cifar* to *Don Quixote,* but it seems to us that the final word has yet to be spoken in this regard, and much remains to prove this assertion. Martín de Riquer, to name but one, flatly states "that no passage of *Cifar* left its trace upon *Don Quixote.*"[4] Later, as though wavering, he wrote, without apparently realizing to what extent he was diluting his earlier pronouncement: "Nevertheless, the character of the Ribaldo (the Knave) and the proverbs which appear in the *Cavallero Cifar* make this novel a book which, except for the three centuries of distance which separate them, suggests to the reader the inventory of the Cervantine masterpiece."[5] But three centuries did *not* separate the two works, for the two known printings make it quite evident that Cervantes would not have had to peruse manuscripts. He would have had access to the published volumes which appeared only a few years before his birth and which probably were available to him while he was penning his masterpiece.

If *Cifar* was among the books he read, why did he not mention it in the famous judgment of the books in

Part One of the *Quixote?* Perhaps because many authors, no matter how honorable, would hardly admit that the focal point of their work had been conceived by an earlier writer. And this same thesis is the axis upon which the development of Cervantes' great book turns. It is fascinating to reflect that Cervantes understood well in advance of his contemporaries that nobles and commoners are mutually dependent and must work together in some sort of communion if the nation is to progress. This realization on his part can, of course, be the inspiration and historical background of the companionship of knight and peasant, an association which is the very crux of his novel. But did he arrive at this conception originally or was it suggested to him by earlier observations on the part of other authors?

When Cervantes wrote, chivalry was quite dead except in the novels of chivalry which so charmed his contemporaries with their derring-do and serialized romantic fantasies. Apparently Cervantes scorned these novels, and yet how assiduously had he read so many of them! Surely no one setting out to satirize a genre ever prepared himself so completely. And yet when in those novels, or indeed in any writings of earlier vintage that he might have encountered, did he read of the unusual communion between a knight (therefore a nobleman) and a squire who was a peasant? Medieval knights did not mingle freely with *villanos,* men of the peasant class, or with commoners from any of the lower strata of their world. In one French twelfth-century geste, it is true, knight and commoner were companions, but not in the essentially polarized and yet symbiotic fashion that characterizes the Knave and the Knight Cifar or Don Quixote and Sancho Panza. Cervantes evidently recognized the value of the rustic foil for his noble knight, and capitalized upon it. But so did the author of the *Cavallero Cifar* much earlier, though not as skillfully nor to such good effect. The latter was incapable of investing the Knave with those qualities of a Sancho Panza, that immortal bumpkin squire who radiates lovable and universally human qualities. But he did create, possibly for the first time in literature, the kind of relationship that later became immortal in *Don Quixote, Lazarillo de Tormes,* and many Golden Age dramas in which noble and *gracioso* (the witty servant) are close companions. Some would attribute the first occurrence of such a fellowship to the author of the romance *Carlos Maynes* of roughly the same period,[6] but even that work falls short of creating anything like the intimate association which obtains between the Knight Cifar and the Knave.

Consider the first part of the *Cavallero Cifar,* which deals primarily with the knight, his wife, and their two sons as they wander about in a long series of adventures encountered and hardships endured, in the course of which they become separated, yet continue to survive, each in his own way. Cifar is a good soldier and military strategist, and his common sense in such matters is both exemplary and admirable. He can lay seige to and storm a stronghold, even a sizable city, with notable success. Yet when it comes to finding food and shelter, he must leave such everyday activities to his thieving, clever, and very roguish squire. Since no noble and villein in earlier literature shared the camaraderie experienced between the Knight Cifar and the Knave, and since the selfsame subjects of satire used by Cervantes are present in *Cifar,* the same sententious discourse, the same symbiotic relationship, we believe it is time to reconsider the question of direct influence.

Nothing is known for certain about the author of *Cifar,* but a good deal can be surmised from his book. He was certainly an erudite and skilled manipulator of the Spanish of his times. Since he probably wrote in the last quarter of the thirteenth century, he would have been cognizant of the reforms in Castilian found in the carefully edited works of King Alfonso X. His obvious morality, especially in the first part of *Cifar,* his occasional insertion of the miraculous in his interpolated tales concerning the Virgin and the Christ Child, and what seems to James F. Burke to be a rather consistent use of figural reference to Jesus,[7] can easily lead to the assumption that he was one of the erudite clergy. But his innate knowledge of military strategy and the tenets of both the old and the new chivalry points also to secular authorship. We lean to the belief that he was actually one of the truly erudite clergy, probably the second or third son of some noble house, and that before he studied for the priesthood he had absorbed a full understanding of matters military and chivalric.

The Prologue of *Cifar* may give a reliable clue to authorship. In it one reads that a certain Ferrand Martínez of Madrid, Archdeacon of the Church of Toledo, journeyed to Rome to obtain and bring back to Spain the remains of a Spanish cardinal, Don Gonzalo Gudiel de Toledo. We believe that this archdeacon may be the elusive author of *Cifar.* He writes in the third person, but this was common among medieval authors when writing about themselves. Toward the end of the Prologue he states that the Archdeacon Martínez (himself?), mindful of the obligations he owed the dead cardinal, reflected that all men should be grateful to those who guide and protect them, and that because memory can be short and people will not recall ancient deeds unless they can see them in writing, the translator of the story to be heard (that is, of *The Knight Cifar*) has had it written down for future generations. He writes also that it has been translated into Latin from Chaldean (which in his times signified Syriac), and from Latin into Romance, which meant Spanish. He adds the ancient and well known directive to the effect that any author who attempts to produce a fine work must interpose in it at times some elements of enjoyment. He sounds the religious note when he reminds his readers that God will help any man who keeps Him in mind, just as He helped a certain knight from India whose name was Cifar. Cifar in Arabic can mean "errant" or "wandering," a most appropriate name for a man who was indeed a knight errant.

If the Archdeacon Ferrand Martínez of the Church of Toledo wrote the *Cifar,* he certainly lived in the perfect milieu for such literary activity. Toledo in this period was at the confluence of Hispano-Christian, Hispano-Arabic, and Hispano-Jewish cultures. In such an atmosphere the author could read French *gestes,* the *matière de Bretagne,* the great compendia of Christian lore, and particularly of pious *exempla;* the miracles of the Blessed Virgin and the saints, both international and local; the fables of Antiquity; fantastic accounts found in such eastern works as the *Thousand Nights and a Night* and *Kalila wa-Dimna,* to name but two; and, not to be forgotten, the lore of the Spanish folk, available in certain books but also very much alive in the popular oral tradition. From these sources and from others not yet identified, the author of *Cifar* produced a remarkable potpourri.[8]

The adventures of the Knight Cifar follow the format of the Byzantine romance, with its shipwrecks, capture by pirates, abduction by wild beasts, separation of family, and final recognition and reunion. All of these elements and others are deftly grafted by the author upon the rootstock of a well-known hagiographical account, the *Life of St. Placidus,* sometimes known as the *Life of St. Eustace,* since Placidus changed his name to Eustace. Though this famous saint's life story was widely dispersed across Christendom, not all scholars today hold that it was the inspiration for parts of the *Cavallero Cifar.* Roger Walker proposes hypothetically a more detailed parallel proto-legend and cites certain oriental possibilities. John K. Walsh prefers Placidus as the source.[9] No matter which is correct, *Cifar*'s author was certainly familiar with the *Life of St. Placidus* and was confident that his audience recognized it, too. We think he realized that a comfortable familiarity is often the best posture to adopt when one wishes to establish rapport with one's read-ers. The universally known life of Placidus was adroitly blended by association with the piety of the principal character, Cifar, thus assuring the reader or audience of the unimpeachable character of the protagonist. If Cifar's reward for his labors was to be glory and happiness in this world, always with the expectation that good works and piety would eventually gain him heaven, such earthly felicity was a fitting parallel to the heavenly bliss of the martyred Placidus.

This balanced formula of earthly saintliness and saintly earthliness produced a story well calculated to satisfy ecclesiastics on the one hand and lay readers on the other, making *Cifar* possibly one of the most successful fusions of the pious and the secular. Readers would not fail to find in the errant knight, just as they had in Placidus, the figural interpretation of Job or even of Our Lord. Readers and audiences whose tastes were more mundane could also savor *Cifar* for the sheer pleasure and excitement it provided. Even a rough knight whose interests lay primarily in battles, booty, and seduction could identify with the adventures of the brave Knight Cifar or with his son Roboán, and could thrill to the harrowing escapes of Cifar's wife Grima. The novel, a strange transition between the saint's life and the Byzantine novel, is a *refundición,* a true recasting of the life of Placidus combined with episodes from oriental and Celtic fantasies and other known and unknown books.

Perhaps no writer ever refurbished a model as much as did the author of *Cifar.* Placidus and his wife were Romans of noble birth living as pagans in the time of Trajan and Hadrian. Early in their hagiographic history they are miraculously converted to Christianity and change their names to Eustace and Theospita. Jesus himself informs them that they must undergo intolerable suffering, just as Job had, but that in the end, if they are able to survive the pain and anguish, they will either regain their former earthly position, or, if that is not to be, will be taken to heaven. A few days later all their servants and animals die and they leave their home, since Eustace must resign his post as an imperial Roman officer. Their adventures, which often find a parallel in those of the Cifars, eventually lead them to martyrdom and a place in Paradise.

The author of *Cifar* alters his characters so that they are citizens of India. We say he changes them, but we are not certain. It is possible that he did indeed, as he states, translate the story from an unknown eastern work, just as did the translator of *Barlaam e Josafat,* whose original characters were all of Indian origin. However this may have been, the Cifars are Hindus and therefore exotic folk from a land most Europeans believed to be inhabited by strange peoples, fabulous monsters, and a variety of demons. The Cifar family, having fallen on hard times and out of royal favor due to the sin of an ancestor, may only be restored to grace when some descendant of that sinner has performed sufficient good works. We are constrained to ask if this particular motif may not derive from vaguely understood or poorly translated implications of Indic belief in the reincarnation of souls through which the sinner, reduced in status or even in physical form through sin, can in successive lives of increasing morality, be reborn on a higher plane. If such influence is present, one might veer indeed toward far-eastern origins.[10]

The life of Placidus contains no elements of chivalry, as does the *Cifar,* wherein two varieties of chivalry play an important role. Cifar himself is true to the tenets of the old chivalric code practiced by the Cid in the famous epic of that name. He meets no monsters, engages in realistic battles, is faithful to his wife, and indulges in no romantic dreams of either attainable or unattainable princesses. Later in the book certain characters, among them Cifar's son Roboán, partake of the new chivalry as embodied in *Amadís de Gaula,* a work much loved by Don Quixote.

The miniatures of *The Book of the Knight Cifar* are found in a manuscript archived at the Bibliothèque Nationale in Paris. Charles P. Wagner, who edited *Cifar,* considered this illuminated codex, on the basis of style, to be of the fifteenth century. A very convincing dating comes from the wide knowledge of medieval costume of María Elena de Arizmendi, who states that the costumes belong to the period between 1470 and 1480. Her contribution is great, for it definitely fixes the date of this second manuscript of *Cifar.* Wagner's dating of the earlier unillustrated manuscript around 1301 has been accepted by most scholars.[11]

The Paris codex, known as MS Espagnol 36, contains 192 folios, or 384 pages, each of which measures 397 by 270 mm (15.62 inches high by 10.62 inches wide). Such a lavishly illustrated volume is unique and must have required the expenditure of much time and effort, not to mention a great deal of money. Only the *Cantigas de Santa Maria* possesses a greater wealth of pictures, and it is therefore a pity that none of Cifar's miniatures have been published in color reproduction until now. It is also unfortunate that we know neither the patron nor the artist or artists.

Of the 241 illuminations, some one dozen visualize the content of brief narratives. Of the remainder, 45 are miniatures in which the Knight Cifar, who has now become the King of Mentón, teaches his two

sons, leaving the surprising number of 184 to illustrate the longer novelesque sequences describing the adventures of the Cifars. It will be recalled that in the *Cantigas* and the *Castigos e documentos,* only brief narratives are illustrated, and that even in *Calila e Digna* the line drawings portray but a few novelesque sequences. The *Cifar,* then, may be the earliest example of illustrated Spanish novelesque fiction.

Though not sectioned into separate divisions, the work may nevertheless be seen as consisting of four distinct parts whose unity is preserved and maintained by the charaters themselves.[12] Part I treats the adventures of the Cifar family before fate separates its members. Following that separation, the narrative focuses on each individual, featuring variously the adventures of Grima, Cifar's wife, and Cifar's own adventures and his association with the Ribaldo, or Knave, which continue until he wins favor at the court of the King of Mentón by saving that land from is enemies. Part II deals with the fortunes of the Knave, who has attained knighthood and is now known as the Cavallero Amigo or Friend Knight, and with the manner by which the Cavallero Cifar marries the Princess of Mentón but avoids consummation of the marriage when he wonders if Grima is still alive. Part III is made up of the teachings which Cifar, the new King of Mentón, relates to his sons, the greater part of which comes from the thirteenth-century *Flores de filosofia.* Part IV recounts the adventures of Roboán, Cifar's son, who goes forth on a knightly quest, eventually returning to his parents.

The pages of *Cifar,* with their measurements of 15.62 by 10.43 inches, are not as large as those of the *Cantigas de Santa Maria,* which measure 19.09 by 13.14 inches. This means that in general *Cifar*'s miniatures are smaller, too. On the other hand, some illuminations in *Cifar* reveal larger human figures for the simple reason that more space is given to them than was possible in the miniatures of the *Cantigas.* Some miniatures in *Cifar* are small enough to be encompassed in one of the two columns of calligraphy, and therefore measure no more than two inches in width, while others, spanning both columns, may measure as much as 8 inches wide by 4 inches high.

The art displayed in the illuminations of the *Cavallero Cifar* is of very high quality in execution and application of color. If the miniatures of the *Cantigas de Santa Maria* are the illustrations par excellence of thirteenth-century art, those of *Cifar* must indeed be viewed as the cream of fifteenth-century secular book illumination. That they have been so utterly neglected as monuments of pictorial art history is as lamentable as the disregard and indifference which until very recently surrounded the miniatures of the *Cantigas de Santa Maria* and the *Castigos e documentos. Cifar* probably owes its beautiful illustrations to royal patronage. We must remember that nearly two hundred years had elapsed since the time of the *Cantigas,* during which art had evolved and borrowed from abroad on a much larger scale. Miniatures from France, Italy, Germany, the British Isles, and probably even Greece, the Islamic East, and Africa may well have played important roles in fifteenth-century Spanish book illustration. We hope that our efforts, which we believe are the first to reproduce miniatures from *Cifar* in full color, will make students of medieval art cognizant of hitherto unrecognized accomplishments in peninsular iconography. We hope, too, that within a few years we may be able to obtain an entire set of color reproductions of *Cifar* and will be able to undertake a comprehensive investigation of its treasure trove of visual narrative techniques.

The world as painted by the artist of the *Cavallero Cifar* is a far cry from that of either the *Cantigas* or the *Castigos*. Landscape and seascape are far less conventionalized than those in King Alfonso's great Marian anthology or those found in *Castigos,* which are much closer chronologically. *Cifar's* illuminator lavished much greater attention on landscape and seascape, which he made more expansive, more detailed, more colored by love of depth and perspective, and apparently imbued with a finer feeling for more realistic and exact reproduction. In the *Cantigas,* for example, mountains are more often suggested than exactly portrayed, while in *Cifar* they tower above plain and seacoast in truly impressive loftiness and grandeur.

Architecture as painted in *Cifar* is not only strikingly beautiful but of great historical interest. All the castles, fortresses, churches, and other buildings are of western European vintage, even though the events of *Cifar* are said to take place first in India and subsequently in various parts of Asia. In several scenes the reader will discover castles belonging to periods earlier than the fifteenth century, which is perfectly natural. Others, especially those castles with the majestic towers and peaked turrets we find exalted in the beautiful Alcázar of Segovia (a structure Walt Disney chose to typify as the quintessence of the fabled "Castle in Spain"), are from an age when esthetics mattered quite as much as military strength. These fortifications closely resemble the truly delicate and beautiful structures found in the *Belles Heures* and the *Tres Riches Heures* of Jean Duc de Berry of the same chronological period.[13] Few such edifices existed in Spain, even in the fifteenth century, so that their presence in a Spanish manuscript of that time is surprising, to say the

least. They suggest that *Cifar's* artist had either traveled to lands where such buildings stood or studied the illuminations of such strongholds in books from abroad.

With regard to the human figure, especially in the realm of facial expressions, *Cifar's* artist surpasses the painters of the Learned King and parallels fairly closely the skill and refinement of the *Castigos,* which belong to the same general period. Human figures in *Cifar* emerge from the artist's brush with heightened grace and poise, and with less stiffness. More attention is also paid to proportion, and there is a rather constant insistence upon true skin coloration.

Since the subject matter of *Cifar* varies so greatly from that of the *Cantigas* and also, though to a lesser extent, from that of the *Castigos,* there is much less emphasis on religious topics. The Virgin, though she speaks, does not appear in either the verbalization or the visualization of *Cifar,* and though Jesus is seen in the sequence of Grima's adventures, he is always the Child Jesus, perched in several instances on the mast of her ship. The supernatural—the world of demons and monsters—is confined in *Cifar* to the adventures of the Cavallero Atrevido in the underwater realm of the Lady of the Lake, who is in truth a demon if not perhaps the devil himself, and to the rather bizarre events and relationships which surround Roboán, Cifar's son, in the Yslas Dotadas, a never-never land of either oriental or Celtic provenance, or of both. The world of nature interested the artist greatly and led him to some noteworthy depictions of plants and animals. But though in *Cifar* the artist painted with a slightly more realistic touch, he does not stray far from the style of animal portrayal found in the *Cantigas de Santa Maria* and often falls short of the latter's accomplishments.

In the discussion to follow, we stress pictorial art in the miniatures, for some of which we were fortunate enough to obtain color reproductions from the Bibliothèque Nationale. The number is lamentably small due to the prohibitive cost, but the illuminations we have chosen are representative of the narrative techniques in which color figures prominently. The black-and-white reproductions serve well enough as the framework for discussion of the nine basic elements of the classic design of narrative, and enable us to parallel visualization with verbalization.

The initial folio, 1r, of the *Libro del Cavallero Cifar* presents the first visualization even before the text begins. The miniature (Plate 51), which is quite small, spans only one column. On this first page, the two columns of text are narrower than anywhere else in the book due to a band of very ornamental artwork which separates them. In this small but most brilliant illumination the artist illustrates, we believe, an important event related in the Prologue—the petition of Archdeacon Ferrand Martínez to Pope Boniface VIII for permission to remove the body of the Spanish Cardinal Gonzalo Gudiel of Toledo from his resting place in Santa Maria Maggiore so as to take it to be buried in Toledo. Earlier in the Prologue the Cardinal had exacted a promise from his former student Martínez to arrange for the transportation of his body to his native soil. The archdeacon managed the arduous and perilous journey.

In the first illumination, then, we see Pope Boniface seated on his golden throne as he receives the archdeacon. He holds audience in a beamed chamber painted in robin's egg blue. In his crimson cope, from which samite sleeves and collar protrude, and his three-tiered tiara of the same brilliant hue, the pope cuts an imposing and colorful figure. He wears papal garments, identified as of the very late fifteenth century, and the two cardinals standing just beyond wear the caps and copes of this period.[14] The archdeacon kneels at the pontiff's feet, his hands extended in prayer, as he asks permission to remove the body of his mentor and take it to Spain. His flowing robe of cream, from which the green sleeves and collar of his cassock project, offers great contrast to the robes of the three high ecclesiastics. The pope's face is benign, the archdeacon's intent and serious.

Framing the entire column—text and miniature—is a highly decorative band composed of human figures, animals, birds, flowers, fruits, vines, and leaves. It is quite as ornate and many-hued as similar designs found in contemporary books of hours. If the characters are indeed Pope Boniface and Archdeacon Ferrand Martínez with two cardinals, then the artist has portrayed in his pictorial introduction a crucial incident from the verbal prologue. It is a remarkable opening for a series of illustrations and is representative of the close parallel of visualization and verbalization which characterizes the entire volume. If Ferrand Martínez is the author of *Cifar,* as we opine, then the artist has portrayed an author (one he had not seen, of course, for much time separated artist and writer) as he might have looked in the clerical costume of the artist's own time, not that of Ferrand Martínez's era.

Moving beyond this introductory miniature, we treat first the visualization of four brief narratives selected from the dozen scattered through the work. The first is the by-now familiar story of the half-friend, also found in the *Castigos* and there illustrated by a single miniature.[15] Plate 52, from folio 6r, appears in the left-hand column of the text. The verbalization reveals that the author of *Cifar* has added to the age-old tale of the half-friend. In this version the father tells the son that he has had to kill one of the son's enemies, who was lying in wait for him. The father then puts the dismembered body of a pig into a sack, so that the son, as he test his friends, does not have to pretend that the body is that of a man, as in other versions, but really believes it. As in the other versions, the son is rejected by all his friends.

The miniature shows a room in the father's house, where he can be seen killing the pig prior to cutting it into pieces. He wears a short-sleeved shirt of scarlet with a robin's egg blue cuff just above the elbow. His vest is buttoned from the V of the neck to his waist. He wears either short trousers or more probably a skirt or an apron which cannot be seen, since it is hidden by the table upon which the pig struggles. One can see both his legs, which are bare from the knee to the calf-high boots. The floor is handsomely laid in terra cotta tile put down in a diamond-shaped design. Two blue door frames behind the man rise to a vaulted and ribbed ceiling. The wooden table or workbench is so detailed that one can see its knotholes and the four round legs, which, due to poorly indicated perspective, make the table appear to float. With his left hand the man grasps the pig's forelegs firmly, while his left arm holds the hind legs close against his body, thereby controlling the animal's struggles. With his right hand he plunges a silvery blade into the beast's throat, and two streams of crimson blood gush forth over the table's surface and to the floor.

The entire miniature is framed by a simple oblong, which at the top curves inward on each corner, enclosing the scene in a kind of romanesque arch with a roselle motif in the upper corners. Clusters of golden-brown leaves and berries or fruits are painted outside the frame. Without the accompanying text the picture would have meant little to one who was not familiar with the story.

The second incident, seen in Plate 53, from the right-hand column of folio 6r visualizes the moment when the son, carrying over his shoulder the sack containing the body of the pig, approaches the first of his friends. It could almost have been copied from the miniature in the *Castigos,* leading to the suspicion that both books used some earlier illustration as a model, perhaps some lost text of the *Disciplina Clericalis,* the book which introduced the story into western fiction.

Scene here is detailed and costumes carefully delineated. Across the top of the miniature is the skyline of a substantial city partially concealed by rocky brown hills. To the city's left, green slopes topped by a grove of trees appear, and behind both hill and slopes can be seen the turrets and battlements of a castle. Characterization is expressed in the two men as they face one another, just as in the verbal account. The young man's serious expression shows concern, and the uncooperative friend grasps his arm vigorously with his right hand to arrest his progress, while holding the pommel of his sword with his left.

Costumes are particularly well adapted. The bareheaded, close-cropped young man with the sack wears a blue robe near knee-length, caught at the waist by a belt from which hangs a sword in its scabbard. His legs are bare and his shoes of brown leather and laces can be seen. His friend wears a blue robe and a scarlet cloak with a figured border and a peaked scarlet cap. They are obviously people of consequence, perhaps even wealthy.

Considerable conflict is evident, and the theme, which is the undependability of friends in time of need, is bitter and as well presented artistically as it is verbally. The realistic style is portrayed by a confident and skilled artistic hand. Only the simplest framing device is used, clusters of golden circles at each corner and at the middle of each of the miniature's sides.

Some part of the verbalization merits inclusion:

"Surely, father," said the son, "I am pleased [by the father's plan mentioned earlier in the story] and you will now see what friends I have gained."

And he took that sack on his shoulders and went to the home of a friend he trusted most; and when he reached him, the other marvelled because it was so late at night, and he asked him what it was he carried in that sack, and he told him everything and asked that they bury it in a garden he had there; and his friend replied that since he and his father had committed the folly, they should abide by it and that he [the son] should get away from his house; and he did not wish to see himself endangered for them.

The story goes on to relate that all the other friends reply in kind and that the son returns to his father with his sack and tells him how none of his friends wish to take a chance for him in his danger. The scene visualized illustrates perfectly the instant of time it portrays.

In all other versions we have encountered, the story ends when the half-friend buries the sack and the father proves to his son that the world contains very, very few true friends. But the author of *Cifar* was not content with so simple a dénouement and added from his own imagination, or perhaps from some unknown version, new and peculiar incidents which the artist

illustrates with a miniature found on folio 6v (Plate 54), set into the test of the right-hand column. This part of the story was anticipated earlier when the father persuaded the son that the body in the sack was that of a slain man, not a pig. The father now tells the son to go to the half-friend and tell him to dig up what is in the sack, and that they will join the friend for dinner when the sack's contents have been properly roasted. The son is at first dubious about eating human flesh, but once he has tasted the flesh of the roasted pig, thinking it to be that of a man, he delights in the savor and remarks, "and surely, since an enemy's flesh tastes so good, my other enemies shall not escape." Then the father and the half-friend decide they had better tell the young man that he has eaten pork, lest he become a confirmed cannibal.

The visualization of this preposterous finale is framed only by the walls and beamed ceiling of the half-friend's dining room. The three sit around a large square table covered with a white cloth. Three round loaves, the hindquarters of the pig, and a knife to cut them with lie on the table. The gentlemen drink from tall goblets and might be speaking of anything. We see no table legs and wonder if the table, like the benches upon which the men sit, is fastened to the walls of the alcove. The gray-haired, gray-bearded father sits at the right in a puce robe and is barefooted, as are his table mates. He is about to put a morsel of bread into his mouth, but seems to have paused to speak, for his left hand is raised in a gesture of some sort. Across the table from him sits the half-friend, also middle aged, in a robe of burnt orange. He is about to drink from a goblet. His hair is light brown, but his sideburns and the hair at the nape of his neck are gray. His face and the father's bear wrinkles and other marks of age.

The son faces the viewer, about to take a bite of bread. His lime-green robe sets off his light chestnut hair. His face is young and reveals none of the wisdom of his elders. Such a face becomes perfectly the inexperienced and headstrong character that is his.

The ancient *exemplum,* also in *Disciplina Clericalis,* of the man who caught a lark and freed it on the condition that it give him three pieces of invaluable advice, appears on folios 98v and 99r. It forms an integral part of the teachings that Cifar, the King of Mentón, offers his sons. In the first illustration of the story, from folio 98v, framed by no more than a simple oblong, the scene is limned in intricate detail and may be viewed in Plate 55. Under a bright blue arched porch of the house, whose flat roof, ornate with a carved frieze, is supported by four round, slender columns with lathed capitals and pedestals, stands the hunter. Through the arches the terra cotta tiled walls of a fine house appear, and above these, in still deeper perspective, rise four groves of trees, the foliage of each blending into a single canopy.

The hunter is garbed in a tunic of darkest cobalt, the broad hem of which is decorated with an attractive motif in goldwork; his legs, in hose of brilliant green, flow naturally into ankle-length boots, and he wears a turbanlike green headdress. In his left hand he holds the lark captive, grasping it by its wings. This "lark" is so detailed in presentation that the viewer can distinguish even the smallest individual feathers. But its size—as large as a good-sized hen—and its long snipe-like beak are not those of a lark, a bird no larger than a robin. The hunter has drawn from its scabbard of tooled leather a long curved knife and has raised it preparatory to killing the bird. His visage is swarthy and bearded. It is a dark and merciless face, and one not denoting high intelligence. He seems to raise his brows as though considering the bargain offered by the bird. The hunter's net lies where he has dropped it on the floor of the porch, which is sprinkled with what appears to be a design of golden aspen leaves. Scene, though beautiful and most attractive, is certainly not truly sylvan. Characterization of the hunter seems well developed, and also conflict.

The verbalization of this fine old story in *Cifar* is well worth translating, as much for its excellent narrative technique as for its clever handling of the elements of the classic design.

The story goes that a fowler went hunting with his nets and caught a lark and nothing more. And he returned to his house and put hand to knife to behead it and eat it. And the lark said to him: "Alas, friend, what a great sin you commit in killing me! Do you not realize you cannot sate yourself with me, since I am a very small morsel for a big body like yours? Therefore, I consider it better to free me and let me live, for I will give you three pieces of good advice from which you can derive advantage if you wish to follow it."

"Certainly," said the hunter, "I am very pleased, and if you give me one piece of good advice, I shall free you from my hand."

"Well, I give you the first counsel," said the lark, "that you not believe anything which you see and realize cannot be; the second is that you do not seek after what is lost, if you understand that you cannot regain it; the third, that you do not strive for something you understand you cannot obtain. And I give you these three similar pieces of advice, one after the other, where you demanded only one."

"Surely," said the hunter, "you have given me three fine admonitions." And he loosed the lark and let it out of his hand, and as the lark flew above the hunter's house she saw that he was going hunting with his snares, and she flew right in front of him in the air, watching out to see whether he would follow her. And as the hunter went along spreading his nets and calling birds with his sweet decoys, the lark, who was in the air, spoke to him: "Oh, wretch, how you were deceived by me!"

"And who are you?" said the hunter.

"I am the lark whom you freed today for the advice I gave you."

"As I see it, I wasn't deceived," said the hunter, "for you gave me good counsels."

"That is true," said the lark, "if you learned them well."

"So," said the hunter, "tell me how I was tricked by you."

"I'll tell you," said the lark. "If you had known that I have a precious stone which is as large as an ostrich's egg in my belly, I am certain you would not have let me go, for you would have been rich forever if you had kept me. I would have lost the power of speech and you would have obtained greater strength had you carried out what you wished."

The hunter when he heard it was very sad and grieved, thinking it was as the bird said, and he went after her to snare her again with his sweet decoying. But the lark, since she was wary, protected herself from him and refused to descend from the air, saying, "Oh, fool, how badly you learned the counsels I gave you."

"Surely," said the hunter, "I remember them well."

"That may be," said the lark, "but you didn't learn them well, for if you did learn them, you do not know how to use them."

"And why not?" asked the hunter.

Said the lark: "You know that I said the first counsel was not to believe anything you see and know cannot be."

"That is true," said the hunter.

"Well, how," asked the lark, "are you to believe that in so small a body as mine there could fit a stone as large as the egg of an ostrich? Well should you have understood that it is not a thing to be believed. In the second counsel I told you not to strive after something lost if you understand that you cannot recover it."

"That is true," said the hunter.

"Then, why," said the lark, "do you strive in thinking that you can catch me again in your snares and with your sweet whistlings? Do you not know that from the experienced are fashioned the wise? You surely should have understood that since once I escaped your hands, I would keep myself from falling into your power, and it would be very just if you killed me as you desired to the other time if I did not protect myself from you. And the third counsel was that I told you not to follow after something you realize you cannot get."

"That is true," said the hunter.

"And," said the lark, "since you see that I go flying wherever I please through the air, and that you cannot rise after me nor do you have the power to do it, for it is not your nature, you should not attempt to follow me, since you cannot fly as I do."

"Surely," said the hunter, "I shall not rest until I catch you through trick or force!"

"You speak madly," said the lark, "and may God preserve you, for God makes the proud fall from on high."

The story in all the other versions we have read ends here with the bird's departure. But again, as was the case with the story of the half-friend, *Cifar*'s author embroiders upon the age-old tale, providing it with a new and extravagant ending. On folio 99r appears an illustration of the revised dénouement (Plate 56). The hunter has gone to a magician who equips him with the plumage and pinions of a bird, probably of an eagle or vulture, since the wings are large. He has climbed up into a high tower, and the miniature now captures him in his headlong fall to earth and to his death. The lines of the text visualized in the illumination read: "And the hunter did so, [clothed himself in feathers], and when he leaped from the tower, thinking to fly, he did not know how and could not, for it was not in his nature, and he fell to the earth and was crushed and died."

The illumination in its simple oblong frame occupies the lower half of the right-hand column of the folio, and is of remarkable color and detail. Much of the classic design is reflected here. Scene, conflict, characterization—indeed, all or the greater part of the nine elements can be distinguished. Very few of the larger miniatures excel this one in arrangement and in the use of a variety of hues. Scene is lavish in detail. In the background is a skyline composed of rocky, conical hills, which rise above slopes green with agricultural activity. The characteristic groves appear, the many boles of trees supporting the blended leafy treetops. A very ornate blue castle with needle-like spires rises into the sky. In the foreground at the left we see a house whose walls are of bottle green slabs of masonry. The doorway is a yellow oblong in which is an arch, and above it rises the angle of a thatched roof, with a dormer window to let in light. At the far right towers a truly beautiful piece of medieval architecture—a tower of pale pink stones, its base decorated with circles, as is the upper portion just beneath its crenelations. Four stories, each with two arched windows, and one with double doors and a landing and two steps, complete its design.

The magician who has assisted the fowler in his mad preparation for flight stands within the doorway wearing a scarlet robe. His face surely expresses sorrow at the failure of his client's attempt to fly. His hands in unmistakable sign language are raised in a gesture of amazement and consternation. But it is the fowler who occupies the center of this remarkable scene, as he hurtles earthward, having cast himself

from the top of the tower. One is reminded of the heretical Samaritan magician Simon Magus of the first century, who according to legend attempted to fly from a tower in Rome and was dashed to death. The author of *Cifar*, as well as the artist, would have known the story of Simon and may well have seen depictions of his fall, for they were available. The fowler has covered himself from neck to toe with slate-blue plumage, so detailed that scores of individual feathers are visible. The pinions of an eagle are affixed to his arms and shoulders, leaving only his hands showing. He pulls back his head as though to avoid the oncoming contact with the ground. He has closed his eyes, or at least is squinting as one would surely do under such circumstances.

The effect and tone of this miniature blend to produce a theme well calculated to evoke the essential imprudence, the audacity, and the blind impetuousness of a foolish man who has repeatedly spurned the good advice given him by his feathered counselor. Medieval man would have had no sympathy for this unheeding fellow and would certainly have understood the moralization embodied in the story and the visualization. This miniature is probably one of the most beautiful and well proportioned in the entire manuscript.

The peculiar and macabre motif of the bitten-off lips[16] is visualized for the viewer in two graphically executed miniatures, which may be the first pictorial representation of this grim tale to be found in any Spanish manuscript. Cifar, as the King of Mentón, recounts the events within the context of educating his two sons. It is an unusual narrative:

The story tells of a lady who was happily married to a very good and wealthy knight and when this knight died, he left a young son whom he had by this lady, and no other. And the lady so well loved this son, because she had no other, that whatever he did, either of good or evil, she praised and gave him to understand that she was well pleased. And when the lad grew up, there was no work of the devil which he did not undertake since he wished to do them all, stealing on the highways, killing many men without cause, and raping women wherever he found them and it pleased him.

And if those who had to maintain the laws arrested him for some of these reasons, his mother immediately got him out of prison, paying something to those who demanded his arrest, and taking him home, and saying not a word of chastisement nor about the evil he had done. Instead she enjoyed the most pleasant times in the world with him and invited knights and squires to dine with him as though he possessed all good things and had gained all the prowess that a man could have.

So it was that in the wake of all these crimes which he

committed the emperor came to the city where that lady dwelt, and quickly those who had received dishonor and evil at the hands of that squire came to the emperor and complained to him of them. And the emperor was astonished at these ugly things which the squire had done, for he had known his father who had been his vassal a long time and he spoke well of him. And because of these complaints he sent for the squire and asked him if he had done all the evil those plaintiffs said about him and reported. Now he knew he had, but he always excused himself that he had done it due to his youth and lack of understanding.

"Surely," said the emperor, "for the least of these things a thousand men who had done them would deserve to die, if it were proven, and if my own son should fall into these errors I would order him put to death for it. And since you are so cognizant of what you did, it is not necessary that we make any other inquiry, since for what is manifest there is no need of proof."

And he ordered his constable to take him off to be executed. And as they led him off to die, the lady, his mother, followed behind him, wailing and clawing her face with her nails and making the loudest laments in the world so that there was not a man in the city who did not greatly pity her. And the good men went to beg mercy of the emperor so that he would pardon him, and even some of the plaintiffs grieved for the lady. But the emperor, as one pleased to carry out justice, did not wish to pardon him, but rather was all the more adamant in his determination.

And as he arrived at the place where he was to die, his mother asked the constable that for mercy's sake he might allow her to embrace and kiss her son on the mouth before they executed him. And the constable ordered the guards to halt and not to slay him until his mother came up and embraced him. The guards halted and told him that his mother wanted to embrace and kiss him on the mouth before he died, and the son was very happy and immediately said in a loud voice: "Let my mother be welcome, for she desires to help me carry out justice as she should, and well do I believe that God can wish nothing save that the one who suffers pain deserves to suffer it."

All were amazed by those words which that squire spoke and they waited to see what would happen. And as that lady reached her son, she opened her arms like a woman most concerned for him. And they had loosed his hands, though they guarded him well so that he would not escape.

"Friends," said the squire, "do not think that I am going anywhere, for I desire my death and am pleased that justice be carried out, and I consider myself a great sinner in committing so much evil as I have committed, and I wish to begin with the one who deserves it."

And he went up to his mother who wanted to kiss and embrace him, and he seized her with both of his hands by the ears and her hair, and placed his mouth against hers, and he began to gnaw and chew both her lips in such a way that he left nothing up to her nose, nor of her lower lip down to her chin, and all her teeth were showing and she was hideous and terribly mutilated.

All there were horrified by this terrible cruelty which that squire had committed and they began to hurl insults at him and to beat him. And he said: "Good folk, do not berate me nor lay hands on me, for it was God's justice and He commanded me to do it."

"But why to your mother?" the others said. "Is she to suffer for the evil you committed? Give us a reason that moved you to do it."

"Surely," said the squire, "I will tell no one but the emperor."

Many went to the emperor to tell him the cruelty which that squire had committed and told him how he would not tell anyone why he did it except him. And the emperor ordered that he be brought before him, and he would not even sit down to eat until he had been apprised of this strange act and why it had been done.

And when the squire came before him along with the lady, his mother, most ugly and disfigured, the emperor said to the squire, "Say, false traitor, did not all the sins you committed in this world satisfy you? And that you should oblige your mother who bore you, and reared you in luxury, and lost on your account all she owned, paying for the sins you committed, to appear in a way that is unseemly before the eyes of men? And did you not fear God or the vengeance of men who hold you to be so evil and cruel?"

"Sire," said the squire, "what God considers worthy of being done no one ought to keep from being done. And God Who is the justice-giver over all the judges of the world wanted justice to be manifest in the person of her who was the cause of the sins I committed."

"And how can this be?" said the emperor.

"Surely, Sire, I shall tell you. This lady, my mother whom you see, even though she was well bred, the doer of good to those in need, giving alms very freely and hearing her hours most devoutly, considered it good not to chastise me by word or act when I was small nor after I was grown, and she praised everything I did, whether it was good or evil. And, curse it, she spent more on evil deeds than on good ones! And now, when they told me she wanted to greet me and kiss me on the mouth, it seemed to me that someone descended from heaven who put it in my mind that I should gnaw the lips of the one who had not been able to punish me and did not wish to. I did so, believing that it was God's justice. And He knows well that she is that thing in this world which I love most. But since God wanted it to be so, it could not be otherwise. And, Sire, if greater justice is to be done here, order it done to me, for much I deserve it, to my misfortune."

And the plaintiffs present pitied the squire greatly and the lady, his mother, who was very sad because the emperor was having him executed; and seeing that the squire recognized the errors into which he had fallen, they begged the emperor for mercy's sake to pardon him, since they pardoned him.

"Certainly," said the emperor, "God has done me much grace in this case in His desire to carry out justice on the one He knew for certain was the occasion of all the sins which this squire committed. And since God so wished it, I pardon him and acquit him of the sentence I ordered done, not knowing the truth of the matter as did that One who showed it. And blessed be His Name forever!"

And immediately he made him a knight and received him as his vassal, and he was thereafter a fine man and much honored; and justice was carried out on that lady who deserved it, as an example to those who must rear children so that they will not allow themselves to fall into the danger of failing to punish their charges.

The verbalization is typical of *Cifar*'s careful narrative techniques. The style is clear and direct, presenting the necessary details, yet sustaining a definite economy with those particulars needed to create an atmosphere which will support the rather unexpected ending. Though a macabre story, it fascinates and is apparently deathless.

The miniatures previously discussed were small, appearing within the columns of the text. Both the illuminations of this story are much larger, spanning both columns of the page. The first (Plate 57), from folio 106r intercepts that moment in the narrative when the squire is on his way to execution. The simple gallows, made from the boles of two trees, with forks to support the crossbar from which pieces of rope hang, rises from stony ground over what may be a manmade structure, perhaps for the purpose of burial. A herald in a blue tunic, gold hose, and green boots marches along blowing a long trumpet to announce the event. Behind him on foot come five guards with colorful shields and long spears, and behind them the squire mounted upon an ass, since condemned criminals were not allowed to ride horses, with only a blanket under him in lieu of a saddle. His naked legs protrude from his scarlet tunic and his bare feet hang free, for there are no stirrups. He bends low over the neck of his mount, while his mother in a full-length, colorfully figured gown and a cloak leans to kiss him, her arms around his shoulders. A white wimple frames her haggard face. Four mounted guards carrying spears sit on their horses behind her, one of whom appears to be a constable. The scene is starkly portrayed, with rocky escarpments rising along the sides of the road, while in the distance the skyline is a flat horizon whose monotony is relieved only by an occasional grove of trees. It is a perfect setting for a hanging, created skillfully by an artist who knew quite well how to produce the necessary mood.

In the verbalization the mother does not approach her son as he rides, but waits for him to dismount. Here in the visual representation of the event she certainly clasps him in her arms while he is mounted. The viewer can see him bending forward and twisting

his head to place his face against hers. The artist even reveals his open mouth as he makes ready to bite his mother. Conflict, which is the strongest element portrayed here, is thus clearly in evidence, together with suspense and characterization, starkly depicted in the action of the lady and the faces of the escort, both mounted and on foot. Pictorial style conceals nothing, and the effect is one of grimness and horror.

Plate 58 presents the miniature found on folio 109v, illustrating a scene from the dénouement of the story. This miniature, like the former, runs the full width of the page and occupies, as did the previous picture, about one-third of the page. The scene takes us to the emperor's court and a roofless walled enclosure of pink masonry which encompasses most of the available space. At the far left stand two great towers whose carved tops on either side of a tall gate rise against a skyline of rocky hills and groves of umbrella pines. Beyond the wall rises the gallows. The emperor sits on a dais, his scepter over his left shoulder, his right hand extended in a gesture demanding reply. His black velvet cap with a brim and a peaked crown, with its row of tiny golden crosses, his brilliant robe with its neckline, hem, and broad sleeves ornate with golden design, and his golden scepter render him a very distinguished and compelling figure. The artist has successfully captured his expression in such a way as to depict that grave, uncompromising character which is invested in the verbalization.

Standing before the monarch we see a group composed of the disfigured lady, her son—whose crossed hands are securely bound with a rope, while another rope, no doubt the hangman's noose, is fastened around his neck firmly and held by a guard—, two other guards, and an old man, probably the constable. These officers seem to be members of the emperor's guard, for they carry shields emblazoned in one case with a lion rampant and in the other with fleurs-de-lis. The emperor appears to be asking the squire why he has bitten off his mother's lips. The young man has adopted a forthright stance, gazing directly into the emperor's face, his expression clearly contrite. He now wears a bottle-green tunic and yellow hose, but is still barefoot—this in contrast to his costume in the previous miniature. His mother, no doubt unable to speak, since her wound is so recent, gesticulates with her hands as though trying to prompt her son as he addresses the monarch. The viewer is not denied the sight of her mutilation, for he can see that her nose is gone and her lips damaged, but he cannot see her teeth, which the verbalization states were visible. Blood from her face drips onto her white collar.

Harmonious blending of colors makes this miniature most attractive to the eye. The artist has depicted in a very special and tasteful style a scene with inherent topical interest to his viewers, that is, a royal courtroom; though he has gone much farther than did the writer, who provided no details whatsoever concerning the site of the trial or of the ultimate acquittal of the squire. The style possesses great originality, but one of many such examples.

The last brief narrative we discuss comes, as did the previous one, from that extensive section of the manuscript devoted to the teachings of the King of Mentón, and appears on folio 138r (Plate 59). It typically involves a story within a story, which we translate in its entirety. The King of Mentón has just related the account of a Moorish ruler who apprehended several of his men in the act of stealing from the royal treasury. When he accosts one of them, the thief, in his defense, recounts the story of the wolf and the leeches:

"Sire, I tell you what has happened to you is even as that which happened to a wolf who, passing through a field, met some sheepdogs. And the dogs went after him and because he did not see a place where he could hide or take refuge, he plunged into a rather large lake which was in the field and passed over to the other side. Now in that lake were many leeches and they clung to the wolf so that his whole body was covered with them and they were filled with the blood they had drawn from him. And he began to pull them off with his teeth and to cast them away from him while the dogs rounded the lake toward him. And when he had plucked off all the leeches, he saw the dogs were near and leaped into the water again and passed over to the other side, finding himself again covered by other leeches which were full of his blood. And he began to tear them off, although he was quite weak due to the great amount of blood they had sucked from him.

And while he was in this travail another wolf came up and asked him what he was doing. He told him that he was pulling off leeches and that he was very weak from the blood they had taken from him and he feared that in his weakened condition he would not be able to cross the lake should the dogs again circle around it.

"Friend," said the other wolf, "since the dogs are coming I do not want to linger, but I advise you if again you cross the lake, not to pull off the leeches which stick to you and are sated and should not be pulled off since they are full; and if you take them off and have to go across the lake again, other hungry ones will stick to you which will try to fill up on your blood like these and you will lose strength and will not be able to swim. And if you had left on the first which stuck to you, since they were full, you would have done better, for the hungry ones would not have had a place to stick and thus you would not have lost so much blood from your body."

The miniature which illustrates this story belongs to the larger variety of illuminations, spanning as it does the width of both columns. It is a brilliant and entertaining miniature into which the artist has attempted, we believe, to inject to a fair degree the elements of the classic design.

The scene most colorfully portrays the land on both sides of the lake and the lake itself. The background is a profile of sere and brown rocky hills crowned by very thick groves and by a most military looking castle with surely four gray towers, although one of them is concealed by another. The banks of the lake are steep and brilliant green, while the water is blue, with lines to indicate waves, but is clear enough to allow the viewer to see the lower legs and feet of the wolf beneath the surface in a kind of perspective all its own and most intriguing. On either shore sit two dogs, one brown, one gray, illustrating that they have pursued the wolf to one side of the lake and then have rounded it to assail him on the other. Here is a definite double action of the type previously seen in *Calila e Digna,* the *Cantigas de Santa Maria,* and *Castigos e documentos,* for there are not two separate pairs of dogs but rather the same two dogs in two sequential incidents. The dogs are huge, wolflike creatures capable of fighting wolves. In the center of the lake the gray wolf stands snarling with blazing eyes and teeth bared. Black leeches, depicted with unmistakable realism, cling to his neck, body, and upper legs.

Here characterization is well visualized. The dogs are distinctly aggressive, with bared fangs and fierce eyes, and one can easily understand why the wolf fears them. The wolf is a wild and fearsome looking animal, as one might expect. Conflict is evident, while suspense is created by the wolf's situation on the horns of a dilemma, in the middle of the lake with the dogs a constant threat and the leeches clinging to his body. It is an incident alive with action. Style leaves nothing to the imagination and makes clear exactly what is taking place. The mood is one of potential violence. This is surely the best portrayal of the long-lived fable to be found anywhere in medieval books.

The *Libro del Cavallero Cifar* may be the first illustrated novel in Spanish literature, and in this context represents an important step in the development of both art and narrative away from the short, didactic *exemplum* or miracle, with its relatively simple visualization of the entire action, often contained within a single frame, toward the elaboration of complicated episodes with their accompanying serialized illustrations. The miniatures next to be observed illustrate the adventures of the Cifar family during and after its departure from a city whose inhabitants, ruled by a noble lady, have just been liberated by Cifar from a series of protracted sieges, punctuated by numerous

Figure 30

skirmishes, battles, and invasions of enemy lines. Because there are many miniatures in this sequence, we present the most interesting in color and round out the events of the series with black and white plates for the less moving and less unusual illuminations.

On folio 32r (Figure 30) the Cifars—Grima and the two sons riding, Cifar on foot—take their leave of a loyal citizen who had hoped to persuade the family to take up residence in that city. One of Cifar's sons looks back toward the town as though reluctant to forsake the comforts they have known there and plunge into unknown perils and adventures. The text reads: "And so they traveled until they reached a kingdom called Falac." There, when the ten days have passed since Cifar mounted the horse given him by the lady of the city, and it has died (as must all horses he rides, due to the curse he bears), he and his family stop to rest at a spring in a beautiful *locus amoenus*. It is not far from the city of Falac that tragedy again strikes; it is a two-fold tragedy and heralds the separation of the family. (*Falak* in Arabic means "separation," but since there is to this day a city of that name, there may be no symbolism involved.)

"Dear husband," said Grima, "let us dismount at this spring and assuage our thirst."

"Very well," said the knight. And they were close to that spring and were eating at leisure, since they had come on their journey near to a city named Mella. And after they had eaten, the Knight lay down for awhile and placed his head in his wife's lap, and as she plucked off fleas, he fell asleep. Now his sons were playing about in that meadow and were getting close to a small grove when a lioness emerged from it and seized the older boy. At the screams of the other child as he fled, the lady turned her head and saw how the lioness was carrying off her little son, and she began to cry, "An animal is carrying off your elder son, and I know not whether it is a lion or a lioness, and it has gone into the forest."

The knight mounted the lady's palfrey and rode into the woods, but he found nothing and returned to the lady downcast and very sad. "Let us go to the city which is nearby," he said, "for we can do nothing here save thank God for what He does for us and accept it as His will."

On folio 32v (Plate 60) the artist has depicted most of what the text relates. The abduction of the child unfolds in a series of actions, as the eye moves from left to right. At the far left a recumbent Cifar, lying on his side, his face supported by his hand, is seen in the moment after the plucking of the fleas, for Grima no longer holds his head in her lap. The arrival of the child who has escaped has distracted her. Apparently Cifar is about to wake up. At the right, the lioness—identified as such by her teats—bounds nimbly away with the little boy dangling from her jaws. She realistically holds her head high, as an animal would when carrying such a weight, in order not to drag its prey and stumble over it. Grima's hands are almost vocal in

Figure 31

their gestures of despair. Seldom do we find in any miniature so much action, suspense, conflict, or setting.

This illumination is one of the brightest in color in *Cifar,* and has the greatest number of details. The skyline reveals the turrets, towers, and walls of Falac, which sits on a low hill with many groves of flowering or fruiting trees. A stream flows between the Cifar family and the fleeing beast, and its almost white surface reflects the sky, whose pale blue is muted. The green groves lend a brilliance to the scene, and the castle is even more colorful in its deep but bright blue, set off by crimson and pink towers and turrets. This castle is one of the most brilliant depicted in the miniatures of *Cifar.*

The Knight Cifar is clothed in a brilliant cobalt robe with a rust-red collar, and Grima in a peach-colored gown which flows across the greensward. The remaining son is in a blue robe like his father's.

Scene is highly detailed and sometimes ingenuous, as proportion is sacrificed in favor of detail and action. Here the meager verbal description has been superbly expanded and amplified into several moments of time and several aspects of scene—Cifar's awakening, Grima's alarm, and the lioness with the child in her jaws.

Readers of the text must surely have enjoyed the marvelous visual amplifications.

Folio 33r (Figure 31) attempts, though not with great success, to visualize the action following the arrival of the Cifar family in Falac and the events which take place thereafter. The miniature is quite large, occupying nearly half the page, yet the artist has somehow failed to cope with all the elements he felt it necessary to portray. Even so, with some interpretation, it is an effective illumination. The city is depicted in extreme detail—walls, crenelated parapets, turrets, gates, windows and doors, streets—all blended into the considerable confusion characteristic of medieval towns. Scene, then, is stressed. Action concentrates upon the movements of Grima as she makes her way through the city. Cifar has left her with the child while he goes to seek out sustenance and shelter for the family and fodder for the palfrey. He has hardly left when the horse frees itself and wanders off into the maze of streets. At once Grima sets out to find it while her remaining son, without her knowledge, sets out after her, takes a wrong turn, and becomes lost. We see Grima as she searches for him. In the foreground, she has stopped two passersby to ask if they have seen the lost child. In the upper half of the miniature,

Figure 32

she may be seen in her fruitless search through the city.

Yet Lady Luck has reserved for Grima an even blacker fate, quite in keeping with the truest traditions of the Byzantine romance. On folio 34r (Figure 32) Grima has boarded a ship the Cifars hope will take them to the city of Orbin, where they have reason to believe their fortunes will take a turn for the better. Because of insufficient space in the small boat for Cifar and his horse, he must await its return. In the illumination, the ship, without Cifar, steals quietly out of the harbor with Grima a captive on board. This vessel appears no larger than a coracle, but had it been drawn to scale the viewer could not have seen Grima surrounded by the crew, her hand extended in a gesture of helplessness. In a scene following the ship's departure, still in the same miniature, Cifar speaks with two bystanders, who tell him that the ship will not return and offer their sympathy for his wife's kidnapping. Modern readers would not easily accept the celestial pronunciation which comforts Cifar, the bereft husband: "Good knight," says the heavenly voice, "do not be distraught, for you will see in time to come that no matter how many misadventures befall you, much joy will come to you and great happiness and honor; and do not fear that you have lost your wife and children, for everything will turn out as you desire." Jesus, in the *Life of St. Eustace,* had so reassured that recently converted devotee.

Folio 34v (Plate 61) shows Cifar riding away, with the receding ship now barely visible on the horizon. The artist has depicted the grief in his face as he rests a despondent cheek on his hand. The harbor of Falac curves far beyond him, the city's walls and towers forming a distant background. Cifar, deeply grieved, rides slowly, not using the bridle at all but merely holding it languidly with his left hand. With his right hand he supports his head. No artist could have better portrayed his deep sorrow.

In this miniature pigments tend toward the pastel, except for the brilliant blue of the horse's accoutrements. Cifar wears a peach-colored tunic and a matching cloak spangled with four-petaled flowers. In the center of each flower sparkles what appears to be a pearl; the border of his robe and its hem also seem to be sewn with seed pearls. Under the broad brim of his hat one can catch a glimpse of a peach-colored kerchief or scarf which completely covers his hair.

Behind him stretches the harbor with three brown ships, whose rigging is seen in great detail. These ships are at different distances from one another, offering a remarkable attempt at perspective. Along the bay and also inland from it rise castles, three in number. The large one to the right is multi-towered; a smaller one to the left, which seems to be a church with fortifications, is less impressive; the third, of a different color, tops a promontory above the bay. Here and there fruit trees appear in groves, either in fruit or in flower.

Folio 35v (Figure 33) discloses a group of burghers and other gentlemen in conversation, with a view of

Figure 33

the harbor and a ship. One burgher explains that Cifar's sons are not dead or lost at all, and that it is a pity it is too late to overtake and inform him of that fact. The man reports that as he was hunting that day his dogs chased a lioness carrying a small boy, that the animal dropped the child unharmed, and that he and his wife have taken him in. Moreover, later that afternoon as his wife and child sat looking out of the window of their house, they noticed a little boy wandering and weeping in the street, who turned out to be the brother of the boy rescued from the lioness. The couple also adopted this second child, so that the brothers would not be separated and could grow up together. Scene predominates in this illumination and the picture merely serves as a transitional step to the next miniature.

The story now focuses upon Grima and her traumatic adventures aboard ship. She is portrayed as a remarkably courageous and imaginative woman who, through her faith in heaven, with the aid of the Blessed Virgin, and by dint of her own independent actions, manages to escape. Fearing rape, she attempts to fling herself into the sea, but her belt catches on a rope and the sailors capture her. Though they speak to her kindly, she fears the worst and begs the Virgin to save her. "Holy Virgin Mary," she cries, "You who succor the troubled and those in peril, succor me, if

You see I have need." The Virgin, heeding her plea, arranges for a devil to provoke the sailors to drink and lust, leading them to fight among themselves, so that they prefer violence to sharing the charms of Grima with each other. And so it is, we are told, that all on board from the youngest to the eldest are seized by their evil desire to such a degree that they lay hands to swords and wound one another until not one remains alive.

The miniature found on folio 36v (Figure 34) depicts the ship on the high seas, yet still not far from land, for rocky cliffs and the towers of a city may be seen on the skyline. The ship, fashioned of shingle-like planks, floats with its sails furled, while the sailors, swords bare and upraised, attack each other as Grima stands unharmed in their midst.

Grima's uncommon bravery, her wisdom and discernment, combined with a strength of character rare in females other than saints in medieval literature, radiate from the next miniature, found on folio 37r (Figure 35). She may, in fact, be the strongest figure in the entire novel, for the author has achieved in her a degree of characterization unequaled by any other personage, including the protagonist, Cifar.

The verbalization tells us that Grima hides below decks as the battle rages all day and through the night. At dawn she hears a voice from heaven which says,

Figure 34

"Good lady, arise and come up on deck and cast into the sea the wicked things you find there and possess for yourself all the goods you find on board." When she has convinced herself that the voice is divine and not that of some sailor trying to lure her out of hiding, she emerges from below and, still guided by the voice, takes the dead and bloated corpses by their heels and throws them all into the sea. They feel as light to her as so many straws, reads the account, and she fears nothing, for God strengthens and comforts her.

The illumination depicts her in the very midst of clearing the ship of dead bodies. Standing at the rail, she is seen in the act of dropping one of the dead sailors into the water. She lifts him by one of his hips and one knee. His dead hands dangle toward the waves. Her head, covered with a white wimple, reveals a calm and placid face. On the very top of the mast stands the figure of the Christ Child.

Much later the vessel, having drifted for some two months, is wafted miraculously to the harbor of a substantial city, whose great walls and towers crown rocky hills all around the water. Scene here is impressive, and we do not hesitate to categorize this miniature as one of the most outstanding representations in the entire work. The miniature on folio 37v, one of the most ample in spatial extent, occupies nearly half the page, running from margin to margin. We read that after Grima has washed the dead sailors' blood from the deck, she explores the ship's hold and discovers a cargo of the finest fabrics, great quantities of gold and silver, and many precious stones— in short, a king's ransom, and she lays claim to it all. It is only at this point that she becomes aware of the Christ Child atop the mast. The miniature (Plate 62) reveals how the ship, unmanned and with no human navigator at the helm, has come to a mooring in the harbor of

Figure 35

Orbin, the Christ Child still on the mast blessing her.

Color in this illumination, which is framed in a narrow band of gold, is as brilliant and as well harmonized as in any illustration in *Cifar*. We are thankful that we were able to obtain the transparency for this truly delightful picture. The background against which the human figures move rises from the harbor on sloping hills. At the left, forming a part of the skyline, is a substantial city with a road running up to and through its open gate between crenelated fortress towers and walls. One tower has a pointed turret. Behind the walls and fortifications one can see a large white church with a roof of terra cotta colored tiles. The roofs of the other buildings are also brightly colored. Gardens grow to the right of the city's gate, while on a terraced hill rises a grove of flowering or fruiting trees. To the right in this detailed landscape another hill, divided into plots of brown plowed earth,

sweeps down almost to the harbor. Above the fields and toward the left we see another castle, this one pale gray, with turrets and walls all crenelated. Diminutive human figures in scarlet holding long lances lend reality to the distance between them and the people at the harbor. Above the gray tower at the very top of the hill is a castle in terra cotta color with a white church inside the walls. And at the far right one sees a pure white castle with one of its towers topped by an azure dome. A red church rises from behind its fortifications.

The human figures in the foreground overshadow all else, however. At the left and on the edge of the rockbound harbor stand five people. The man in the orange tunic and blue cap points toward the ship, in which sits Grima with the same knight after he has gone on board. The device is, of course, related to the "double action" seen in the *Cantigas de Santa Maria* and the other works discussed above; it also serves to

Figure 36

indicate transition from one event to another. Behind the knight on shore stands the King of Orbin, beautifully crowned in gold and wearing an azure robe with a collar made up of three bands—one of pearls, the second of designs in gold, and the third of designs in silver. The side of his robe is slashed to reveal a scarlet underrobe whose hem is bordered in golden motifs. Resting his right hand on his hip, he points toward the ship with his left, as though ordering the knight to go on board. His queen stands just behind him, her left hand holding him by one arm, her right also pointing toward the ship. She wears an identical crown, a green gown which flows gracefully across the earth, and over her gown a peach-colored cape with golden designs at the collar and along the border. The facial expressions of these people are interesting: the knight's is clearly one of inquiry; the king's is decisive as he gives orders; and the queen's is calm, passive, expectant. Behind the queen stand colorfully dressed ladies-in-waiting.

To the right the ship floats, anchorless but miraculously kept stationary. On the bow is a sail which seems to be held taut by the wind. The dark brown timbers of the ship's side are clearly indicated, and the mast rises high above Grima and the knight, who faces her. In the crow's nest stands the Christ Child, his right arm raised in benediction. So detailed is the scene that we even see the rowboat in which the knight has made his way to the ship. He speaks seriously to Grima, using his right hand to drive home his message from the king. She, clothed in a bright azure gown and a white wimple, gesticulates, her face intent.

The knight realizes that a miracle is taking place, since the wind does not control the ship and since it has arrived with no crew. Moreover, the text tells us that the ship has arrived in the midst of a feast of the Virgin, a very important omen.

Folio 38r (Figure 36) also offers an extensive illumination, centered in the middle of the folio. The artist has now enlarged and even changed our view of the city with a proliferation of minutiae—the crenelations of towers, window panes, and even the fruit or blossoms of trees. As mentioned above, the skyline of the city is now vastly altered with buildings present not seen in Plate 62. The artist obviously created what he wished to create, possibly not even considering what he had painted in the previous scene.

The king has reached Grima's ship in another rowboat and stands facing her on board, his hands joined

Figure 37

She told him more, and at last the king lifted his eyes and saw the Christ Child and knew he was right to protect such a pious person.

In the illustration the queen seems to be speaking to Grima and articulating those words attributed to her in the text:

"Lady, if it pleases you, you will lodge in our home with me so that we may see one another daily and converse together." And so Grima lived in high honor in the royal palace of Orbin, and all believed that God had sent her to them for the weal of the kingdom, since crops grew more bountifully than ever before from the time she set foot on those shores.

Folio 40r (Figure 37) reveals Grima, who has used her wealth wisely and shown herself to be a great philanthropist, standing before the monarchs begging their permission to leave the realm, telling yet another lie to convince them of her need to depart. (Intriguing is the author's repeated description of Grima as a prevaricator, though perhaps he pictured her thus in his desire to render her all the more real, unless unkinder motives prompted him to stress the medieval belief in the basic duplicity of the female sex.) She reminds the king and queen that she has been in Orbin nine years, and says that she wants to return to her native land to see her relatives and friends before they die. Grima wisely asks for a new ship, remarking that "mine is old and rotting." She also has the foresight to require other necessities: "Sire," she says, "order that I may be given with the ship reliable men to accompany me in it, since, praise God, I have so much wealth." The king does all she asks and more. The author waxes poetic as he describes the monarch's distress: "Oh, God! How discomforted were the king and queen and all the others of that land when they beheld the ship depart! For they had felt great joy the day they received her and very deep grief and great sadness at her departure."

The miniature is one of the severest and most unadorned in the book, for it presents no more than a room in the palace. At the left stands Grima, chaste and pure in a dark robe and wimple, almost nunlike in their simplicity, while the queen stands nearby, her head very obviously downcast in sadness and her hands expressive in their message of grief. The king on his throne looks despairingly at Grima, his hands also suggestive of the deep feelings he bears for her.

In folio 40v (Figure 38) Grima has boarded her new vessel, whose far larger and grander dimensions are highlighted by an elevated poopdeck, a soaring bow, and a crew of the finest sailors the king could provide. Again she espies the Christ Child in his cus-

in prayer, his face a study of concern and reverence, for he too has decided that the visitor is heaven-sent. He marvels, too, at the fact that the ship remains steady with no anchor. Grima also prays, and the men in the rowboat await the king's pleasure. On shore, the queen points toward her husband and Grima, her face serious and questioning.

Grima, again vividly characterized by the author, is telling the king a blatant falsehood with just enough truth to make it plausible. Surely heaven has not so instructed her. Rather, she is influenced by an innate sense of survival which motivates both cleverness and guile, for she fully realizes that her very life may depend upon duplicity. This dishonesty on Grima's part provides a realistic touch in the midst of the sheer romance of the story. "And she told him," runs the verbalization,

that she was a lady from the land of India and that she had been abandoned by her husband and did not know whether he was alive or dead, and that for a long time the king of that land was very cruel and unjust and that she feared he would take her wealth; and because she had heard tell that he, the king she is speaking with, was a wise and good monarch and known to be just, that she desired to live under his protection and had laden that vessel with all the possessions she owned and had come to him.

Figure 38

tomary post atop the mast, and is confident in the knowledge that it is he who has made the wind to fill the sails and propel the vessel forward on its voyage. According to the verbalization, the pilot has attempted to turn the tiller but finds it fixed so firmly that all his efforts to budge it are for naught. Therefore, since they cannot control the ship, pilot and crew resign themselves and settle down to an uneventful trip. In the miniature, we see the Christ Child aloft, pointing with his hand and apparently directing the ship's progress on the proper course. Grima kneels in thanksgiving at the base of the mast, and three sailors pray with her. On the skyline, we can still see the outline of the city of Orbin.

At last, on folio 41v, the story shifts from Grima to Cifar and the adventures of our undaunted hero which will eventually reunite him with his wife and sons. "The story leaves off speaking of the lady," the author declares, "and speaks of what happened to her husband, the Knight Cifar and the hermit." Thus, simply, directly, and sensibly is the transition effected from the Grima episodes to the adventures of Cifar.

We draw the reader's attention again to the extensive sequence of *Cifar,* which differs so markedly from the previous shorter stories whose illuminations we have studied. This transitional work evinces quite as much accomplishment in the visualization of longer scenes as it did with regard to the short interpolated tales. The technique involved bears attention. In a long chapter or section of the novelesque first division

of the book, the artist in eleven separate miniatures has related the episode of Grima and has manipulated therein the nine basic elements of story, concentrating in some illuminations upon setting, often lavishly treated, in others focusing on action and conflict, or on character, mood, or tone. The style in all the miniatures is strikingly similar, probably indicating that one artist executed the entire work. He seems to have been capable of instilling the appropriate mood throughout. Theme is never neglected and the topic never lost from sight—the divided family, its acceptance of Fate's vicissitudes, and its conviction that eventually, with God's help and by dint of the individual members' own determination and patience, all will finally be reunited. Characterization in the visualized portions aptly parallels the verbal development, and, as we shall see in other long narrative sequences, the artist maintains his visualized transitions and attempts to provide full inclusion of the basic narrative elements.

Interestingly and realistically, too, the artist has deftly paralleled the efforts of the author of the book by stressing the highpoints of each narrative event or sequence within the overall novelesque section. No writer can effectively sustain the element of suspense page after page but must produce plains of action as well as peaks, rolling hills as well as precipices. The artist, by following the author's lead, has successfully depicted the same variety and incidence of action.

In describing the adventures of Grima from that point in time when she is separated from her husband up to the moment she sets sail from Orbin toward Mentón, where she will eventually be reunited with the Knight Cifar and their two sons, we have deliberately dwelt upon the verbalization and the accompanying visualizations of this entire sequence of events, adopting a holistic approach, no matter how intrepid or prosaic these events may be. In subsequent sequences we shall place less emphasis on minor incidents, and present illuminations which we believe are particularly beautiful or significant.

On Folio 41r, Figure 39, spanning a column and a half of text, depicts Cifar standing before the hermit's abode, his horse behind him stomping with one foot most realistically, as though to drive off flies, or perhaps impatiently waiting to be stabled. The illumination reveals the usual scenic skyline of rocky hills topped by the turrets of a city. In the very center, out of a mass of foliage formed by a considerable grove, there rises a tall, crenelated tower, and above it, higher still, a lesser tower topped by a pointed spire. As is his custom, the artist creates scene, costume, expression—in short, all those elements of vital concern to

Figure 39

plot unfolds. It shows what a fisherman's hut might have been like in those times—a conical affair with thatch or straw as its outer covering—and it also serves to introduce the fisherman, while functioning as a visual transition from one sequence to another. Note also the rather interesting attempt by the artist to provide perspective. The Knave holds a pole as he speaks over his shoulder to the hermit standing behind him; this pole and the line danging from it form a triangle which frames the ships in the distance and another almost at the fisherman's feet.

The verbalization tells us that the Knave slips away from his chores to visit the hermit. His conversations with that pious man set the tone of his new character as it is to be developed throughout a good part of the book. The Knave, like Spanish servants through the ages, speaks with great familiarity to his betters, first to the hermit and later to Cifar, even after the Knight has become his master. He is brash, ambitious, and very intelligent in the process of sounding out the Knight as a prospective employer. Moreover, he is endowed with the low cunning of the peasant, a deep folk wisdom, and an innate knowledge of human psychology. He is presumptuous and unabashed as he speaks to the hermit, who knows him for what he is and tells him so.

On the day the Knight arrives at the hermitage and takes his ease with the old man, writes the author, the

our visualization of the Knight that are omitted in the verbalization, which consistently neglects to include such details. The scene, though of no particular artistic merit, is nonetheless crucial to the story, for it introduces the hermit and sets the stage for future incidents of greater importance which revolve around the anchorite and his dwelling.

Cifar's robe, even in black and white, is still impressive. His horse's accoutrements are quite ornate, and his long lance has, in the original, a shining blade. His conversation with the hermit is intended, we believe, to be both serious (from the knight's point of view) and possibly amusing from the reader's angle: when the hermit regrets the fact that he has no fodder for the knight's horse, Cifar replies: "Don't let that concern us, for it will be dead tonight."

"How can you know that?" asked the hermit.
"Surely," said the knight, "because the ten days I've owned it are running out, and it can last no longer without dying."
And even as they were talking, the horse fell dead to the ground, and the hermit was astonished at this.

What a pity that the artist chose not to depict this at once grim and humorous instant. Knowing how hard it is for a knight to be compelled to travel on foot, the hermit hospitably invites him to stay a few days, and Cifar willingly accepts.

Folio 41v (Figure 40) reveals the *choza* or fisherman's hut where the Ribaldo (Knave) has gone to work. Though the miniature is of minor merit, we include it because it helps to situate the reader as the

Figure 40

Knave appears and inquires as to the stranger's identity. The hermit replies that he is a knight errant (*cavallero viandante*) who has come there by chance, and that no sooner did he arrive than he averred that his horse would die, since no mount lasted him longer than ten days, and that his words were fulfilled yesterday, for the horse indeed dropped dead on the ground.

"Surely," said the Knave, "I believe he is some unfortunate knight and one with little gumption, so I'd like to go speak with him and say some harsh and sharp things to him and I'll see if he is moved to anger or how he'll answer me."

"Get thee gone, rash knave!" said the hermit. "Do you think to find in all men what you find in me, since I endure patiently all you wish to say?"

"What you say is true," replied the Knave, "if this knight is addled in his wits, but if he is sane and of right understanding, he'll not answer me idly. For what in this world most proves if a man is mad lies in this, that is, that when one says something biting and objectionable to him, he is quickly enraged and angrily answers, but not so the sane man. For when the latter is spoken to improperly, he knows how to endure it with patience and to reply wisely. Now perchance this knight is more patient than you suspect."

The hermit hopes it will turn out well, to which the Knave replies: "Amen, but it is quite all right to attempt it, for it does a man no harm to test matters unless the test is harmful."

The hermit opines that a fool will often try to please his betters and fail miserably, as was the case of an ass who tried to emulate a lapdog. We include from folio 42v this story and its illustration (Plate 63) to underscore the ease with which long narrative and interpolated tale are interwoven. This miniature depicts one crucial moment, or perhaps even two, of the age-old tale (which is treated below in the discussion of *La vida del Ysopet con sus fabulas hystoriadas,* and illustrated in Figure 52.) Much action has been crowded into this page-width illumination, for the artist surely recognized both the story's importance and its popularity. At the left we see the handsomely dressed master of the house with the fluffy little dog seated in his lap. His concern for the little creature is by far the strongest element depicted in his character. His left hand strokes the dog's head or covers it as he seeks to protect it from the hooves of the ass. His right hand may even be raised to fend off the larger animal. According to the story, the ass, having watched how its master delighted in the lapdog and was pleased when the animal placed its little feet on his shoulders, resolved to gain affection in the same way. In the miniature he is in the act of rearing up on his hind legs and placing his front hooves on the shoulders of his master, who has called for assistance. At the right are two servitors who beat the ass with clubs. The alcove, or perhaps doorway, in which the master sits is an oblong of three heavy wooden beams. Several steps beyond him is another such doorway, and deeper still into the hall is still a third aperture. Here, we believe, is as good an example of perspective as any one could need to prove that artists of this time used it.

The master, seated on a stool, wears a full-length robe. The dog, to judge by its ears and long blond curls, is a spaniel, though its tail has not been clipped in the way of a modern spaniel.

The ass seeking the caresses of its master is well depicted, with a mane, its mouth open, and its eyes wild, with the whites showing. Its fully developed genitals reveal that it is an ass and not a mule.

To the right is a scene out of doors with a steep green hill in the background topped by one of the most beautiful and complex castles in the entire set of miniatures. So substantial is it that it might well be a city, for in addition to turrets, battlements, and crenelated walls, one can see a large church within the enclosure and several other buildings.

Returning to the mainstream of the Knight Cifar's adventures, we omit the miniature on folio 43v, a picture of the Knave as he attempts to anger Cifar with impertinent questions, which, together with the Knight's calm and patient answers, run on for pages. Cifar's polite replies reveal his strong sense of *mesura,* a quality highly esteemed among nobles of the Middle Ages. The Knave quotes many proverbs and maxims, all intended to provoke angry reactions, but to no avail, for the Knight is exceedingly self-contained. At last the Knave announces to Cifar that the King of Mentón has proclaimed that he will give his daughter in marriage to any knight who can lead his troops to victory against the enemy who is at this very moment besieging his capital. Cifar modestly disavows any ability he may have to accomplish such a feat, but the Knave manipulates him to a point where he agrees to attempt it. Finally the Knave begs Cifar to allow him to be his squire, for he believes in the Knight's prowess and trusts in his gratitude, which would not permit him to forget his faithful attendant. "I shall guide you to Mentón," says the Knave, "for I know where this king is besieged, and from here to there it is no more than a ten days' journey. And I will serve you very well so that when God gives you high estate you may repay me, for I am certain that God will lead you if you will take Him as your companion, for gladly does God guide and accompany the one who accepts Him as a companion."

All this greatly disturbs the hermit, for he firmly

Figure 41

believes that the Knave is not the kind of squire a knight like Cifar should have. But the Knight feels that the Knave is wise and clever, and as unusual as such a companionship is for those times, he accepts him into his service. Evidently, like Don Quixote with Sancho Panza, Cifar senses the young man's limitations, but he believes in spite of them that he can be a good squire.

We pass over the miniatures on folio 45v, which reveal two men in conversation; folio 46r, where the Knave takes leave of his former master, the fisherman; and folio 46v, wherein the hermit tells Cifar of his vision predicting that the Knight will be successful in this venture. But folio 47v (Figure 41) creates a scene not to be overlooked. The Knave and Cifar lodge at an inn where two robbers, posing as pilgrims, lie in wait for unsuspecting travelers. The miniature shows Cifar in bed, bare to the waist, while the thieves take up the attack. But the Knave, ever alert, has heard them. At the left one of the brigands, whom the Knave has slain, lies on the floor, while in the center the Knave has raised his sword against the other, who counters with

his own sword at the ready. The room is large and has a paneled ceiling. Cifar's bed appears to be above the combatants, though this is but a problem of perspective, which would seem to have the Knight observing what transpires below. At the right, the innkeeper in a nightrobe and with rumpled hair, makes ready to leap to the Knave's assistance. Together they capture the villain, who is summarily executed on the following day.

On folio 48r the artist depicts the departure of the Knave from the fisherman. We omit this miniature, passing on to one of the very best in the entire work, found on folio 48v (Plate 64). The colors here are some of the most delightful among all these miniatures. Cifar has sent the Knave with a few of his last remaining coins to shop for food. The Knave has managed to purchase a pheasant and is returning with it when a robber who has stolen a sack of gold coins runs up and asks him to hold the sack while he saddles his palfrey. With the Knave literally left holding the sack, the robber flees on foot and the constabulary arrest the Knave and take him to court, where the

Figure 42

judge sentences him to die on the gallows the very next morning. Cifar, unaware of what has befallen his companion, is most grieved, for he has become fond of his servant. He therefore sets out to try to find him and to forgive him for having, he thinks, absconded with the money he was given to buy food.

As the Knave rides toward the execution, bareback on a mule, his hands bound in front of him, many people sorrow for him, for—and here the author gives his first description of the Knave—he is young and comely and speaks well. The artist depicts the very moment when the ass stops beneath the gibbet, while on its back the Knave, stripped almost naked and wearing no more than a breechcloth, waits for the hangman's noose to tighten when the bailiffs drive the ass from him. The Knave under the artist's brush emerges quite as well favored as the author has described him. His head, rendered slightly larger than might be natural, is nonetheless well portrayed, and his face is handsome, with a good forehead, a shapely nose, a full-lipped mouth, and a well molded chin and jaw. His hair is russet and styled in the manner of the early fifteenth century, somewhat resembling the hair of King Henry V in some portraits painted of him at the time of the Battle of Agincourt in 1415. His eyes, deep brown and large, are quite naturally filled with concern, but not with terror, for what they behold and cling to is the eyes of his master, who has come up to the gallows.

The Knave sits upon a saddle blanket of fawn-colored leather or cloth to contrast with the chocolate brown of the ass's hide. The ass rolls its eyes and lifts one forefoot as though prepared to bolt, and this injects an element of suspense into the incident. The gallows makes a perfect frame for the principal action, just as some of the arches did in the *Cantigas de Santa Maria.* Through the square provided by the gallows, and beyond the Knave on the ass, hang green and brown hills, groves of trees, and a fine three-towered and turreted castle, while at the far left rises another castle with a central domed tower flanked by pointed towers. At the far right stands a grim fortress with three crenelated towers, each surmounted by a red watchtower.

The assembled human figures are no less colorful. At the far left, a gray-bearded judge in a cobalt robe speaks to a bailiff dressed in gold and pink. Both judge and bailiff sport stylish hats. At the far right we see three men. Two are constabulary and one, resting his sword point on the earth while facing the viewer, is an impressive personage in a scalloped kiltlike tunic with wide-mouthed sleeves, a white turbaned headgear, and knee-high ruby-red boots. Behind him we can make out another figure whose fascinating face features a gray beard and wide-set eyes. The third man is Cifar. The artist depicts him in the very act of saving his squire. His left hand grasps the gallows and his right is upraised with his great sword, its blade an almost electric blue, as he prepares to cut the hangman's rope. He is simply dressed for travel. Cifar stares straight into the eyes of his squire as though to reassure him. Skin tones of all present in the miniature are natural and of the kind one would find in western European types, even though Cifar is from India.

Amusing, in spite of the perilous circumstances, is the conversation overheard between the Knight and his servant in the verbalization. Once Cifar is convinced that the Knave is innocent, he says he will go to the judges, revealing that his mind still moves in legalistic and formal ways. To this, the Knave, who is desperate and also practical, shouts: "That's a fine and lordly service for one in straits like mine! Don't you realize that my life is under the foot of this ass and that one 'gee up' will move him, and you talk about going off to seek legal counsel?" At this, Cifar cuts the rope just before the ass is driven from under the gallows, and for this he is arrested and taken with the Knave to prison. It is only when the real thief carelessly lets himself be seen by the Knave that they are saved, for the thief under torture confesses and is executed. We omit the miniatures on folios 49r and 50v dealing with this episode.

Rather than enter a city on foot, which would be disgraceful for a knight, Cifar and the Knave take refuge in a ruined tower, and the Knave, who pities his master's plight, goes for food and saves Cifar from great embarrassment. But that night a large pack of wolves attacks them, and one even snatches Cifar's sword from his hand. The Knave's quick thinking and great courage save them both, for he uses straw and sticks of burning wood to hold the wolves at bay until he can retrieve the sword. In the miniature on folio 50v, one that spans both columns of text, we encounter a gripping scene (Fig. 42). The artist has frozen the action just as the Knave, with both hands clutching torches of straw, moves toward the wolves. Cifar stands at the left, hands open in a gesture of helplessness, while before him his squire faces the wolves. Outside the ruin which half shelters them lies the sword. In the background, hills and the towers of a city rise in the distance.

Folio 51v, through its humor, deserves to be reproduced. As Cifar and the Knave approach a village not far from the besieged city, the Knight spies turnips growing in a field and expresses a desire to have some. The Knave, leaving Cifar at an inn, goes to the field, scales the fence, and fills a sack with turnips, but is forwith challenged by the owner. The passage represents one of the few outright and intentionally comic occasions in the book.

"Certainly, wicked thief," said the owner, "you shall go under arrest with me to court and they will give you the

Figure 43

penalty you merit because you entered over the walls to steal turnips."

"Alas, sir," said the Knave, "as God gives you good fortune, don't do it, for I was forced to enter here."

"How forced?" said the owner of the garden. "For I see nothing to reveal how anyone could have forced you, unless your own wickedness did not make you do it."

"Sir," said the Knave, "the wind was so strong and forceful that it was lifting me up from the earth, and out of fear that it would hurl me into some bad spot, I clung to the turnips and many were pulled up."

"Well, who put the turnips in the sack?" asked the owner.

"Really, sir," said the Knave, "this puzzles me greatly."

"Since it puzzles you so," said the owner, "you clearly give me to understand that you have no blame in this. I forgive you this time."

"Alas, sir," said the Knave, "what need is there of pardon for one not guilty? You would surely do better in letting me have these turnips on account of the suffering that I experienced in pulling them up."

"It is my pleasure," said the owner of the garden, "since you defend yourself so well with clever lies. So take the turnips and go your way, and see to it that hereafter this does not happen to you again; for if so, you shall pay for it."

The miniature (Figure 43) depicting these humorous incidents covers a column and a half of text and is charmingly droll. In a well-defined frame limned with black ink, we can discern a considerable degree of landscape drawn up into two low hills in the background, their bases covered with trees, shrubs, and garden vegetables. Behind their grove-topped summits may be seen a city rising within its walls. In the

Figure 44

immediate foreground, and in the actual garden itself, stands the owner at the left facing the Knave at the right. Between them slumps a sack with the tops of turnips visible in its open mouth. The owner shakes his finger at the Knave, who stands with one hand on his chest, expounding his farcical tale of woe, while gesturing in explanation with the other. The farmer's face is disdainful and his expression condescending, while the Knave's countenance is a frozen study of mock-fear and mock-piety. Both scene and characterization under the artist's skillful brush match the verbalization well.

We pass over a small miniature revealing Cifar and his squire in conversation, this on folio 52r, but offer in Figure 44 what appears on folio 53r, for it is a true gem of visualization. Cifar, as a strange knight, could never penetrate the enemy lines and enter the city. The Knave solves the problem by suggesting a very clever ruse: Cifar will change clothes with him to conceal his knightly person and, placing a garland of ivy on his head, will pretend to be a madman. Thus he will be able to enter the city and seek out important people to whom he can offer his services.

The miniature reveals the gateway of the city to the left, with twin towers looming on either side of the entrance, while walls mounted at regular intervals with other towers—much like what one still sees at Avila and Lugo—retreat into the distance. Above the portal stands a soldier conversing with the disguised Cifar, who indeed appears in the Knave's rough garments, his head crowned with ivy. To the right may be seen several fine campaign tents belonging to the besieging forces, while two men stationed at the entrance of these pavilions deride the antics of the supposed "lunatic." Characterization is strong, for the staid Cifar can, under the pressure of need and guided by his roguish squire, sink even to playing the fool in public. Naturally the ruse succeeds and Cifar enters the city without mishap, quickly establishing contact with the necessary authorities, who bring him before the King of Mentón himself.

Cifar, named by the king of Mentón to lead his armies, wins victory after victory, vanquishing the enemy King of Ester, while slaying his two sons and a nephew. The Knave is not forgotten, for this series of battles serves to establish him as a valiant knight in his own right. The grateful King of Mentón calls upon his daughter to marry Cifar, who is now called the Cavallero de Dios, or "God's Knight." A good many miniatures were executed to illustrate these events. One extremely fine battle scene deserves to be presented for its outstanding detail, vigorous action, and stark realism. On folio 60v (Figure 45) the artist has rendered a scene of extraordinary power and impact, which occupies fully one-third of the entire folio. The two hosts, in serried ranks on opposite sides of the

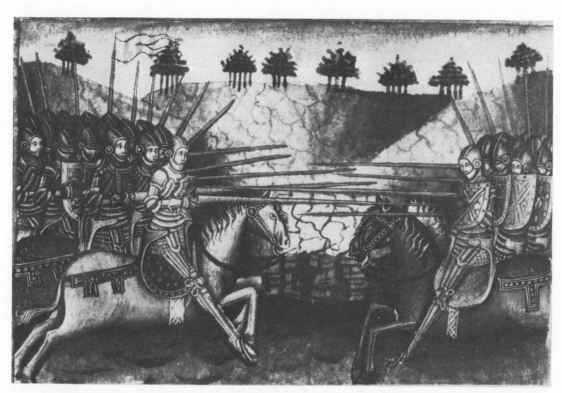

Figure 45

page, tilt at each other in full charge: the first rank of knights rides with lances couched, and so close are the two armies that the shafts of their weapons already overlap. Behind them stands the second line of knights with lances raised, awaiting the proper moment to lower them and charge. The horses closest to the viewer leap forward in dauntless array, martial accoutrements fully displayed. Every detail of flashing armor shines forth from helm to toe, as the viewer revels in the minutiae of the fray: truncheons, the hooves of the horses, swords, shields, armorial designs, and above all, the knights' faces. The armor here portrayed possesses elements of the fourteenth century as well as those of the fifteenth. Perhaps some of these components stem from both centuries. It is hard to date incidents by armor, for good armor was not cast aside to meet new styles, except by the very rich, but was handed down from father to son. In some miniatures of *Cifar* one sees definite examples of fifteenth-century mail with the foot armor tapering into severely elongated points. It is quite possible that this trend followed the same exaggerated length and pointedness of stylish civil footgear. *Cifar*'s illuminator, then, was familiar with more than one period of armor upon which he drew as models for his miniatures.

The second part of the *Cavallero Cifar* concludes with the marriage of the victorious Knight to the daughter of the King of Mentón, the arrival of Grima in the city, Cifar's realization that his first wife is still alive, and his ruse to escape consummation of his new marriage with the princess of Mentón. He employs the same pretext formerly used by Tristan, who, forced to flee Cornwall and the arms of his mistress, Isolde, wife of King Mark, subsequently marries Isolde of the White Hands, telling her he must maintain his chastity for a certain period of time.

In due time, Cifar's sons arrive, having been reared as knights by the burgher who adopted them years before. They meet Grima and are reunited with her; and she, having but one bed, lets them sleep in it with her. When they are observed thus, Cifar condemns all three to death, until he is brought to realize that they are the poor woman's sons and not two lovers. Folio 70v (Figure 46) reveals a scene of double action: at the left we see Grima's bedchamber and in it, in bed, covers pulled up to their necks, Grima with a son on either side. At the right under an arch stands the majordomo who has seen them as he reports to Cifar.

Grima, of course, is able to substantiate her maternity and Cifar's paternity, and joyfully he receives the young men. Shortly thereafter, he knights them. This scene from folio 72v we offer as Plate 65. It is a beautiful illumination, running the full width of the two columns and divided into two distinct parts, each framing a portion of a related action. At the left is

Figure 46

an open room of the royal palace. A pale green brick wall frames it on the left, while on the right is the inner wall of the room. The ceiling, with walnut-colored beams, blends delightfully with the terra cotta of the bricks that line the wall and with the floor made of white and terra cotta bricks in a checkerboard design. This room is a foot or so higher than the patio seen at the right, but the artist does not seem to have worked out the correct perspective for the dividing wall.

Cifar, now the King of Mentón, stands in the center of the room. He is no longer the young and valiant knight we saw earlier. He now has gray, shoulder-length hair and a gray beard. He wears a crown and a long robe reaching almost to the floor, its border a design worked in threads of gold and echoed in a thinner band of similarly wrought material midway between his waist and the hem of his robe. In a pious gesture with his left hand, no doubt connected with the ritual, he appears to be blessing both sons, while with his right, he taps one son on the shoulder with a sword. The young men kneel before him. Their armor, most carefully depicted in all its intricate detail, glows with a silver light, as do their pointed helmets. They pray, with their hands forming steeples and their faces are set in expressions of true piety, while behind them the dark scabbards of their swords point floorward.

The scene on the right is outside the room, perhaps a palace patio, and is outlined in the background by a handsome wall of cream stone cut into perfect squares not much larger than bricks. Above the wall are low hills whose slopes seem to be divided into green and brown garden plots, and whose crests are capped by a variety of trees. The patio floor is etched in shades of deepest brown. Here three gentlemen, probably courtiers, observe the ritual. The one at the far right reflects the king's dress in every detail, save for a conical hat. The man nearest Cifar sports waist-high stockings with a pleated green doublet and a skirt which barely covers the separation of his legs. On his head he wears an attractive turban which appears to be evolving into a *capuchón*. Behind these two men, and concealed by them save for his head, stands one who, to judge by his conical cap, may be a cleric.

Part II contains a long and interesting sequence of the adventures of the Cavallero Atrevido, or Bold Knight, in the underwater realm of the Lady of the Lake, featuring a series of incidents having nothing to do with the lives of the Cifar family. It is yet another example of the author's propensity for inserting a good story into the stream of the main plot, while presenting the protagonist of that story as one of the characters in *Cifar* itself. The adventures of the Bold Knight in the kingdom of the Lady of the Lake merit the two miniatures we offer here in color. The Bold Knight has come to view the accursed lake after the ashes of the wicked Count Nason have been cast upon its waters. He camps there for some days observing the several marvelous things that take place, until one day a beautiful lady appears in the water, her feet just beneath the surface. Lifting her foot, she leads him to believe the lake is quite shallow, whereupon he enters the water and is immediately snatched down by her into the depths below. There at the bottom he encounters a strange underwater land with a populace that does not speak.

On folio 86v is a charming scene (Plate 66), which occupies nearly half the page and runs the full page width. The lake predominates, and is surrounded by rather steep mountains or high hills topped with groves. Between two of these hills rise the towers of a beautiful castle, and behind its walls stands a church with a pink roof. At the left, calf-deep in water indicated by wavy lines, stands the Lady of the Lake, draped in an undecorated lime-green robe. She beckons to the Bold Knight, who stands in front of a handsome pavilion upon which Arabic characters (among them the words "God is Great") are inscribed in circling bands. We can see into the interior, since the tent flaps have been drawn back to provide a doorway. Through the opening we can see the points of the tent stretched taut by pegs driven into the earth. The knight is clad in a long blue robe, from beneath which projects the scabbard of his sword; the collar of his robe is apparently of white lace. He lifts his hands in a signal suggestive of welcome as he speaks to the Lady of the Lake. The lady, together with all the denizens of her realm, possesses a pair of curved horns sprouting from her head, perhaps to indicate her supernatural or even demoniacal character. If the Bold Knight has seen these horns, no mention is made of it, and indeed the horns, drawn in the shape of a crescent, may have been painted on the various heads to indicate to the viewer the nether-world nature of these creatures. As the reader can readily appreciate, this illumination is executed in vivid colors, thereby contributing measurably to the story's impact and providing us with a very fine sample of the dramatic effects of visualization.

Plate 67 also illustrates the adventures of the Bold Knight. At this point he has married the Lady of the Lake and has fathered a son. Since in that land children once conceived are born in seven days and advance to maturity in another seven, the Bold Knight soon has a grown son whom he names Alberto Diablo. But soon the Knight, who has been forbidden by his new wife to speak to another woman, is deceived by a fair damsel, bringing down upon himself and his son the wrath of his demon spouse. In a framework reminiscent of Cupid and Psyche or the Swan Knight (Lohengrin), we come to folio 91v, where father and son and another

man ride in to see the Lady of the Lake and find her seated on her throne, surrounded by two traitors, Count Nason and his great grandfather, both of whom appear more like naked children than grown men. This type of representation was customary when depicting the soul in medieval art, yet the artist in this visualization has strayed from the text, for the Lady still looks like a human being and not the hideous devil who, the author recounts, has her arms around the two men and seems to be tearing out and eating their hearts.

In the miniature, the artist again divides the scene into two parts. At the left sits the Lady of the Lake. The demon lady sits on a dais enclosed in an arch of golden bricks within a brick wall of various colors. Her full gown flows over the step to the dais and covers her feet. Her long blue cape partially shelters the two childlike figures. Her countenance, lined and wrinkled, is ugly, and there are flushes on her cheeks, which we take for signs of rage, since they are not seen in her other depictions. A dark area following the line of her jaw may indicate a beard. Her long blond hair looks more like a mane. The traitors lean against the lady, whose hands hold them close to her. Both are well proportioned, actually more like adults than children save for their size. Their faces, too, are more mature than children's faces should be. Both turn their heads toward the Bold Knight and his companions, and their faces wear expressions of anger. To the right the Bold Knight, his son, and another gentleman are mounted on their horses, while in the distance may be seen the usual tree-topped hills. The three men, with hands raised in alarm and with grim expressions, face the three apparitions.

According to the verbalization, the transformed queen shrieks: "Oh, mad and daring knight, go with your son from my realm, for I am the Lady of Treachery!" At the same moment the watery realm is rent by a fearful earthquake which seems to topple every palace in the city, and a great whirlwind seizes the knight and his son, hurling them from the lake and depositing them near the tent. This earthquake, we are told, is felt a distance of two days' journey around the lake, and many towers and houses fall to the earth as a consequence. The Bold Knight, escaping from the accursed lake, leaves the region and returns with his son to his former lands, where he and his son Alberto subsequently give rise to the bold and valiant line of the knights of Porfilia.

Thus we reach the end of this long interpolated tale, after which the author continues with the story of the King of Mentón. Good and truthful king that he is,

Figure 47

Cifar-Mentón has acknowledged the existence of his family and they are all readily accepted by the people of his realm. In time, the queen and former princess of Mentón dies, leaving Cifar as king and Grima as queen, and they live happily ever after.

The reader will recall that Part III, dealing exclusively with Cifar's instructions to his sons, was represented by the miniatures illustrating certain short narratives: plates 55 and 56, about the hunter and the lark; plates 57 and 58, from the story of the bitten-off lips; and plate 59, which visualizes the story of the wolf and the leeches.

Part IV, the adventures of Cifar's son Roboán, is a tale of derring-do. The young man sets out on a quest, accompanied by the Cavallero Amigo, the erstwhile Knave, who has been knighted following his conversion into a responsible citizen. Together they help a lady named Siringa, whom Roboán nearly marries, but he decides to leave her and continue his quest. They are now in Greater Asia and before long arrive in the land of the Emperor of Tigridia, whose name derives from the Tigris River in the Fertile Crescent. After some time spent in this monarch's service, Roboán rises to such favor that jealous nobles resolve to destroy him. They hit upon a novel method to dispose of the young man: the emperor never laughs, and it is well understood in that land that no one must ever ask him why, for those who have dared to inquire have been immediately beheaded. This story, of which a

version may be found in the *Thousand Nights and a Night,* is no more bizarre in its oriental counterpart than here in *Cifar.* Young Roboán poses the fatal question, the emperor realizes someone has put him up to it, and, rather than oblige the intriguers by beheading his young friend, he confronts him in a most mysterious way: "Let us go to the seashore," he says to Roboán, "and I shall place you in such a situation that perchance you will be better off dead than alive, or it may be that great will be your good fortune and your honor, if you happen to be a man of sufficient gumption and if you know how to take care of yourself. But, curse it, few are those who know how to endure good fortune, and they fall into misfortune and endure it though they do not wish to!"

The emperor takes Roboán to a fortress on the shore of the sea, and after he has unlocked the door, he makes Roboán enter a boat without oars. The moment he sets foot in it, it moves rapidly out and onto the high seas.

The miniature on folio 170v (Plate 68) reveals much of this action. It is a large illustration containing much that is impressionistic. The emperor stands in the fortress to the left, looking over its wall at Roboán, whose boat floats out to sea. The fortress is depicted with only three walls of stone, and the sea flows right up to the aperture which one would expect to be the fourth wall. The arched gates of the fortress seem to be made of metal and are thickly studded. Behind the fortress hang the ubiquitous hills, on one of which a grim, crenelated castle may be seen. The fortress has no roof, since we must see the emperor as he stands inside, one hand placed on the wall, the other raised in farewell to Roboán. His face is sad, for he knows to what Roboán is sailing and what sad fate will probably be his. Roboán sits in the boat, which is no larger than a coracle, although it is intended to represent a larger craft. His hands are extended toward the emperor in farewell and his face is sad. The brown and green of the hills and groves, the pale blue of the sky and water, and the blue and green robes of the emperor and Roboán make this illumination attractive, although it is far less brilliantly pigmented than most of those in the book.

Roboán floats to the Blessed Isles, where he is soon taken before its queen, Nobleza (Nobility), whom he subsequently marries, for they fall in love at first sight. They are happy for nearly a year, until the devil in the form of a comely lady thrice tempts Roboán, each time persuading him to ask his wife for some new gift. First it is a hunting dog from which no prey can escape; next, a hawk "which pleased him even more than the hound, and he loved the empress so

Figure 48

much after he had hunted with the hawk that he stayed with her day and night and took great solace in her company." Last, the devil persuades Roboán to ask for a certain horse the lady owns, and of course she gives it to him willingly out of the great love she bears him. But once he has the horse, he wants to ride away, and does so. The horse goes like the wind to the shore, where the oarless boat floats, and there the horse leaves him. Entering the boat, Roboán is soon wafted back to the emperor's grim fortress, where he is so filled with sadness that he weeps and longs for his lovely empress, whom he will never see again.

To illustrate these adventures, the artist paints a number of miniatures. The one on folio 171r, which we offer as Figure 47, finds Roboán in the boat headed out to sea and toward the Blessed Isles. Folio 176v (Figure 48) depicts Roboán with the empress and hunting dog, and astride the magic horse, with the falcon on his wrist. The empress either wears a crescent headdress or has, like the Lady of the Lake, a set of strange horns. On folio 78r (Figure 49), the miniature presents Roboán's departure on his new mount, carrying the pennant the empress has made for him. The setting here is lavish. Roboán rides away against a background of pleasant landscape, while gazing back at the empress, who stands in the doorway of a beautiful castle, framed on either side by intricately decorated and detailed towers. In a scene suggestive of Dido and Aeneas, she clutches her robe to her mouth,

her face the picture of grief, for she knows she will not see her beloved husband again.

Upon his return, Roboán seeks out the emperor, knowing now why he never laughs, for he has had the same adventure. They remain fast friends until the emperor dies, bequeathing to Roboán the empire of Tigridia. Roboán's story draws to a close as he defeats a rebel king with the aid of the Cavallero Amigo, the erstwhile Knave, and at length he has his worst enemy, Count Farán, beheaded. This act appears in the last miniature which we present from folio 188r (Plate 69).

In this miniature, which extends the full width of the folio and occupies approximately the bottom third of it, nothing is left to the imagination. The foreground appears to be paved in diamond-shaped paving stones. The skyline is made up of green and brown hills and scattered trees, single or in groves. At the left rises a fine manor house with a tower. The Cavallero Amigo, who serves the emperor (Roboán), has just struck off the head of Farán. The scene is realistic to a marked degree. The Cavallero Amigo stands at the far left, wiping the blood of Count Farán from his sword with the hem of his cloak. The deep blue of this garment, the silver of the blade, with the barest tinge of blood still upon it, his bright green hose and his high stiff collar in red render him a colorful figure. His face reflects the seriousness of the moment, for his eyes are grim, his forehead frowning, and his mouth set.

Figure 49

Count Farán's body lies supine on the pavement, blood gushing from his severed neck toward his head, from which blood is beginning to pool on the stones. His green tunic and scarlet hose draw the eye to the remainder of the scene. The young emperor stands above him, holding a golden scepter with the orb as its head. His brilliant blue collar, stiff and high, and his cap with a brim embellished with spikes of gold make him an imposing figure. He points with his right hand at the corpse, and his face, depicted by the artist as grim and stern, is one of the best facial depictions in the book. So detailed is the portrayal that we can see just a tip of his brown hair, which is confined by a bright red kerchief. The two men standing behind the emperor wear the stylish high, stiff collars, and both grimace at the execution.

This might have been a good place for the writer to end the novel, but Roboán has no wife and his thoughts return to Siringa, whom he had once thought to marry but had left to continue his quest. At length he seeks her out, makes her his wife, and together they ride with the former Knave to visit Roboán's parents and his brother, Garfín, in Mentón. There they all hold high festival for a week, after which Roboán and Siringa return to rule their empire in peace and happiness.

We have treated the *Libro del Cavallero Cifar* in such great detail because we consider it to be one of the most important books in the history of medieval literature, as well as of medieval pictorial art. Surely no other lengthy prose work was so handsomely illuminated, indicating to us that in its own time it was regarded as a very precious story.

# La vida del Ysopet con sus fabulas hystoriadas

fitting *terminus ad quem* for our study of the art of narrative fiction in Spain is a post-medieval book, yet one which contains many of the techniques and devices of visualization found in previous centuries, revealing that medieval practices continued into later times. This book, *La vida del Ysopet con sus fabulas hystoriadas (The Life of Aesop with His Fables Illustrated),* was published in Saragossa in 1489 by the German book-maker Johan (or Hans) Hurus. It was the first collection of Aesopic fables published in Spain and one of the first books printed there. It brought to the corpus of Spanish letters a cornucopia of Aesopic tradition. The *Ysopet,* as it is often referred to, became the ancestor of subsequent Spanish collections of fables, and in most cases remained the actual source, with few changes apparent in later editions. In 1929 the famous scholar Cotarelo y Mori edited it in facsimile for the Royal Spanish Academy and made the woodcuts available to the public.

The *Ysopet* was not originally composed in Spanish but was a translation from a well-known collection of Aesopic material in German which had been published in Ulm in 1474 by Johannes Zeiner, based upon a translation from the Latin and Italian by Heinrich Steinhöwel. The printing of 1473 in Augsburg contained a Latin text paralleling the German, and the German here was based upon Steinhöwel. The Spanish translator followed the Ulm printing of Steinhöwel fairly faithfully, although he inserted a few fables and several short stories not present in either the German or the Latin texts. Both the translation printed in Saragossa and the one printed in Toulouse trace back directly to one of the volumes printed in Germany, and both use woodcuts which are copies of those in the German editions.

We have used the Saragossa edition of the *Ysopet* in preference to the translation done from French by Julien Macho and published in Toulouse in 1488.[1] We feel that Macho's translation is inferior and we also believe that a book printed outside Spain would not have been as available as one published there, especially one published in Saragossa, a city noted for printing and for the dissemination of its books.

The history of Aesopic fables, insofar as that mysterious tradition can be unravelled, has been discussed too frequently for inclusion here, but far less is known about the history of Aesop in Spain, and therefore the rise and development of the tradition there may justifiably be treated here. Aesop had been familiar to Spaniards since the Roman conquest, if not earlier, and he was no stranger to medieval people. Two famous literary figures who recognized the value of his fables were Juan Ruiz, Archpriest of Hita, and Don Juan Manuel. The former, the author of the renowned *Libro de buen amor (The Book of Good Love),* included in that lengthy work no less than twenty-five fables from the Aesopic tradition, and Don Juan Manuel used several.[2] Other writers also drew from that tradition, notably in *El libro de los gatos (The Book of Tales* [not of

# La vida del yſopet con ſus fabulas byſtoriadas

Enel año del señor de mill,ccccbxxic,

Figure 50

cats, as the word *gatos* might suggest]), and *El libro de los exenplos por a.b.c. (The Book of Moralized Tales by A.B.C.)* by Clemente Sánchez de Vercial, Archdeacon of Valderas in León.[3] But nothing like a comprehensive collection was forthcoming until the *Ysopet* made its appearance in print, which assured it a much wider dissemination than fables had hitherto enjoyed. This book, illustrated with woodcuts, made a considerable contribution to brief narrative in the Spanish language.

Fables and other brief narratives make up the greater part of the *Ysopet,* but they are preceded, as the title indicates, by a strange and almost novelesque life of Aesop written originally in Greek by a monk named Maximus Planudius, who around 1327 went to Venice as ambassador from Constantinople. Toward the middle of the fourteenth century, his fables and his life of Aesop were translated into Latin by one Rinuccio d'Arezzo, and dedicated to the Spanish cardinal Antonio Cerdá of Mallorca. Without the efforts of Planudius, who brought the Greek fables to Italy, the Aesopic tradition in the West would have suffered considerably or been significantly delayed.

Steinhöwel's translation, as published in Augsburg and Ulm, was illustrated by some of the best woodcuts created in Germany and the Netherlands, where that art had reached its zenith with Dürer and the "little masters," Altdorfer, Behams, and Pencz, all of whom forsook religious topics, preferring to produce, with a touch of that decorative quality learned from Italian masters in the art, the humor and studied debauchery of everyday life, a practice to be followed in Spain a few decades later.

The Spanish woodcuts which we reproduce from the 188 in the book utilize narrative techniques and devices of visualization already well known in other parts of Europe, for these devices belonged to a very old medieval tradition prevalent across much of Christendom. Indeed, the Spanish woodcuts of the *Ysopet* may actually be faithful copies of the German or may possibly even have been made in Germany and imported into Spain by Hurus, who surely must have seen them before he left his native land. He may well have brought copies with him to Saragossa. These Spanish woodcuts stemming from German originals, or possibly from French woodcuts from the same tradition, represent some of the finest concordance between text and illustration ever conceived, before or since. The pages measure ten inches high by eight wide, and the woodcuts are generally three inches high by four wide.

The techniques of narrative art found in the *Ysopet,* and by extension in the German editions, also form the basis of the French and English editions, and thus were of pan-European constitution. Apparently, since these techniques had existed in Spain for centuries, they were understood by Spaniards and can be considered an integral part of the Spanish tradition. That the art of woodcuts did not have to evolve in Spain slowly, but sprang into being fullblown through German models does not weaken our reasons for including the *Ysopet* here, since to all intents and purposes the illustrations are Spanish and therefore comprise a most appropriate finale for the art of medieval narratives. Those Spaniards who read the fables and viewed the woodcuts understood the narrative techniques of visualized story, and could smile or laugh or grimace in perfect comprehension.

The *Ysopet* is divided into eight separate sections, labeled "books" in a table at the end of the text which lists the titles of all the fables. Books I, II, III, and IV contain twenty fables each. Book V has seventeen, and these are given the title *Fabulas extravagantes,* possibly because they are tales from less familiar collections, such as the *Roman de Renart,* the French *fabliaux,* and certain folkloristic sources. Book VI also contains seventeen fables and bears the title *Las fabulas de Remisio,* a misspelling or distortion of Rinuccio d'Arezzo. Book VII, *Las fabulas de Aviano,* from fables written by one Avianus, who flourished between the second and fifth centuries, contains twenty-two tales. Book VIII, *Las fabulas de Alfonso,* that is, of Pedro Alfonso, is based upon that author's *Disciplina Clericalis,* a work which had appeared in Latin toward the end of the eleventh century.[4]

Each fable or tale in the *Ysopet* has its own illustrative woodcut, giving us 158 in all. But since the introductory *Vida* itself contains another 30, the grand total comes to 188. The frontispiece (Fig. 50) depicts Aesop. For the life of Aesop, Planudius utilized an unknown and ancient tradition and possibly embroidered upon it, presenting Aesop as an ungainly, dwarfish, and hideous slave who served a harsh master named Xanthus. This bizarre story derives a certain unity from the series of tricks played by the slave on his master and at times on his master's equally hateful wife. Some of these pranks are obscene, as are the woodcuts which illustrate them. Each is of a single action, with only one moment of time depicted, and is therefore not easily interpreted without the text, since the episodes in Aesop's life are not nearly as familiar as the fables themselves for which the illustrations often contain the double-action technique.

We offer now a selection of representative woodcuts from each book of the *Ysopet,* together with either a translation or a suitable paraphrase to provide a

La .viij. del lobo z dela grulla.

Figure 51

means of comparison between text and illustration.

A single woodcut presenting but one crucial incident of plot accompanies Fable 8 in Book I, *"Del lobo e dela grulla"* *("Of the Wolf and the Crane"),* and can be seen as Figure 51. We translate the text in order to show the parallels between the content of the printed word and the illustration.

Whoever does good to one who is evil can receive harm from it and not good. And this is to be heard in the *exemplum*[5] of how the wolf was eating and a bone became lodged in his throat and he begged the crane, since she had a long neck, to please apply a remedy and free him from that peril, promising her for it a great reward when the bone had been extracted. She, through these requests and promises, removed the bone, and with the wolf thus saved, asked him to pay her for her labor and to fulfill what he had promised her. It is related that the wolf responded, "Oh, unpleasant and ungrateful one, don't you realize that you had your head in my mouth so that I could have beheaded you had I desired? And I let you draw it out without doing you any harm. Doesn't it seem to you that I did you a great favor in this and that you are demanding more?"

This fable shows us that doing good to the evil is of no advantage because they never remember the good they receive.

The Spanish here is far from spritely and is clearly unequal to the masterly visualization. With a few strokes of the woodcutter's chisel, the artist has presented remarkably well and with perfect clarity more elements of the classic design than one would have expected to see in a single illustration. A considerable portion of plot is evident by virtue of the fact that both protagonists appear in action. The evil wolf holds the head of the trusting crane deep in his mouth while the crane probes for the bone. The wolf's very stance, his forelegs planted firmly with the claws visible and his

La .xvij. del asno z dela perzilla.

Figure 52

hindlegs tense, as though in pain, reveals the apprehension and discomfort he feels. The guileless crane lifts one foot, a seemingly innocent and impotent gesture made as if to support her attempt to delve deeper.

Setting is clearly rural, with a tree at the left depicted with hardly more than a few strokes of the blade, while at the right still another tree stands to balance the first. Wavy lines indicate furrows of plowed land. Conflict is obvious, for both characters seem tense in their postures, which indicate that the outcome is uncertain. Characterization, particularly in the case of the wolf, is forceful. His long fangs are quite capable of snapping off the crane's head, but the bird's rather perilous position underlines its simple trust. Theme, unless the viewer knew the story, would not be clear, but style is so artless and direct, so concise, even stark, that it closely parallels the terseness of the printed word. Effect is strong because so much latent possibility is encapsulated in so unqualified a portrayal of action. Point of view is that of the artist, just as the printed word represents the author's. Mood or tone is at once didactic and recreational, for the lesson is clear and the story possesses a wry humor all its own. Probably the nine elements of brief narrative found sparsely in the verbalized account are as well presented as they could possibly be.

Another fable found in Book I is Fable 17, "Del asno e dela perrilla" ("Of the Ass and the Lapdog"), whose moralization appears in the first line: "No one should stray from his proper profession so as to enter better ones." The woodcut of this humorous fable (Figure 52) all but relates the entire story.

About this [the matter of abandoning one's proper role] is told a suitable story. An ass continually saw how his master

patted and delighted in a lapdog, and was accompanied by her. Seeing this, the ass said to himself, "If my master holds this tiny and dirty creature in such affection and esteem, how much more would he love me if I should do him some service. I am better than she is and I am superior to this little bitch for many things and duties. In this way I'll be able to live better and attain to higher honor."

And the ass, thinking this, saw that his master was coming home and was entering his house, and he left the stable and ran braying to him, launching kicks and leaping upon him, and he placed his front hooves over the shoulders of his master and with his tongue, like the lapdog's, he began to lick him. And he oppressed him with his great weight and got his clothes filthy with mud and dust.

The master, frightened by those tricks and fawnings of the ass, called out and asked for help and assistance. And his household, hearing his cries and clamor, came and beat the ass with sticks and whips, breaking his legs and ribs, and took him to the stable and hitched him to the plow.

This fable signifies that no one ought to involve himself in matters which are not proper, for what nature does not give or dispose one cannot easily do, and thus the foolish ass, thinking to please, displeased and rendered disservice.

The woodcarvers were not able to depict all the elements of the classic design here, but they conveyed some of them exceptionally well. Plot and conflict stand out in the woodcut, which may depict a single action but is more likely a double event. If single, then the gentleman is sitting with the lapdog on his lap as the ass leaps upon him and places one of its hooves on his knee and the other on his shoulder. If, however, it contains two separate incidents occurring at different times, one may regard the master as fondling the dog at one moment and contending with the ass in the next. The scene is in the master's house, for the gentleman is sitting in a chair whose size would preclude an outdoor setting. He tries to push the ass away and we can see his fingers on one of the animal's legs, while with his other hand he seems to pet the dog or perhaps protect it from the weight of the ass. Facial expression tells little, an unfortunately common aspect of the woodcuts of the *Ysopet*. The lapdog expresses its character as an affectionate pet, standing on its hind legs so as to lick its master's chin. The ass's stupidity is evident in every line of the illustration. Style in both words and woodcut is straightforward and simple. Effect is amusing, and this time the humor is not wry but of a more boisterous nature. Point of view, as in all the woodcuts, is that of the illustrator. The mood or tone of the woodcut is humorous.

Figure 53 narrates, this time in true double action, the two high points of the famous fable of Jupiter and the frogs who desire a king. It is the first story in Book II and bears the title "De Jupiter e de las ranas" ("Of

Figure 53

Jupiter and the Frogs"). In its woodcut the artist has actually portrayed all the elements of the classic design to a greater or lesser degree. There are two actions, both primary to the fable's argument. At the left one sees Jupiter, who, having been petitioned by the frogs for a ruler, and "seeing their innocence," is in the act of casting a log into their habitat. The King of the Gods sits crowned on his throne, clothed in flowing robes and holding his sceptre in his right hand while using his left to fling the log into the swamp. The story recounts that the frogs, frightened by the great splash, dive under the water, but later a frog raises its head above the surface to see what kind of ruler they have been given. Soon all the frogs lose fear and emerge to sit on the log, and they see that it is only an inanimate object. In disappointment they complain to Jupiter and ask for a better king.

The artist picks up the story just at the moment in which Jupiter has raised his arm to throw the log toward the frogs. There is a visual transition between this scene and the sequel at the right, wherein the stork has been sent as the second king and is now attacking his subjects mercilessly. Here, although the stork is the principal figure, one frog faces Jupiter, perhaps one of those who has petitioned the god a second time, or possibly even the first. If this is so, then there may even be triple action in this single woodcut. The artistic interlocking of the two or three episodes forms a most moving picture of the fable's several events. The god, the stork, and the frogs are all realistically portrayed, except for the webbed forefeet of the frogs, whose hindfeet alone are usually webbed in nature.

Plot and conflict make up but two actions in the verbalized fable—the log sent as king and later the stork—and the artists have presented both these events. Setting in the left-hand part of the illustration

is meant to give the impression of the god on his throne in heaven. At the right, the scene is more specifically depicted, and here we can see the frogs in their home with the stork. Characterization is less well presented, due to the absence of any expression on Jupiter's countenance, but if one knows the fable, one gleans the fact that the god is both generous and vindictive, since he punishes the poor frogs who have dared petition a second time. The very moralization serves to show how hard life is in a world governed by the gods: "This fable signifies that man does not recognize good except when he suffers harm." Theme would be difficult to identify from the illustration alone. Style, as always in the woodcuts, seems direct and to the point, paralleling the qualities of the printed version. The effect of this fable and its woodcut stresses the necessity of man's accepting whatever Fate may send him. Point of view is the same as in the other illustrations. Mood or tone is serious and is calculated to instill in the reader and viewer a kind of pessimism and some degree of wariness toward life's harsh rules, which must often be accepted with a grain of sardonic humor.

One of the most popular and widely known of all the fables in Aesopic lore is found in Fable 13 of Book II, "De la raposa e de la cigüeña" ("About the Fox and the Stork"). The woodcut (Figure 54) offers another example of double action and, like the fable of Jupiter and the frogs, comes very close to illustrating all that the verbalization contains. In the woodcut both plot and conflict are superbly indicated. The order in which the two events are to be viewed moves from bottom to top. The fable relates that the fox first invites the stork to dinner and sets before her a plate of food from which the long-beaked bird is unable to pick up even the smallest morsel. The stork goes

Figure 54

## La.xiij.dela rapoſa ⁊ dela ciguena.

home hungry, and later invites the vixen, serving her food in a long-necked vase from which she cannot eat. The illustration shows in the first episode the fox greedily gulping food while the scissors-like beak of the stork fails to seize a bite. Above, in the second sequence, the stork has plunged her long beak deep into the vase, one eye fixed upon the hungry fox, who vainly licks the vessel's side.

We select from Book III two very different stories. The first, a fable in the true Aesopic tradition, is Fable 4, bearing the title "Delas bestias e delas aves" ("About the Beasts and the Birds"). It tells an ancient tale of conflict between the beasts and the birds, and how the bat, then a feathered creature and definitely belonging to the race of birds, believes the beasts will win and goes over to their side. But the eagles eventually lead the birds to victory and in revenge they deplume the bat and relegate him to nakedness and darkness. The illustration (Figure 55) displays a stag, a doe, a unicorn, a hare, a fox, and one other animal whose head is hidden but which is most likely another deer, while the birds are represented by a stork and two eagles. Above the raging battle we see the bat with its featherless wings outspread. In viewing the woodcut, we are aware of multiple action: the fight is in full swing and yet the bat, according to the verbalization, is not transformed from bird to winged beast until after the conflict ends. We may therefore assume that two moments of time are depicted. All the birds and beasts are true to life, and even the unicorn looks as unicorns were supposed to look, but the bat excels them all for its remarkably well-portrayed form, especially its wings and tail.

Fable 9, "Dela muger e del marido muerto" ("Of the Woman and the Dead Husband") is a story rather than

Figure 55

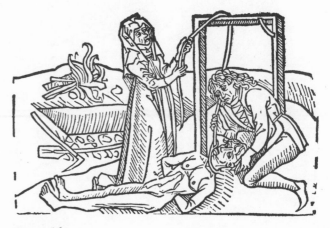

Figure 56

a true fable, and comes directly from *The Golden Ass*, written by Apuleius in the second century. The story is generally known as "The Matron of Ephesus." It is a strange tale, strong in characterization, especially of the matron, and evocative of a kind of macabre and very heartless humor. Apuleius in his inimitable style relates the events unforgettably. In the *Ysopet* it is far more unvarnished and ingenuous. We translate it to illustrate its verbalized components and to compare them with the woodcut. (Figure 56).

Dripping with irony, as the reader will soon perceive, the tale opens as follows: "For womankind is chaste, as I believe, nor is she overcome by importunements and solicitations of a lover, as the fable proves." The effect of this contradiction of what the author actually believes is startling at the end, and makes the lesson unusually bitter, even cruel:

A woman, when her husband died, went to the tomb where he was buried so as to spend her days in mourning and grief. While she was there, a man committed a crime and wickedness for which he was hanged by the court, and a knight was placed on guard so that his relatives would not take him down from there. This knight, suffering from thirst, came to the tomb where that woman was and begged her to give him a little water to assuage his thirst.

And because the knight had seen the woman, he went back again to the tomb to see what sort of woman she was. And becoming acquainted with her, he began to console her and to converse with her, and from there, as the friendship continued, he went back to her more times and to such a degree that one day while he was at the tomb, they stole the hanged man.

When the knight returned and did not find the hanged man, he comes[6] fleeing to the feet of that woman and in great travail commences to complain to her.

Aqui comiença el quarto libro del yfopo.
La primera fabula dela rapofa z delas uvas.

Figure 57

She says to him: "Your trouble disturbs me, but I don't know what I can do about it."

The knight replied: "Please help me! And I seek counsel from you."

Taking pity on him, she disinterred her husband and put him on the gallows and thus she concealed the knight's failure through pity. He seeing so great a love in the woman for him, courted her and at last she yielded to his plea. And although she had been chaste until that time, she committed theft and fornication, one crime after the other. And thus the dead do not lack those who mourn them and the living those who fear for them.

A remarkably vivid woodcut illustrates this anti-feminist story by seizing upon the pivotal incident, but goes farther than the story, offering us a considerable degree of characterization, setting, and the very climax of the plot, the essence of theme in its stark portrayal of the fickleness of the female sex. The decidedly masculine point of view is most certainly the author's, but that attitude was not out of step with the times. Setting is depicted well. At the left a fire burns near the open grave from which the corpse has been exhumed, and at the grave's edge lie a pick and shovel and clods of earth to make it plain that the excavation is recent. The characterization of the two people could hardly have been visualized with greater effect, especially with regard to the matron. Smitten at last by the knight's allure, the once mourning widow has actually seized the rope and is hoisting her late husband's body onto the gallows. Nothing she could have done could be more damning to or revealing of her character. Her new lover has adjusted the noose around the dead man's neck and is in the act of lifting the corpse from the ground. The amorous pair have even divested the body of its winding sheet, allowing it to go to the gallows undignified and stark naked. We may assume that sufficient passage of time has elapsed to render the body unrecognizable.

This version omits the final macabre touch found in the original of Apuleius. There the lover recalls that the criminal lacked front teeth and points out that the matron's dead husband has all his teeth intact. At this, the lady picks up a stone and remedies the defect forthwith.

From Book IV comes woodcut number 1 (Fig. 57), in which can be seen the famous fable of the fox and the grapes. The vineyard and the leaping fox are so charmingly portrayed that they deserve inclusion, even if the illustration captures but a single facet of the action. The scene is certainly one of the most delightful in the collection.

Another from Book IV is Fable 5, "Del lobo cerval e delos labradores" ("Of the Lobo Cerval and the Farmers"). The illustration of the *lobo cerval* may remind readers of the variety of animals to which that term was applied. In *Calila e Digna* this term referred to the protagonists, who were jackals. In the woodcut illustrating the story here (Fig. 58) the animal is a hybrid monstrosity, fire-breathing, with the head of a bull, the body of a horse though spotted like a leopard, and the feet of a bird of prey. According to the story, a *lobo cerval* falls into a pit and is injured. Some farmers find it and beat it savagely until others persuade them to spare it. Later, when it has recovered, it lays waste the land and slays many people, sparing only those who have saved its life. The moralization seems to stress that people should be kind to travelers and pilgrims.

Figure 58

La.v.del lobo cerual z delos labradores.

**La.xvij.dela formiga: z dela cigarra.**

Figure 59

From the *Fabulas extravagantes* comes the woodcut illustrating the well known Fable 17, "Dela formiga e dela cigarra" ("Of the Ant and the Grasshopper"). In the woodcut (Figure 59) the artists have depicted a reasonably realistic ant and a perfect cricket rather than a grasshopper, both with the correct number of legs and other appendages. Setting is especially well portrayed here, with an accurately scaled landscape, including a city in the distance.

Figure 60 illustrates Fable 17 from the *Fabulas de Remisio,* whose title is "Del labrador e sus fijos" ("Of the Farmer and His sons"). A farmer has told his sons that after he is dead they should dig for a treasure in the vineyard. The woodcut reveals the three sons hard at work with mattock and spades. More than the usual amount of detail appears in their garments, in the furrows of the field, and especially in the staked vines. They find no buried treasure, but their digging does cultivate the vines, which through their unsuspecting efforts bear a great harvest.

From the *Fabulas de Aviano* comes Fable 8, "Delos dos compañeros" ("Of the Two Companions"). In its woodcut (Figure 61) the artist concentrates on characterization and setting but does not neglect conflict and a crucial incident of plot. This story is perhaps more artistically told in picture than many are in words. Two travelers who are virtually strangers are making their way through a hilly and forested area when they see a bear approaching them. The more agile traveler climbs a tree. In the woodcut, we see him there terrified, and here even his face seems to reveal his emotions, a rare occurrence in the woodcuts of the *Ysopet.* Behind the tree and its occupant rises a mountain, on which grow other trees, and between the mountain

and an upthrust rock can be seen plowed fields and the roofs and towers of a town. The man in the tree kneels in a crotch and clings frantically to the branches.

The less agile traveler resorts to a ruse. He falls to the earth as though dead. In the woodcut he lies supine, one arm thrown back over his head while the other in a very natural way protects his genitals. His eyes are tightly shut, his legs outstretched. The bear's body all but covers his, and its open mouth, teeth displayed, looms not far from his face. The fable relates that the animal sniffs him all over especially his face, mouth, and ears, while the traveler carefully holds his breath and remains motionless. Since his flesh is icy with terror, he seems dead to the bear, and since, according to folk belief, bears do not eat dead bodies, it leaves him and goes to its lair.

The traveler in the tree descends at last, and from what he has observed is curious to know if the bear has spoken to his companion, for so it seemed to him. His partner replies that it has indeed given him many lessons, but especially one to the effect that people ought always to avoid bad company and that once a man discovers that a companion has deceived him or otherwise failed him, he should part company with him. And so he leaves his cowardly fellow traveler.

The last book of the *Ysopet* has a rather long title, "Aqui comiençan las fabulas collectas de Alfonso e de Pogio e de otros en la forma e orden seguiente" ("Here Begin the Collected Fables of Alfonso and of Poggio and of others in the Following Order"). Most of the "fables" are in reality *exempla* found in Pedro Alfonso's *Disciplina Clericalis,* though toward the end of the book several are taken from Poggio's fables and tales,[7] as well as from other sources. The *Disciplina Clericalis,* certainly not a "discipline of the clergy" but rather a quasi-serious wisdom book, was one of the

Figure 60

Figure 61

most popular works in the Middle Ages. More than sixty extant manuscripts are distributed from Iceland to Constantinople. Its influence since the time of its composition in the first quarter of the twelfth century has been enormous, for scarcely a collection of stories has been written that has not drawn from it. Its own sources are for the most part Arabic and Hebrew *exempla* and *sententiae,* some extracted from *Kalila wa-Dimna,* others from *The Books of Sindibad,* later to be rendered into Spanish as *El libro de los engaños,* and still others from a multitude of mideastern wisdom tales and jests. Figure 62 illustrates Fable 1, "En que Alfonso amonesta las personas a la sabiduria e verdadera amistad" ("In Which Alfonso admonishes People to Wisdom and True Friendship"). It stems directly from the *Disciplina Clericalis.*[8] This was one of the most highly prized stories from the Middle Ages and appears in Don Juan Manuel's *El Conde Lucanor,* in a much expanded and altered version in *Castigos e documentos,* in the *Libro de los exenplos por a.b.c.,* and in *El Cavallero Cifar.* The story is told by an Arabic father who offers his son firm counsel concerning friends. We discuss this tale above in the chapter on *Castigos e documentos.*

A comparison of the woodcut illustrating the moment when the son with the sack on his back arrives at a friend's house to ask for help, with the painting of the same incident in *Castigos* (Plate 50) reveals considerable similarity, even if, as we believe, there could have been little or no influence from the manuscript on the printed book. It is simply an example of two artists' interpretations of the same material, although there remains the possibility of some common illustration with which both may have been familiar.

Facial expression in this woodcut actually reveals the characters' emotions. In the young man's countenance one sees concern as the friend turns his face away, thrusting out both hands in refusal. The door of his house, with four tiny windows much like the panel lights of some modern doors, is shut. Since this story was quite well known in the fifteenth century as a truly Aesopic fable, the single woodcut must have been sufficient to illustrate it.

One of the most amusing stories in the *Fabulas collectas* comes also from the *Disciplina Clericalis* and is Fable 5, "Dela fe o engaño de los tres compañeros" ("Of the Faith or Deceit of Three Companions"). It is famous enough to merit full translation rather than paraphrase. The woodcut (Figure 63) captures one moment in time, but since the story was so familiar, the viewer needed no more. It illustrates the climax of the story and the very crux of its humor.

Often a man falls into the net which he sets for another, according to what is contained in this fable. There were three companions of whom two were merchants and city-dwellers and the other a villager. Due to their devotion, they were going on a pilgrimage to the city of Mecca and provisions failed them on the road to such an extent that they had nothing to eat except a little flour which was only enough to make one small loaf of bread. When the deceitful burghers saw this, they spoke to one another: "We have little bread and our companion is a great eater, so it is necessary for us to think of how we can eat this little loaf without him."

After this agreement had been agreed upon and consented to between them, they went to sleep. The villager, understanding his companions' deceit, took the bread half-cooked and ate it by himself and went back to sleep. After a little while, one of the merchants, as though frightened by a marvellous dream, started to get up, and his companion asked him, "Why are you startled?"

He replied, "I am startled and terror stricken by a wonderful dream. It seemed to me that two angels, opening

Figure 62

**La .v. dela fe/o engaño delos tres cõpañeros.**

Figure 63

the gates of heaven, took me before the throne of the Lord God."

In great joy, his companion said, "That is a wonderful dream, but I have had one even more marvellous, for I saw two angels who carried me over the firm earth and to hell."

The villager, hearing all this, pretended he was asleep. But the city-dwellers, desiring to finish their trick, awakened him, and the rustic artfully, as if startled, responded, "Who are those calling me?"

They said to him, "We are your companions."

And he asked them, "So you are back?"

They replied, "We never left here. Why do you speak of our return?"

The rustic said, "It appeared to me that two angels, opening the gates of heaven, took one of you before the throne of the Lord God and took the other, dragging him across the earth, to hell. And I believed you would not return here. Until now I haven't heard that either one has come back from paradise or hell, so I arose and ate the bread myself."

This fable shows that sometimes when someone thinks to deceive some ignorant person he is himself deceived by him."

The woodcut is delightful. Plot and conflict, even in one encapsulated moment, are deftly handled. All three protagonists are present. Characterization is nicely achieved as the two deceitful townsmen lie in feigned slumber, their eyes shut tight, their limbs arranged in attitudes of sleep. One lies supine, the other on his side with his head resting realistically on one hand. The latter has even removed his cap. The rustic, his feet almost touching them, sits and greedily crams the loaf into his mouth with his right hand while his left holds a cup. His eyes are on the faces of his companions. Behind the group the fire burns merrily. The woodcut's style is straightforward, omitting nothing found in the verbalization. The effect is humor-

ous, while point of view is, as usual, the artist's. The mood is conducive to laughter. In sum, the ancient motif of the cheater cheated was never more skillfully depicted.

Another story, famous long before the *Ysopet's* printing and made so in the West by Pedro Alfonso, Fable 10, is "Dela muger moça e su marido e de la suegra e del adultero" ("Of the Yong Wife and her Husband and of the Mother-in-law and of the Adulterer."). The woodcut (Figure 64) reflects a very important moment of action while managing to instill a good deal of character into the faces of the four people. The story runs that a young wife, with her mother's connivance, admits a lover into her house and is busily entertaining him when the husband knocks at the door. At first no one knows what to do, but the mother thinks of a clever ruse. She commands the paramour to draw his sword and stand at the door to threaten the husband when she opens it.[9] The husband, naturally curious, asks what has happened, and his mother-in-law tells him that some men have pursued the young man into the house and that she and his wife have protected him. When the husband knocked, the young man thought his pursuers had returned and hence drew his sword and appeared to be angry. The husband then comes in, seats the young man comfortably, and after a cordial conversation, sends him on his way and even plans to keep him as a friend thereafter.

The woodcut cleverly depicts the scene just as the door is opened. The husband places one foot over the threshold and stops, one hand upraised in inquiry, the other on the hilt of his own sword. Facial expressions in this woodcut fairly reveal the emotions of the characters. The husband looks surprised. The young man

Figure 64

**La .t. dela muger moça z su marido**
**z dela suegra z del adultero.**

holding the sword appears to be ready to slash with it, as his eyes meet those of the husband. The older woman stands facing the door, one hand open and stretched toward her son-in-law, the other in a gesture of explanation. Her face conveys her false concern. The wife stands a little behind her, one hand raised as though she too were attempting to explain what has taken place. Her face is serious. It is a most graphic depiction of the story's climax.

The next tale, this one from Poggio, with its scene laid in Italy, is Fable 19, "Del loco e del cavallero caçador" ("Of the Madman and Hunter Knight"). In Milan, the story goes, there lives a physician who cures insane patients by placing them up to their waists in a tank of stinking water and mud, while keeping them on a strict diet until their madness abates. One madman they bring him is placed up to his thighs in the tank for two weeks. At the end of that time he begs to be removed, vowing that he is entirely cured. The doctor pities him and allows him the run of his house provided he does not leave it. One day a hunter arrives with a falcon on his wrist and several dogs, and the madman, who has forgotten that he has ever seen such creatures, speaks to the hunter, asking him about them and about himself and why he has come there. He goes on to inquire how the falcon and the dogs are used and how much money they make for their owner from the hunt. The man replies that he estimates upward of five pounds in gold. The madman inquires how much it takes to keep a horse, falcon, and dogs, and is told around fifty pounds. At this, the madman urges the hunter to flee the premises lest the doctor, learning of his great insanity, throw him into the tank with the other patients. The moralization of this story states that people should not be so insane as to spend

Figure 66

their time on activities such as hunting in which gain is far less then expenses, if they expect to be honored by their fellows.

The woodcut (Figure 65) closely parallels the episode in the printed version, in which the hunter and the madman are talking. Setting is well portrayed, for one sees the front of the house with its arched door in which the madman stands as he converses with the mounted hunter. The dogs, however, are not present. Actually, most of the house is portrayed with both upper and lower stories and many windows. Behind it can be seen the tank and three madmen submerged in its muddy water. This woodcut would be incomprehensible without the accompanying verbalization.

Figure 66 illustrates a story which has gravitated to Aesopic collections although it does not belong to that tradition. Fable 20, "Del padre a fijo que yvan a vender el asno" ("Of the Father and Son Who Were Going to Sell the Ass") may be one of the best known of medieval tales. A father and son set out to sell their donkey, the father mounted on the animal and the boy on foot. As they encounter various people on the road, each protests that either the father should be walking and the son riding, or else both walking or both riding. Finally someone berates them for mistreating the donkey, declaring that they should carry it. This last, in fact, is the moment depicted in the woodcut. We see them staggering along with the animal tied to a pole and dangling between them. When they are ridiculed for such a stupid act, the father, in a rage, hits the ass in the head and kills it. Later, when they take the hide to sell it, some boys drag the father through the mud and all but kill him. The lesson is clear: one must not heed what others advise but do what one thinks best.

The artists depict the most crucial and amusing

Figure 65

### La.rir.del loco.z del cauallero caçador.

episode in the story, for what could be more eye-catching and unusual than a donkey suspended from a pole? Both father and son support themselves with a staff, for it is clear that the beast is heavy. The ass demonstrates his unwillingness to be so conveyed. His mouth is open as he brays in protest, and every line of his body is tense. To the right, three men observe, speak, and gesture. The background scene presents the entire skyline of a good-sized city in great detail, and yet both the scene and the human figures lack the finesse of all the other woodcuts in the book. We have no explanation and can only surmise that the Spanish bookmaker lacked a woodcut from the set he used and had to prepare one.

The *Ysopet,* in its illustrations, carries forward beyond the limits of the Middle Ages those narrative techniques long accepted and understood by Spaniards. It reveals that novelesque pieces—the longish *vida* of Aesop, as well as the shorter fables and stories—were illustrated with sufficient success to assure that the influence of this art and its techniques would carry over into the Renaissance. Similar techniques for presenting narrative fiction visually lived on especially in works of a popular nature. Often subsequent editions continued to use the very same woodcuts unaltered. We hope that the illustrations in such books will tempt investigators to pursue the development of narrative art in later Spanish books.

Plate 40. King Sancho instructs Prince Fernando. *Castigos e documentos*, folio 2r. Authorized by the Biblioteca Nacional (Madrid).

Plate 41. Christ chastises the errant nun. *Castigos e documentos*, folio 74v. Authorized by the Biblioteca Nacional (Madrid).

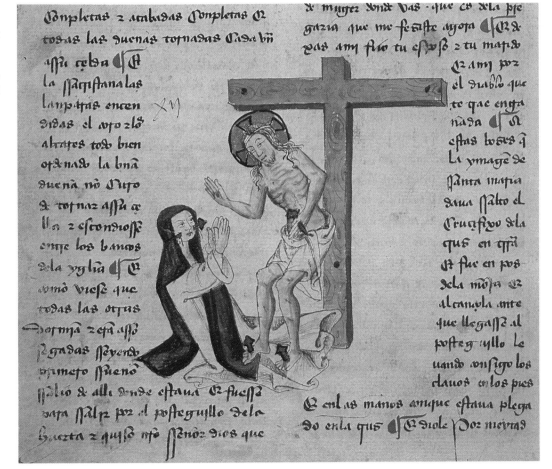

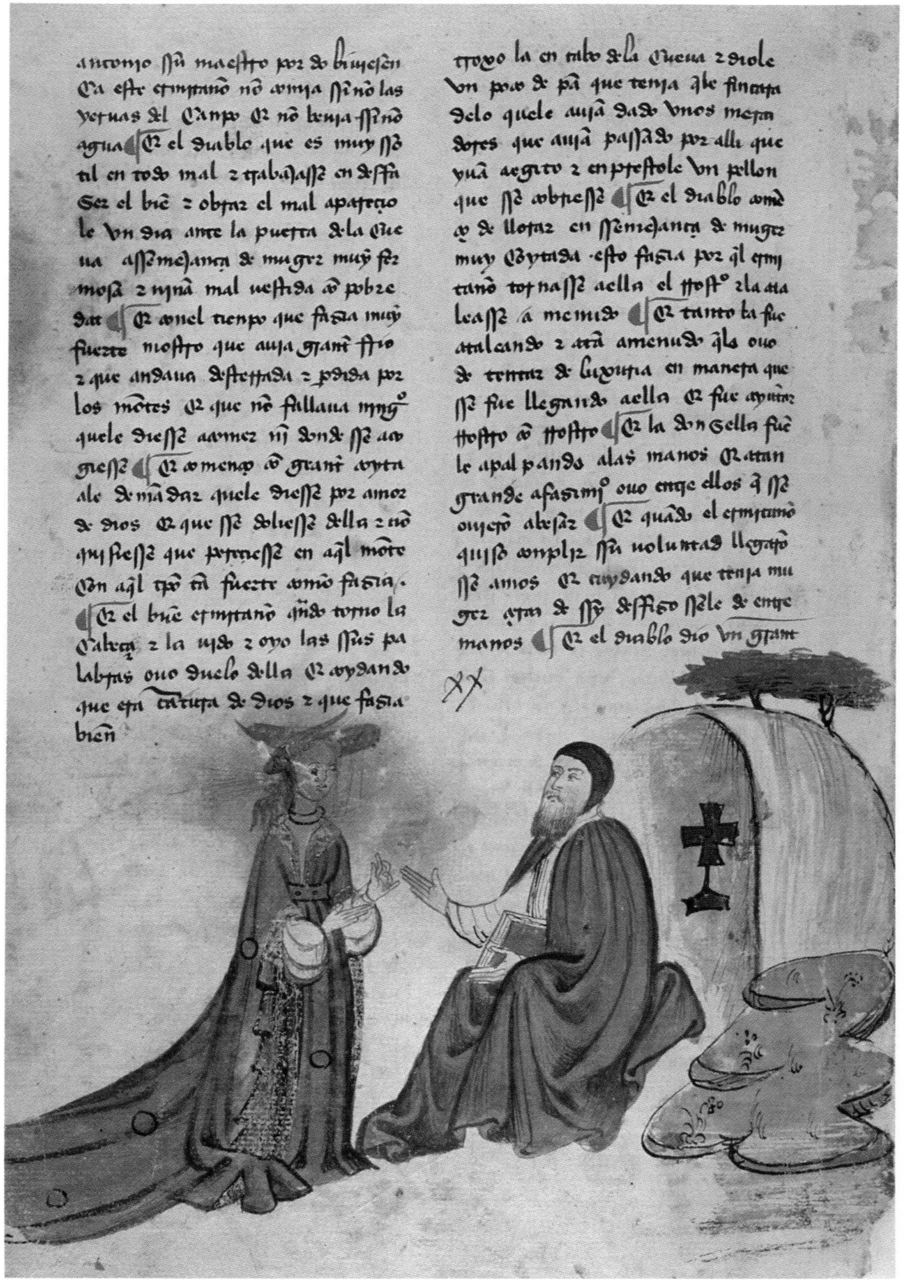

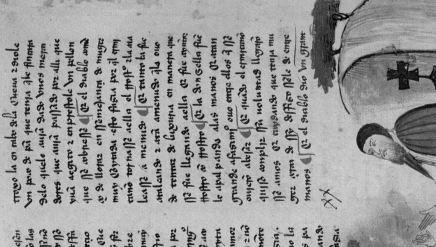

Plate 43. The repentant hermit receives a blessing. *Castigos e documentos*, folio 75r. Authorized by the Biblioteca Nacional (Madrid).

Plate 42. The devil in disguise tempts the hermit. *Castigos e documentos*, folio 74v. Authorized by the Biblioteca Nacional (Madrid).

Plate 44. Marziella confronts Juan Corvalan. *Castigos e documentos*, folio 49r.
Authorized by the Biblioteca Nacional (Madrid).

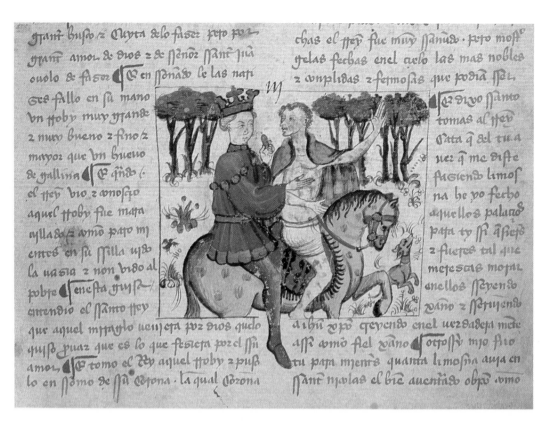

gant busco z curta de lo faser yepo por
gran amor de dios z de señor sant iu
ouelo z fasez  C E en señaço le las nati
ges fallo en su mano
vn ytoby muy yrande
z muy bueno z fino z
mayor que vn hueuo
de gallina  C E esto (.
el yey vio z conoscio
aquel ytoby fue mata
rylla do z amo paro m
entes en su silla uj do
la vazia z non vido al
pobre  C En esta guy sa
enendio el santo yey
que aquel mysaylo veu eta por dios quelo
quiso puar que es lo que fesiera por el su
amor.  C E tomo el yey aquel ytoby z puso
lo en somo de su corona . la qual corona

chas el yey fue muy sanado . yepo mosf
yelas fechas enel cielo las mas nobles
z complidas z fermosas que podia ser.
C E dryo santo
tomas al yey
Certa q del tu a
uer q me difte
fasiendo limos
na he yo fecho
aquellos palacio
paya ty si aseys
z fuerez tal que
metescais mo py
an ellos seyendo
vano z seruiendo
a ihu xpo creyendo enel verdadera mete
asi amo fiel vano C otrosi mio fuo
tu papa mientrs quanta limossia auia en
sant ny ulas el bie auentado obpo amo

Plate 45. (*left*)
King Edward takes
the leper on his horse.
*Castigos e documentos,*
folio 13v. Authorized by
the Biblioteca Nacional
(Madrid).

Plate 46. (*below*)
Noah and his family
view the Flood.
*Castigos e documentos,*
folio 23r. Authorized by
the Biblioteca Nacional
(Madrid).

ha estado no es bueno el miedo esta el
yerro el mesmo sse judga conosçiendosse
E por esto trahe el temor consigo ssegun
que contesçio a ada que desque ovo pesar
de quando passo el madamiento de dios q
luego conosçio q estaua contra el escondi
osse E oyo la bos que dios lo llamo ent
los arboles de parayso quando le dixo oes
adan · como qui dise ado estas tu que
estaste E como ada oyo la bos amysada
que era de ssu sseñor dios z temjola con
grant myedo conosçiendo el ssu grant yerro
E en conosçiendo tomo uerguença dela

Conosçer despues que aua fecho el yerro
ssegunt que te yo agora dixe el yerro el
mal fecho quel ome fase lo mete en
uerguença · luego en pos la uerguença
uiene el temor z el temor judga la pena
que deue auer E por ende quando los
uasallos an estas dos cosas z guarda a
ssu rey z assi sseñor uerguença z temor
el rey es bien auenturado z ellos conel
E por estas dos cosas lo matiene en buen
estado z los guarda que no yerre en di
chos nj en fechos E mucho mejor cosa
es auer el uasallo de poder mejorar al rey

·cosas uergonçosas de ssu cuerpo z cobrie
ron sse el z eua ssu muger conlas foias
delos arboles E estonçe dixo ada sseñor
oy la tu bos que me llamaste z oue de
ty grant myedo z quis me esconder M
podiera E dos cosas sson las q guardan
al ome que no yerre esta primera es uer
guença la ssegunda temor z auer mje
do delas cosas que podrie acontesçer E el
que estas cosas no cata nj guarda an
te que yerre conuiene quelas aya E

quele de galardon por los sseruiçios que
le ha fecho que nol podrie le perdon por los
erores quele ha fecho E Capitulo
de como comjenço asseynar los reys
z los prinçipes z delas herençes dellos

En el primero tienpo quando
fueron asseynar los enperadores
fueron en essa sazon ... el rey ...
de agora ... sson primera mente de dios
fue cada una dellas E esto conuiene que

Plate 47. The expulsion of Adam and Eve. *Castigos e documentos,* folio 21v.
Authorized by the Biblioteca Nacional (Madrid).

Plate 48. Daniel in the lion's den. *Castigos e documentos*, folio 18v. Authorized by the Biblioteca Nacional (Madrid).

Plate 49. Dido leaps to her death.
*Castigos e documentos*, folio 78v.
Authorized by the Biblioteca Nacional (Madrid).

Plate 50. The story of the half-friend.
*Castigos e documentos*, folio 68v.
Authorized by the Biblioteca Nacional (Madrid).

Plate 51. Archbishop Ferrand Martínez petitions Pope Boniface VIII. *Cavallero Cifar*, folio 1r.

All plates from *Cavallero Cifar* courtesy of the Bibliothèque Nationale (Paris).

q esta aqllo q yaya enel saco z el gelo
conto todo z otrogole q aſſeſe q lo su
teuiaſe en buenas oſtal q auia z su amigo
le respondio q amo fiziera el z su pa
dre la locura q se parase a ella z q salie
se fuera de casa q no qua verse en peligro
por ellos / z et eso mesmo le respondi
eron todos los otros sus amigos z torno
pa casa de su padre con su saco z dixole
como ninguno de sus amigos / no se quiſie
ron auenturar por el d este peligro z fijo
dixo el ome bueno mucho me marauille
quido te oy dezir q çient amigos auias
ganado z semeja me q entre todos los de
to no fallaſe un medio z mas vete pa
el mi medio amigo z dele de mi pte esto q
nos auiteso z q el fuego q nos lo enci
bra z el fijo se fue z leuo el saco z
fizo a la puerta del medio amigo de
su padre z fueſo gelo dezir z mando
q entraſe z quando lo vio venir z lo
fallo con su saco acuestas mando a los
otros q saliesen de la camara z fina
ron solos z el ome bueno le pregunto

q esta lo q ffera z q yaya enel saco z el le
conto lo q auiniera a su padre z a el
z q le rogaua de pte de su padre q gelo
encubrieſe z el ome bueno ffeſpon
dio q aqllo z mucho mas fiſie el por

amor de su padre z tomaro una aça
da z fizieron amos a dos un foyo
su el su lecho z metieron alli el saco co
el puerto z cubrieron lo muy bien de ña
z tornose luego el moço pa casa su
padre z dixole en como el su medio
amigo lo ffesçibiera muy bie oto lue
go q le conto todo el fecho z le ffeſpo
dio q aqllo z mucho mas / fiſie por el
z q fizieran amos un foyo su el su le
cho z q lo soterara alli z et pues
fijo dixo el padre q te semeja de aql
mi medio amigo z certo padre dixo
el semejante q este vro medio amigo q
vale mas q todos los mis çiento z fijo
dixo el ome bueno en las obras dela
çura se prueuan los amigos / et por
ende no te deues tu fiar mucho en todo

Plates 52-54. The story of the half-friend.
*Opposite page: lower left* (52): The father
kills the pig; *upper right* (53): The son
seeks a friend who will hide the corpse.
*Right* (54): The banquet with the half-friend.
*Cavallero Cifar*, folios 6r, 6v.

Plate 55. The hunter about to kill the lark.
*Cavallero Cifar*, folio 98v.

Plate 56. The hunter attempts to fly.
*Cavallero Cifar*, folio 99r.

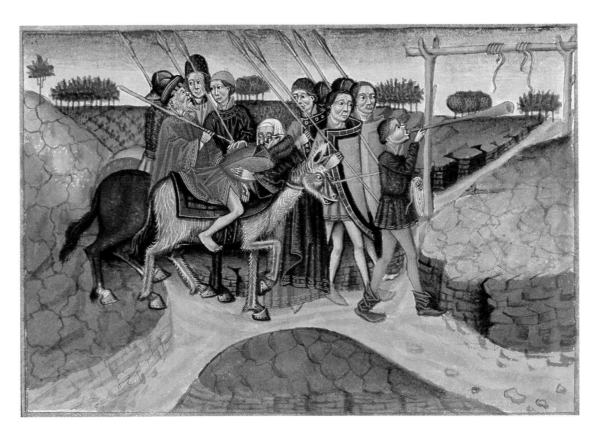

Plate 57. (*left*)
The squire bites off
his mother's lips.
*Cavallero Cifar*,
folio 106r.

Plate 58. (*below*)
The squire pleads
his case before the
emperor. *Cavallero
Cifar*, folio 109v.

Plate 59. The wolf and the leeches. *Cavallero Cifar*, folio 138r.

Plate 60. The Cifars' older son is abducted by a lioness. *Cavallero Cifar*, folio 32v.

Plate 61. (*right*) Cifar grieves
for the kidnapped Grima.
*Cavallero Cifar*, folio 34v.

Plate 62. (*below*) Grima is greeted
by the king and queen of Orbin.
*Cavallero Cifar*, folio 37v.

meter ¶Ca tu sabes bien q̃ no telo
da la natura  ca no fuesse grado en
tre buenos om̃s nj sabes bie Casonar

¶Ca este cauallero paresçe de bue
logar ¶ de buẽ entendimjento ¶Ca
por auentura tu pensaras desir algo
antel ⁊ diras alguno mal ¶Crahbo

¶Jd vos adios om̃e bueno dixo
el sibaldo ca yo sienpre sepa ncao
syno prouase las cosas/ ¶Ca no sa
bedes vos bien dixo el sibaldo q̃ la
Ventura ayuda aqllos q̃ toma osa
dia  ¶Ca por Ventura puedo yo
appender muchas buenas cosas deste
cauallero ⁊ ser bien andante conel

¶Dios lo mande dixo el hermja
no  vete ⁊ sey muy cortes en tus pa
labras ¶Dios me ayude dixo ¶El
sibaldo q̃ asi lo fare ¶Et fuesse
luego pa el cauallero Cafar ¶Et en

logar dele desu dios vos salue
dixo te estas palabras ¶E delas
preguntas que fiso el sibaldo al
cauallo afir ⁊ telo q̃ el lerespodia
atodas ellas ¶

¶Cauallero desauenturado
perdiste tu cauallo ⁊ no
tienes por ello pesar  no
lo perdi dixo el cauallero
por q̃ no era mjo calo tenja acomen
do fasta dies dias ⁊ no mas/ ¶E pu
es piensas dixo el sibaldo q̃ no lo
pecharas aql q̃ telo acomendo  pues
q̃ entu poder murio ¶E testo por la
mala guarda ¶E no lo pechase dixo
el cauallero en aql lo mato cuyo era
⁊ auje poder delo fiser ¶E pues a
sy es dixo el sibaldo  yo te do por

Plate 63. The story of the ass and the lapdog. *Cavallero Cifar*, folio 42v.

Plate 64. Cifar saves the Knave from hanging. *Cavallero Cifar*, folio 48v.

Plate 65. Cifar, now King of Mentón, knights his sons. *Cavallero Cifar*, folio 72v.

Plate 66. (*right*)
The Bold Knight
encounters the Lady
of the Lake.
*Cavallero Cifar*,
folio 86v.

Plate 67. (*below*)
The Lady of the Lake
changed into a demon.
*Cavallero Cifar*,
folio 91v.

Plate 68. (*left*) Roboán is set adrift by the Emperor of Tigridia. *Cavallero Cifar*, folio 170v.

Plate 69. (*below*) Emperor Roboán orders the execution of Count Farán. *Cavallero Cifar*, folio 188r.

# Notes

## Introduction

1. Ernst Robert Curtius, whose work we highly respect, in his *European Literature and the Latin Middle Ages,* trans. Willard R. Trask (New York: Pantheon Books, 1948), in his opening chapter states in essence that literary historians have nothing to learn from art, since we learn from literature primarily. We disagree and place ourselves in the camp of F.P. Pickering, who in an article and a book rejects this thesis. Curtius scorns what he terms a "reciprocal illumination" of the arts (art and literature) and claims that it "befogs the issue by the dilettantism of its efforts" and "then proceeds to apply the art historical sequence of any period's styles in its literary study." For Pickering's rebuttal see "On Coming to Terms with Curtius," *German Life and Letters* 11 (1958): 335–45; and idem, *Literature and Art in the Middle Ages* (New York: Macmillan, 1970), 61ff.

2. Curtius's great importance and influence upon medieval scholarship merits one additional disagreement on our part. Like Curtius, we know and practice the tenets of philology and therefore agree with him that medieval literature can best be understood through that discipline. But we cannot accept his thesis that "the study of art is easier" or that "there is nothing which cannot be understood." He states further that "to understand Pindar's poems requires great intellectual effort." With this last statement we agree wholeheartedly. But we are startled by his statements that "the Parthenon frieze makes no such demands" and that "the study of pictures is effortless by comparison with the study of books" (p. 15). We see in the frieze, from careful study of the Elgin Marbles, a vast panorama of narrative techniques which reflect much of Hellenic life, belief, and understanding of man and nature, and we wonder if even now art historians in collaboration with scholars in other fields have interpreted all that can be interpreted.

3. Alfonso allowed interesting pronouncements about medieval drama to be set down in his *Siete Partidas.* See Samuel Parsons Scott, *Las Siete Partidas* (New York: Commercial Publishing House, 1931), which is a remarkably able translation of the original. In *Partida I,* Title VI, Law 34, appears the discussion of pious and secular drama.

4. In the summer of 1978, working under a grant from the National Endowment for the Humanities, we traveled through much of Spain and, having read the article by Dr. Lázaro de Castro ("Fantásticas leyendas medievales, recogidas en la pintura por un artista mudéjar en Los Balbases [Burgos]," *Minutos Menarini,* Circular 33175, 3–6, Dirección General de Sanidad, August 1975), we traveled to Los Balbases. The *alfarjes* were discovered by the curate of the village, Don Constancio Escolar Royuela, in 1975 when some eighteenth-century plaster was removed from the beams of the church. The *alfarjes,* which date from the fifteenth century, depict the action of what can best be described as medieval tales from literature and folklore. Dr. Castro, now deceased, published another article on the same roof beam paintings, "Algunas notas para la historia del arte burgalés," *Boletín Instituto "Fernán González" de Burgos* (1973), 716–22.

5. For bibliographical data about the *Book of Sindibad,* see p. 107, note 1 below; for the *Libro de buen amor* see page 109, note 2, below.

6. For valuable material on the rise and development of the study of medieval art, we are indebted to Wayne Dynes, "Tradition and Innovation in Medieval Art," in James M. Powell, ed., *Medieval Studies: An Introduction* (Syracuse: Syracuse Univ. Press, 1976).

## Las Cantigas de Santa Maria

1. Perhaps the most sound and comprehensive study of Alfonso's life and works is that of Antonio Ballesteros-Beretta, *Alfonso X, el Sabio* (Barcelona: Salvat Editores; Murcia: Consejo Superior de Investigaciones Científicas, 1963).

2. Fortunately the vast *Siete Partidas* has been translated

into English. See Samuel Parsons Scott, *Las Siete Partidas* (New York: Commercial Publishing House, 1931).

3. A fine interpretive study of Alfonso's many works is that of Evelyn S. Procter, *Alfonso X of Castile, Patron of Literature and Learning* (Oxford: Clarendon Press, 1951). See Also Gonzalo Menéndez Pidal, "Cómo trabajaron las escuelas alfonsíes," *Nueva Revista de Filología Hispánica* 5, no. 4 (1951):363–80.

4. There is no translation of either the *Libro de astronomía* or *Los lapidarios*. See the edition of the former by Manuel Rico y Sinobas, *Los libros del saber de astronomia* (Madrid, 1863). The old facsimile edition of the latter, that of Fernández Montana, *Lapidarios del rey Alfonso X* (Madrid, 1881) has been replaced by *Lapidario de Alfonso X el Sabio* (Madrid: Edilán, 1980), with excellent facsimiles in color. See also the sound edition of Roderic C. Diman and Lynn W. Winget, eds., *Alfonso el Sabio, Lapidary and Libro de las formas e imagenes* (Madison: Hispanic Seminary, 1980).

5. For an excellent study of versification see Dorothy Clotelle Clarke, "Versification in Alfonso el Sabio's *Cantigas*," *Hispanic Review* 23 (1955):83–98.

6. John E. Keller has studied folklore and daily life in the *Cantigas*. See his "A Note on King Alfonso's Use of Popular Themes in His *Cantigas*," *Kentucky Foreign Language Quarterly* 1, no. 1 (1954):26–31; his "Daily Living as Presented in the *Canticles* of Alfonso the Learned," *Speculum* 33, no. 4 (1958):484–89; and his "Folklore in the *Cantigas* of Alfonso el Sabio," *Southern Folklore Quarterly* 23, no. 3 (1959):175–83. See also Frank Calcott, *The Supernatural in Early Spanish Literature* (New York: Instituto de los Españos en los Estados Unidos, 1923).

7. Gonzalo Menéndez Pidal, in "Los manuscritos de las *Cantigas:* cómo se elaboró la miniatura alfonsí," *Boletín de la Real Academia Española* 150 (1962):23–51, rehearses the theories of foreign influence, insisting (we believe with good cause) that Italian as well as French Gothic and possibly German and even Islamic art influenced King Alfonso's artists as they produced the *Cantigas de Santa Maria.*

8. Violence in Spanish literature, especially in the drama of the Golden Age, as contrasted with the amount of violence in French classical plays, has intrigued scholars. A study of violence in medieval Spanish miniatures is a desideratum.

9. *El arte de la miniatura española* (Madrid: Editorial Plutarco, 1932), 6.

10. Paul Durrieu, "Manuscrites d'Espagne remarquables par leur peintures ou par la beauté de leur executions . . . ," *Extraite de la Bibliothèque de l'Ecole de Chartres* 54 (1893):60.

11. *Cantigas de Santa Maria de Alfonso el Sabio, Rey de Castilla* (Madrid: Editorial Patrimonio Nacional, 1974).

12. Menéndez Pidal, "Los manuscritos de las *Cantigas*," 50, lists six separate artists: 1) D. Andrés signs the miniature 156a; 2) Pedro Lorenzo, "who painted well and quickly the books of Holy Mary," 3)Bonamic, scribe of the king of Seville; 4) Juan González, who subscribes the Escorial codex b.I.2.; 5) Martín Pérez de Maqueda who subscribes the Vatican codex of the *General Estoria;* and 6) Juan Pérez, the king's painter in Seville.

13. *Las Cantigas: Estudio arqueológico de sus miniaturas* (Madrid: Consejo Superior de Investigaciones Científicas, 1949), 31–37.

14. Ibid., 36.

15. *Arquitectura civil española* (Madrid: Editorial Calleja, 1922), 1:89, n. 2.

16. Menéndez Pidal, "Los manuscritos de las *Cantigas.*" 23, rightly describes the Florentine codex as a second volume complementing Escorial T.I.j. In the same article he describes in detail the history, series of owners, and final archiving in Italian libraries, and gives dimensions, characteristics, and other important matters concerning this manuscript, archived today in the Biblioteca Nationale in Florence as Ms. Banco Rari 20.

17. See Israel J. Katz, "The Traditional Folk Music of Spain: Explorations and Perspectives," *1974 Yearbook of the International Folk Music Council* (Kingston, Ont., 1974). In his discussion of folk music, he discusses (78) the melody found in the *Cantigas* and in present-day Portugal entitled "Rosas das rosas."

18. *Alfonso X el Sabio, Cantigas de Santa María: Edición facsímil del Códice T.I.j. de la Biblioteca de San Lorenzo el Real de El Escorial, Siglo XIII* (Madrid: Editorial Internacional de Libros Antiguos, 1979).

19. *The Gothic Image,* trans. Dora Nussey (New York: Harper and Row, 1972), 51.

20. Cayetano Rossell, *Crónicas de los reyes de Castilla,* Biblioteca de Autores Españoles, 66:8 (Madrid, 1953).

21. (London: E. Arnold, 1937).

22. See Joseph T. Snow, "The *Loor* to the Virgin in Its Appearance in the *Cantigas de Santa Maria* of Alfonso el Sabio," Ph.D. diss., Univ. of Wisconsin, 1972. An abstract appears in Dissertation Abstracts International.

23. Gonzalo Menéndez Pidal, "Los manuscritos de las *Cantigas*," 33, discusses the poor artistry of some of the miniatures of the Florentine codex.

24. Guerrero Lovillo, *Las Cantigas,* 26, treats some examples of nudity in the *Cantigas.*

25. Gonzalo Menéndez Pidal, "Los manuscritos de las *Cantigas*," 42–43, discusses interesting miniatures arranged in six panels found in manuscripts of the Frankish Kingdom of Jerusalem around 1286, and in the Biblia del Arsenal also illuminated in Acre around 1250–54. He suggests that Alfonsine artists saw Islamic miniatures with six panels which influenced both the Jerusalem and the Acre miniatures, as well as those of the *Cantigas de Santa Maria.*

26. Guerrero Lovillo, *Las Cantigas,* 43–44, discusses this influence.

27. All translations are taken from the typescript of a complete translation of all four hundred-odd *Cantigas de Santa Maria* by Kathleen Kulp-Hill of Eastern Kentucky University. She does not translate the refrain at the end of each stanza, but only gives it at the beginning of each of her translations.

28. At least two articles have dealt with the miracle of the statue bride. See Paull F. Baum, "The Young Man Betrothed to a Statue," *PMLA* 34 (1919):523–79; and John E. Keller, "The Motif of the Statue Bride in the *Cantigas* of

Alfonso the Learned," *Studies in Philology* 56, no. 4 (1959):453–58.

29. See Otto Pächt, *The Rise of Pictorial Narrative Art in Twelfth-Century England* (Oxford: Clarendon Press, 1962). 31ff.

30. See Emile Mâle, *L'Art religieux du XII^e siècle en France,* 4th ed. (Paris: Armand Celins, 1922), 137.

31. Pächt, *Rise of Pictorial Narrative Art,* 14.

32. Ibid., 16ff.

33. Ibid., 19ff.

34. See John E. Keller, "The Depiction of Exotic Animals in *Cantiga* XXIX of the *Cantigas de Santa Maria,*" in *Studies in Honor of Tatiana Fotitch,* 247–53 (Washington, D.C.: Catholic Univ. Press, 1972).

35. Mâle, *Gothic Image,* 264, treats this miracle as depicted in a stained glass window in the Church of Le Mans.

36. Guerrero Lovillo, *Las Cantigas,* 112–34, discusses the armor seen in the miniatures of the *Cantigas* and gives citations about armor from other medieval Spanish manuscripts. Sketchers with labels of the parts of armor, also from the miniatures, appear. Pages 136–62 present sketches of weapons.

37. Charles L. Nelson, "Literary and Pictorial Treatment of the Devil in the *Cantigas de Santa Maria,*" M.A. thesis, Univ. of North Carolina, Chapel Hill, 1964.

38. Mâle, *Gothic Image,* 265.

39. The *Cantigas de Santa Maria* are unusual in the number of times the artists depict the king himself. Evelyn S. Procter, *Alfonso X of Castile* (33) remarks quite rightly on the unheard-of personal element of the *Cantigas,* and lists twenty-eight in which appear Alfonso or members of his family.

40. *Cantigas* 7, 55, 58, 59, and 94.

41. Two miracles with Alfonso's illnesses occur. The other in Valladolid (no. 235) is described by Evelyn S. Procter, *Alfonso X of Castile* (37). She states that "every incident can be identified and dated, and the poem provides an historical epitome from 1272 to 1278." She reveals, too, that this miracle helps "to account for the otherwise puzzling six-months' gap between Alfonso's audience with Gregory X in May and his return to Castile in December 1275."

42. See Antonio Madrigal, " 'El ome mui feo': Primera aparición del salvaje en la iconografía española?" in *Medieval, Renaissance and Folklore Studies in Honor of John Esten Keller* (Newark, Del.: Juan de la Cuesta, 1980.)

43. Several miracles occur in connection with pilgrims. At least two seem to show the rivalry between the shrines of the Virgin and the great international shrine of St. James at Santiago de Compostela. See John E. Keller, "King Alfonso's Virgin of Villa-Sirga, Rival of St. James of Compostela," *Middle Ages-Reformation-Volkskunde: Festschrift for John G. Kunstman* (Chapel Hill: Univ. of North Carolina Press, 1959); and idem, "More on the Rivalry between Santa Maria and Santiago de Compostela," *Crítica Hispánica* 1, no. 1 (1979):37–43.

44. Rocamadour in France attracted many devotees of Our Lady.

45. The culture of silk in Spain can be traced to periods before the reign of Alfonso. The industry was probably established first by the Moors.

46. See the transcription of John E. Keller and Robert W. Linker, "Las traducciones castellanas de las *Cantigas de Santa Maria,*" *Boletín de la Real Academia Española* 54 (1974):221–93. For two other transcriptions of the prose renditions found in T.I.j. see James Chatham, "A Paleographical Edition of the Alfonsine Collection of Prose Miracles of the Virgin," *Oelschläger Festschrift,* Estudios de Hispanófila, 36 (Chapel Hill, 1976); and José Filgueiro Valverde, "El texto, introducción histórico-crítica, transcripción, versión castellana y comentarios," in *Alfonso X el Sabio, Cantigas de Santa Maria: Edición facsímil.* The latter presents a complete transcription of all the *Cantigas* in T.I.j. together with his translation from Galician-Portuguese into Spanish.

47. Actually it may be no more than bullbaiting, yet it depicts much that is present in later bullfighting: the cape, the darts (which must be the ancestors of the *banderillas,* today plunged by hand into the neck of the bull), and the spears, which are not driven into the animal as they are today by *picadores* on horseback. Also the plaza, with its entrances sealed off to form an arena, performs the same functions as plazas do today in towns and villages where there are no true arenas, as for example Chinchón.

48. Irjö Hirn, *The Sacred Shrine* (Boston: Beacon Hill Press, 1957), 466–67, cites Jesus as the sun and the Virgin as a cloud.

49. While viewing the fresco above Mari Saltos's niche in the cloister of Segovia's Cathedral, we eavesdropped on a father as he recounted the miracle to his ten or twelve-year-old son. He knew the story well and even promised to take the boy to the very Cliff of the Ravens from which the Jewess was hurled down. The miracle is documented in the *General Estoria* of Alfonso X, Chap. 80.

50. Merlin was known in medieval Spain from the Arthurian cycle, which made its way there. See Karl Pietsch, *Spanish Grail Fragments* (Chicago: Univ. of Chicago Press. 1924); and William R. Davis, Jr., "Mary and Merlin: An Unusual Alliance," *Romance Notes* 14 (1972):207–12.

51. At present greater attention is being accorded the *Cantigas de Santa Maria.* A significant conference, the "International Symposium on the *Cantigas de Santa Maria* of Alfonso X, el Sabio (1252–1284) in Commemoration of Its 700th Anniversary Year—1981," was held at the Spanish Institute in New York City. Twenty-six papers were presented by scholars in many areas from across the world. In April 1984, to commemorate the anniversary of Alfonso's death, two additional symposia will be held, one at the University of Wisconsin in Madison and the other at the University of Kentucky in Lexington. All of these are described in *Noticiero Alfonsí* 1 (1982), the new Alfonsine newsletter prepared by Anthony J. Cárdenas and printed at Wichita State University.

## Calila e Digna

1. *The Book of Sindibad's* Spanish version has been translated into English by Domenico Comparetti for the Folklore

Society in *Researches Respecting the book of Sindibad*[9] (London: Stock, 1882); and by John E. Keller, *The Book of the Wiles of Women*, University of North Carolina Studies in the Romance Languages and Literatures, 27 (Chapel Hill: Univ. of North Carolina Press, 1956).

2. The two best modern editions of *El Conde Lucanor* are those of José Manuel Blecua, *El Conde Lucanor* (Madrid: Editorial Castalia, 1969); and Reinaldo Ayerbe-Chaux, *Don Juan Manuel, El Conde Lucanor, edición, estudio y notas* (Madrid: Clásicos Alhambra, 1983). A modern translation is that of John E. Keller and L. Clark Keating, *The Book of Count Lucanor and Patronio* (Lexington: Univ. Press of Kentucky, 1977).

3. Agapito Rey, ed., *Castigos e documentos para bien vivir ordenados por el Rey Don Sancho IV* (Bloomington: Indiana Univ. Press, 1952).

4. For a translation into English, see Joseph R. Jones and John E. Keller, *The Scholar's Guide: A translation of the Twelfth-Century "Disciplina Clericalis" of Pedro Alfonso* (Toronto: Pontifical Institute of Mediaeval Studies, 1969).

5. See Stith Thompson, *The Folktale* (New York: Dryden, 1951).

6. Countless studies of the migration of eastern fables exist. We can list only a few, whose bibliographies are copious: C. Brockelmann, "Kalila wa-Dimna," *Encyclopédie de l'Islam* 2:737–41 (Leyden: E.J. Brill, 1927); Clifford G. Allen, *L'Ancienne version espagnole de "Kalila et Digna": Texte des manuscrits de l'Escorial precedé d'un avant-propos et suivi d'un glossaire* (Macon: Protat frères, 1906); Victor Chauvin, *Bibliographie des ouvrages arabes ou relatifs aux arabes*, vol. 2, *Kalila* (Liege: H. Vaillant-Carmonne, 1897); and John E. Keller and Robert W. Linker, *El libro de Calila e Digna* (Madrid: Consejo Superior de Investigaciones Científicas, 1967). For a complete chart of the dispersal of the *Panchatantra* throughout the East and West, see C.H. Tawney, *The Ocean of Story: Being a Translation of Somadeva's "Katha Sarit Sagara,"* 5: 242 (London: Charles J. Sawyer, 1921).

7. The best English translation is that of Arthur Ryder, *The Panchatantra* (Chicago: Univ. of Chicago Press, 1958); the best and most recent translation of *Kalila wa-Dimna* is that of Thomas B. Irving, *Kalila and Dimnah* (Newark, Del.: Juan de la Cuesta, 1980).

### Castigos e Documentos

1. The most scholarly edition is that of Agapito Rey, *Castigos e documentos para bien vivir ordenados por el Rey Don Sancho IV* (Bloomington: Indiana Univ. Press, 1952), but this is of the shorter manuscript. The only edition of the longer one is that of Pascual de Gayangos, *Castigos e documentos del Rey Don Sancho,* in Biblioteca de Autores Españoles, vol. 51:79–228 (Madrid: Real Academia Española, 1952), and this is not edited in accordance with modern norms. For a good edition of another of Sancho's works, or a work under his auspices, see Richard P. Kinkade, *Los lucidarios españoles* (Madrid: Gredos, 1969).

2. J. Amador de los Ríos, *Historia crítica de la literatura española* (Madrid: Rodríguez, 1861–1865), 1:69.

3. *General Estoria: Primera Parte*, ed. A.G. Solalinde (Madrid: Junta para Amplificación de Estudios Imp. de Molina, 1930). *Historia troyana en prosa y verso, texto hacia 1270,* ed. Ramón Menéndez Pidal with the collaboration of E. Varón Vallejo (Madrid: Centro de Estudios Históricos Imp. Aguirre, 1934). *Gran Conquista de Ultramar,* ed. Pascual de Gayangos, in Biblioteca de Autores Españoles, 44 (Madrid, 1958); and Louis Cooper, *La Gran Conquista de Ultramar* (Bogotá, Colombia: Publicaciones del Instituto Caro y Cuervo, 1979), a four-volume text which may be considered the definitive edition.

### El libro del Cavallero Cifar

1. The translation of Charles L. Nelson is being published by the University Press of Kentucky in 1983 in the series Studies in Romance Languages. In the entire medieval Spanish period, ç and z tend to be used interchangeably.

2. Charles Philip Wagner, *El Libro del Cavallero Zifar* (Ann Arbor: Univ. of Michigan Press, 1929); and Joaquín González Muela, *El libro del Cavallero Zifar* (Madrid: Editorial Castalia, 1982). Marilyn Olsen is preparing an edition. A good modern text based upon Wagner is that of Felicidad Buendía in *Libros de caballerías españolas* (Madrid: Aguilar, 1960), 9–294.

3. Juan de Castrogeriz in the *Regimiento de Principes,* which dates from before 1350, rated *Cifar* as equal to *Tristán* (from which some elements of *Cifar* seem to have been drawn) and to *Amadís de Gaula*. A few years later King Pedro of Navarre, in a letter written in Latin and dated October 27, 1361, showed great impatience because his scribe, Eximeno de Monreal, had not finished copying the *Librum Militii Siffar*.

4. *Historia de la literatura universal*, vol. 1, *Antigüedad al Renacimiento* (Barcelona: Editorial Noguer, 1958), 211.

5. Ibid., 212.

6. Eric Köhler develops the role of the commoner in the French twelfth-century *geste* in his excellent article "Ritterliche Welt und *Villano:* Befmerkungen zum *Cuento del enperador Carlos Maynes e de la emperatris Seuilla,*" *Romanisches Jahrbuch* 12 (1961):229–41. Anita Benaim Lasry deals with many important similarities between *Cifar* and *Carlos Maynes* in the introduction to *Two Romances: A Study of Medieval Spanish Romances and an Edition of Two Representative Works* (Newark, Del.: Juan de la Cuesta, 1982). The two edited works are *Carlos Maynes* and the *Santa Emperatriz de Roma*.

7. *History and Vision: The Figural Structure of the "Libro del Cavallero Zifar"* (London: Tamesis, 1972).

8. See Alexandre H. Krappe, "Le Mirage celtique et les sources du *Chevalier Cifar,*" *Bulletin Hispanique* 33 (1931):97–103; and Charles P. Wagner, "The Sources of the *Caballero Cifar,*" *Revue Hispanique* 10 (1903):5–104.

9. Roger M. Walker, "The Genesis of *El libro del Cavallero Zifar,*" *Modern Language Review* 62 (1967):61–69. John K. Walsh, "The Chivalresque Dragon: Hagiographic Parallels in Early Spanish Romances," *Bulletin of Hispanic Studies* 54 (1977):189–98.

10. Books from Sanskrit sources were translated into Persian and thence into Arabic, Syriac, Hebrew, and other languages. *Barlaam e Josafat* goes ultimately back to the life of the Buddha; *Calila e Digna,* through the Arabic *Kalila wa-Dimna,* traces its way through a lost Persian version all the way back to the Indian *Panchatantra;* the *Libro de los engaños,* the Spanish version of the *Book of Sindibad,* came to Spanish from Arabic and thence from Persian probably. The ancestor of sections of the *Cavallero Cifar* may well have gone back through Syriac or Arabic to Persian to a Sanskrit source.

11. Wagner, "Sources," 11.

12. Burke, *History and Vision,* 1.

13. *The Book of Hours with a Historical Survey and Commentary* by John Harthan (New York: Thomas Y. Crowell, 1977).

14. Mary Galaway Houston, *Medieval Costume in England and France* (London: Adam and Charles Black, 1950), 147.

15. For a guide to complete treatment of this tale, see note 8, below.

16. This strange story appears in *Castigos* (where it is not illustrated) and is said to have taken place in Bulgaria; see the edition of *Castigos* in Biblioteca de Autores Españoles, vol. 51:90–91.

It is also *exemplum* 338 in the *Libro de los exenplos por a.b.c.;* see the edition of John E. Keller, 260. Only in *Cifar* is it the mother who spoils her son, for in the other versions the son bites off the nose, not the lips, of his father. All the motifs of brief narrative in *Cifar,* as well as those in the *Disciplina Clericalis, Castigos e documentos, Calila e Digna,* and other collections of brief narratives not studied for visualization, are to be found in John E. Keller, *Motif-Index of Mediaeval Spanish Exempla* (Knoxville: Univ. of Tennessee Press, 1949). They have all been incorporated, too, into Stith Thompson's *Motif-Index of Folk Literature,* 6 vols. (Bloomington: Indiana Univ. Press, 1955–1958).

### La vida del Ysopet con sus fabulas hystoriadas

1. See Theodore S. Beardsley, *Hispano-Classical Translations Printed between 1482 and 1699* (Pittsburgh: Duquesne Univ. Press, 1970), 2–21.

2. The Infante Don Juan Manuel, nephew of Alfonso X el Sabio, wrote many books of various natures—on poetics, on seigecraft, on the estates of society, and the most famous, *The Book of Count Lucanor and Patronio.* This last is in five parts, only the first of which is concerned with brief narratives; the other parts deal with nonliterary subjects. Two translations into English are available. The first is that of James York, *Count Lucanor, or Fifty Pleasant Tales of Patronio* (Westminister: B.M. Pickering, 1968; reprinted privately in Alhambra, California, 1969). The York translation was made from a French translation of the original. The other is that of John E. Keller and L. Clark Keating, *The Book of Count Lucanor and Patronio* (Lexington: Univ. Press of Kentucky, 1977). The *Libro de buen amor* has scores of editions in Spanish and several translations into English: Elisha Kent Kane, *The Book of Good Love,* first privately printed (New York: William Edwin Rudge, 1933) and reprinted (Chapel Hill: Univ. of North Carolina Press, 1968) with an introduction by John E. Keller. See also Raymond S. Willis, *Juan Ruiz Libro de Buen Amor* (Princeton: Princeton Univ. Press, 1972), which presents the original and the translation on facing pages; the bilingual edition of Saralyn R. Daly and Anthony N. Zahareas, *The Book of True Love* (University Park: Pennsylvania State Univ. Press, 1978); and Mack Singleton, *The Book of the Archpriest of Hita (Libro de Buen Amor)* (Madison, Wis.: Hispanic Seminary, 1975).

3. *The Libro de los gatos,* in part a translation and in part a rendition into Spanish of Odo de Cheriton's *Narrationes* or *Fabulae,* contains Aesopic fables, together with stories from the *Roman de Renart* and sundry other medieval books. It is didactic and yet entertaining and contains strong elements of satire. There is no translation into English. The *Libro de los exenplos por a.b.c.* is the only alphabet of tales in medieval Castilian and contains more than five hundred *exempla.* Most of the *Disciplina Clericalis* is contained here in Spanish translation, which makes the *Libro* a predecessor of the kind of material found in the *Ysopet.*

4. A translation into English is that of Jones and Keller, *The Scholar's Guide.*

5. The word *exemplum* signifies a story with a moralization plainly stated, so the author had every right to label this fable an *exemplum.*

6. The change of tense occurs at the same place in the Spanish.

7. Poggio (Gian Francesco Poggio Bracciolini [1380–1456] was a fertile writer born in the territory of Florence who wrote *fabliaux* in Latin as well as more dignified works, such as the *History of Florence* and the *Dialogue against Hypocrites,* a vindictive and vitriolic attack against the vices of ecclesiastics.

8. Kenneth Scholberg, in "A Half Friend and and a Friend and a Half," *Bulletin of Hispanic Studies* 35 (1958):87–98, treats the motif of the half-friend as it appears in very different forms in *La vida del Ysopet, Disciplina Clericalis, Castigos e documentos, Conde Lucanor, Libro de los exenplos por a.b.c.,* and *Cavallero Cifar.*

9. The motif of the drawn sword appears in most of the versions of the *Book of Sindibad* and is generally known as "De gladio."

# Selected Bibliography

### Las Cantigas de Santa Maria

Aguado Bleye, Pedro. *Santa María de Salas en el siglo XIII: Estudio sobre "Las Cantigas" de Alfonso X el Sabio.* Bilbao: 1916.

Aita, Nella. "Miniaturas spagnuole in un codice firentino." *Rassegna d'Arte* 19 (1919):149–55.

———. "O codice florentino de *Cantigas* de Alfonso, o Sabio." *Revista da Lengua Portuguesa* 13 (1921):187–200; 14 (1921): 105–28; 15 (1922):169–76; 16 (1922):181–88; 18 (1923):153–60.

Alemparte, Jaime Ferreiro. "Fuentes Germánicos en las *CSM* de Alfonso X el Sabio." *Grial* 30 (1971):31–62.

Alfonso X el Sabio. *Cantigas de Santa Maria: Edición facsímil del Códice T.I.j. de la Biblioteca de San Lorenzo el Real de El Escorial, Siglo XIII.* Madrid: Editorial Internacional de Libros Antiguos.

Anderson, Flemming G., et al., eds. *Medieval Iconography and Narrative: A Symposium.* Odense, Denmark: Odense Univ. Press, 1980.

Anglés, Higinio. *La música de las "Cantigas de Santa Maria" del rey Alfonso el Sabio: Facsímil, transcripción y estudio crítico,* vol. 3. Barcelona: Diputación Provincial, Biblioteca Central, 1958.

Bagby, Albert I., Jr. "Alfonso X, el Sabio compara moros y judíos." *Romanische Forschungen* 82 (1970):578–83.

———. "The Jew in the *Cantigas* of Alfonso el Sabio." *Speculum* 46 (1971):670–88.

———. "The Moslems in the *Cantigas* of Alfonso X, el Sabio." *Kentucky Romance Quarterly* 20 (1973):173–207.

Ballesteros-Beretta, Antonio. *Alfonso X el Sabio.* Barcelona: Salvat Editores; Murcia: Consejo Superior de Investigaciones Científicas, 1963.

Baraut, Cebrià. "Les *Cantigues* d'Alfons el Savi i el primitu *Liber Miraculorum de Nostra Dona de Montserrat.*" *Estudis Romànics* 2 (1949–40):79–92.

Bell, A.F.G. "The *Cantigas de Santa Maria* of Alfonso X," *Modern Language Review* 10 (1915):328–48.

Burckhardt, Titus. *Moorish Art in Spain.* New York: McGraw Hill, 1972.

Calcott, Frank. *The Supernatural in Early Spanish Literature.* New York: Instituto de las Españas en los Estados Unidos, 1923.

Calkins, Robert G. *Monuments of Medieval Art.* New York: E.P. Dutton, 1979.

Carpenter, Dwayne E. "Christian Attitudes toward the Jewish Sabbath in the Light of Medieval Spanish Legal Texts." *Proceedings of the Patristic, Mediaeval and Renaissance Conference,* no. 4. Villanova, Pa. (1980).

Castro, Américo. *The Structure of Spanish History.* Princeton: Princeton Univ. Press, 1954.

Castro, Lázaro de. "Fantásticas leyendas medievales, recogidas en la pintura por un artista mudéjar en Los Balbases (Burgos)." *Minutos Menarini,* Circular 33175, 3–6. Dirección General de Sanidad, August 1975.

Chase, Gilbert. *The Music of Spain,* 2nd ed. New York: Dover, 1959.

Chisman, Anna Mary McGregor. "Enjambement in *Las Cantigas de Santa Maria* of Alfonso X, el Sabio." Ph.D. diss., Univ. of Toronto, 1974.

———. "The Symbolism of Diseases in the *Cantigas de Santa Maria.*" *La Corónica* 3, no. 2 (Spring 1975):3.

Clarke, Dorothy Clotelle. "Versification in Alfonso el Sabio's *Cantigas.*" *Hispanic Review* 23 (1955):83–98.

Cueto, Leopoldo A., Marqués de Valmar. *Las "Cantigas de Santa Maria" de Alfonso el Sabio,* 2 vols. Madrid: Real Academia Española, 1889.

Curtius, Ernst Robert. *European Literature and the Latin Middle Ages.* Trans. Willard R. Trask. New York: Pantheon Books, 1948.

Davis, William R., Jr. "The Role of the Virgin in the *Cantigas de Santa Maria.*" Ph.D. diss., Univ. of Kentucky, 1969.

———. "Mary and Merlin: An Unusual Alliance." *Romance Notes* 14 (1972):207–12.

———. "Another Aspect of the Virgin Mary in the *Cantigas*

*de Santa Maria." Revista de Estudios Hispánicos* 8 (1974):95–105.

Deyermond, Alan. *The Literary History of Spain: The Middle Ages.* New York: Barnes and Noble, 1971.

———. *Historia crítica de la literatura española al cuidado de Francisco Rico I. Edad Media.* Barcelona: Editorial Crítica, 1980.

Domínguez Bordona, Jesús. *Exposición de códices miniados españoles: Catálogo.* Madrid: Sociedad Española de Amigos del Arte, 1929.

———. *Spanish Illumination.* 2 vols. Florence: Pantheon Casa Editrice, 1929; reprint, New York: Hacker Art Books, 1969.

———. *El arte de la miniatura española.* Madrid: Editorial Plutarco, 1932.

———. "Diccionario de iluminaciones españolas." *Boletín de la Real Academia Española* 140 (1957):49–170.

———. "Manuscritos alfonsíes y franco-góticos de Castilla, Navarra y Aragón." *Ars Hispaniae* 18:111–29. Madrid: Editorial Plus-Ultra, 1962.

Domínguez Rodríguez, A. "Imágenes de presentación de la miniatura alfonsí." *Goya* 131 (March-April 1976):287–91.

Durrieu, Paul. "Manuscrites d'Espagne remarquables par leur peintures ou par la beauté de leur executions. . . ." *Extraite de la Bibliothèque de l'Ecole de Chartres* 54 (1893):60.

Dutton, Brian, ed. *Milagros de Nuestra Señora.* London: Tamesis, 1971.

Egbert, Virginia Wylie. *The Mediaeval Artist at Work.* Princeton: Princeton Univ. Press, 1967.

García Solalinde, Antonio. "Intervención de Alfonso X en la redacción de sus obras." *Revista de Filología Española* 2 (1915): 283–88.

———. "El códice florentino de las *Cantigas* y su relación sobre los demás manuscritos." *Revista de Filología Española* 5 (1918):143–79.

———. *Milagros de Nuestra Señora.* Madrid: Clásicos Castellanos, 1958.

Gudiol, José. *The Art of Spain.* New York: Chanticleer Press, Doubleday, 1964.

Guerrero Lovillo, José. *Las Cantigas: Estudio arqueológico de sus miniaturas.* Madrid: Consejo Superior de Investigaciones Científicas, 1949.

———. *Miniatura gótica castellana: Siglos XIII a XIV.* Madrid: Consejo Superior de Investigaciones Científicas, 1956.

Guiette, Robert. *La Légende de la Sacristine: Étude de littérature comparée.* Paris: Librairie Ancienne Honoré Champion, 1927.

Hauser, Arnold. *The Social History of Art—Prehistoric, Ancient-Oriental, Greece and Rome, Middle Ages.* New York: Vantage Books, 1951.

Heath, Dudley. *Miniatures.* London: Methuen, 1905.

Huizinga, Johan. *The Waning of the Middle Ages.* London: E. Arnold, 1937.

Janson, H.W. *History of Art.* New York: Prentice Hall and Harry N. Abrams, 1963.

Keller, John E. *Motif-Index of Mediaeval Spanish Exempla.* Knoxville: Univ. of Tennessee Press, 1949.

———. "A Note on King Alfonso's Use of Popular Themes in His *Cantigas de Santa Maria." Kentucky Foreign Language Quarterly* 1, no. 1 (1954):26–31.

———. "Daily Living as Presented in the *Canticles* of Alfonso the Learned." *Speculum* 33, no. 4 (1958):484–89.

———. "Folklore in the *Cantigas* of Alfonso el Sabio." *Southern Folklore Quarterly* 23, no. 3 (1959):175–83.

———. "King Alfonso's Virgin of Villa-Sirga, Rival of St. James of Compostela." In *Middle Ages-Reformation-Volkskunde: Festschrift for John G. Kunstman.* Chapel Hill: Univ. of North Carolina Press, 1959.

———. "The Motif of the Statue Bride in the *Cantigas* of Alfonso the Learned." *Studies in Philology* 56, no. 4 (1959):453–58.

———. *Alfonso X, el Sabio.* New York: Twayne, 1967.

———. "The Depiction of Exotic Animals in *Cantiga* XXIX of the *Cantigas de Santa Maria."* In *Studies in Honor of Tatiana Fotitch,* pp. 247–53. Washington, D.C.: Catholic Univ. Press, 1972.

———. *"Cantiga 135:* The Blessed Virgin as a Matchmaker." In *Florilegium Hispanicum: Medieval and Golden Age Studies Presented to Dorothy Clotelle Clarke,* pp. 103–18. Madison, Wis. Hispanic Seminary, 1972.

———. "An Unknown Castilian Lyric Poem: The Alfonsine Translation of *Cantiga X* of the *Cantigas de Santa Maria."* *Hispanic Review* 43 (1975): 43–47.

———. "Verbalization and Visualization in the *Cantigas de Santa Maria."* In *Oelschläger Festschrift.* Estudios de Hispanófila, 36 (1976):221–26. Chapel Hill, N.C.

———. *Pious Brief Narrative in Medieval Castilian and Galician Verse: From Berceo to Alfonso X.* Lexington: Univ. Press of Kentucky, 1979.

———, and Linker, Robert W. "Some Spanish Summaries of the *Cantigas de Santa Maria." Romance Notes* 2 (1960):63–67.

———, and Linker, Robert W. "Las traducciones castellanas de las *Cantigas de Santa Maria." Boletín de la Real Academia Española* 54 (1974):221–93.

———, and Nelson, Charles L. "Some Remarks on Visualization in the *Cantigas de Santa Maria." Ariel* 3 (April 1974):7–12.

Kulp-Hill, Kathleen. "The Three Faces of Eve: Women in the Medieval Galician-Portuguese *Cancioneiro." Kentucky Romance Quarterly* 16 (1969):97–107.

Lampérez y Romea, Victor. *Arquitectura civil española.* Madrid: Editorial Calleja, 1922.

Le Gentil, Pierre. *La Poesie lyrique espagnole et portuguaise a la fin de Moyen Age.* 2 vols. Rennes: Plihon, 1949.

London, Gardiner. "Bibliografía de estudios sobre la vida y obra de Alfonso X el Sabio." *Boletín de Filología Española* 6 (April 1960):18–31.

López Serrano, Matilde. *Cantigas de Santa Maria de Alfonso X el Sabio, Rey de Castilla.* Madrid: Editorial Patrimonio Nacional, 1980.

Mackay, Angus, and McKendrick, Geraldine. "Confession in the *CSM." Reading Medieval Studies* 5 (1979):71–88.

Mâle, Emile. *L'Art religieux du XII<sup>e</sup> siècle en France.* 4th ed. Paris: Armand Celin, 1922.

————. *The Gothic Image: Religious Art in France in the Thirteenth Century.* Translated by Dora Nussey. New York: Harper and Row, 1972.

Menéndez Pidal, Gonzalo. "Como trabajaron las escuelas alfonsíes." *Nueva Revista de Filología Hispánica* 5, no. 4 (1951):363–80.

————. "Los manuscritos de las *Cantigas de Santa Maria*: Cómo se elaboró la miniatura alfonsí." *Boletín de la Real Academia Española* 150 (1962):23–51.

Menéndez Pidal, Marcelino. "Las *Cantigas* del Rey Sabio." *La Ilustración Española y Americana* 39 (1895):127–31, 143–46, 159–63. Reprinted in *Obras Completas,* vol. 1: *Estudios y discursos de crítica histórica y literaria,* 161–89. Madrid: Consejo Superior de Investigaciones Científicas, 1941.

Mettmann, Walter, ed. *Cantigas de Santa Maria.* 4 vols. Coimbra: Acta Universitatis Conimbrigensis, 1959–1972.

Montoya Martínez, Jesús. "Crítico agrupador de las *CSM.*" In *Estudios literarios dedicados al profesor Mariano Baquero Goyanes,* 285–96. Murcia: Univ. de Murcia, 1975.

————. *Las colecciones de milagros de la Virgen en la Edad Media (el milagro literario).* Granada: Univ. de Granada, 1981.

Nelson, Charles L. "Literary and Pictorial Treatment of the Devil in the *Cantigas de Santa Maria.*" M.A. thesis, Univ. of North Carolina, Chapel Hill, 1964.

Pächt, Otto. *The Rise of Pictorial Narrative Art in Twelfth-Century England.* Oxford: Clarendon Press, 1962.

Pietsch, Karl. *Spanish Grail Fragments.* 2 vols. Chicago: Univ. of Chicago Press, 1924.

Post, Charles R. *A History of Spanish Painting.* Cambridge, Mass.: Harvard Univ. Press, 1930.

Procter, Evelyn S. *Alfonso X of Castile, Patron of Literature and Learning.* Oxford: Clarendon Press, 1951.

Rafols, J.F. *Historia del arte.* Barcelona: Editorial Ramón Sopena, 1949.

Rey, Agapito. "Correspondence of the Spanish Miracles of the Virgin." *Romanic Review* 19 (1928):151–53.

Riquer, Martín de. *Historia de la literatura universal,* vol. 1. Barcelona: Editorial Noguer, 1957.

Robb, David M. *The Art of the Illuminated Manuscript.* New York: A.S. Barnes, 1973.

Rossell, Cayetano. *Crónicas de los reyes de Castilla.* Biblioteca de Autores Españoles, vol. 66 (Madrid, 1953).

Sánchez Cantón, F.J. "Seis estampas de la vida segoviana del siglo XIII." *Correo Erudito* 1 (1940):332–34.

Scarborough, Connie. "Verbalization and Visualization in Ms. T.I. I of the *Cantigas de Santa Maria.*" Ph.D. diss., Univ. of Kentucky, 1982.

Smith, Bradley. *Spain: A History in Art.* With an introduction to the history of Spain by the Marqués de Lozano. New York: Simon and Schuster, 1966.

Snow, Joseph T. "The *Loor* to the Virgin and Its Appearance in the *Cantigas de Santa Maria* of Alfonso el Sabio." Ph.D. diss., Univ. of Wisconsin, 1972.

————. *The Poetry of Alfonso X, el Sabio.* London: Grant and Cutler, 1977.

Tavani, Giuseppe. "Reporterio metrico della lirica galego-portoghese," *Officina Romanica,* vol. 8. Rome: Edizione dell' Ateneo, 1967.

Torres Balba, Leopoldo. "Miniaturas españolas medievales." *Al-Andaluz* 15 (1950):191–202.

Trend, J.B. *The Civilization of Spain.* Fairlawn, N.Y.: Oxford Univ. Press, 1944.

Trens, Manuel. *María: Iconografía de la Virgen en el arte español.* Madrid: Editorial Plus-Ultra, 1946.

Warner, Marina L. *Alone of All Her Sex: The Myth and Cult of the Virgin Mary..* New York: Knopf, 1976.

Werner, Alfred. *Medieval Miniatures.* New York: A.A. Wyn, 1951.

## Calila e Digna

Alemany Bolufer, José. *La antigua versión de Calila e Dimna cotejada con el original árabe de la misma.* Madrid: Sucesores de Hernando, 1915.

Allen, Clifford G. *L'Ancienne version espagnole de "Kalila et Dimna": Texte des manuscrits de l'Escorial precedé d'un avant-propos et suivi d'un glossaire.* Macon: Protat frères, 1906.

Amador de los Ríos, José. *Historia crítica de la literatura española.* 7 vols. Madrid: J. Rodríguez, 1861–1865. See vol. 1 for *Calila.*

Ayyar, A.S.P. *Panchatantra and Hitopadesa Stories.* 2nd ed., revised and enlarged. Madras: V. Ramaswamy Sastulu and Sons, 1960.

Blecua, José Manuel, ed. *Don Juan Manuel: El Conde Lucanor.* Madrid: Clásicos Castalia, 1969.

Brockelmann, C. "Kalila wa-Dimna." *Encyclopédie de l'Islam* 2:737–41. Leyden: E.J. Brill, 1927.

Chauvin, Victor. *Bibliographie des ouvrages arabes ou relatifs aux arabes.* Vol. 2: *Kalila.* Liège: H. Vaillant-Carmonne, 1897.

Cheiko, P. *Kalila et Dimna d'après le plus ancien manuscrit arabe daté.* Beirut, 1905.

Crane, Thomas F. *The Exempla of Jacques de Vitry.* Publications of the Folklore Society. London: Nutt, 1890.

Derembourg, Joseph. *Johannis de Capua Directorium Vitae Humanae.* Paris, 1887.

Gayangos, Pascual de. *Calila e Dimna.* In *Escritores en prosa anteriores al siglo XV.* Biblioteca de Autores Españoles, 51:1–78. Madrid, 1965.

González Palencia, Ángel. *Versiones castellanas del "Sendebar."* Madrid and Granada: Consejo Superior de Investigaciones Científicas, 1946.

Hauser, Arnold. *The Social History of Art—Prehistoric, Ancient-Oriental, Greece and Rome, Middle Ages.* New York: Vantage Books, 1951.

Huizinga, Johan. *The Waning of the Middle Ages.* London: E. Arnold, 1937.

Irving, Thomas B. *Kalila and Dimnah.* Newark, Del.: Juan de la Cuesta, 1980.

Janson, H.W. *History of Art.* New York: Prentice Hall and Harry N. Abrams, 1963.

Keller, John E., ed. *El libro de los engaños*. Romance Monographs. University, Miss., 1983.

———, and Linker, Robert W., eds. *El libro de Calila e Digna: Edición crítica*. Madrid: Consejo Superior de Investigaciones Científicas, 1967.

———, and Linker, Robert W., eds. *Barlaam e Josafat*. Madrid: Consejo Superior de Investigaciones Científicas, 1979.

Knust, Hermann, and Birch-Hirschfield, Adolph, eds. *Juan Manuel: El libro de los exienplos del Conde Lucanor et de Patronio*. Leipzig: Dr. Seele, 1900.

Lacarra, María Jesús. *Cuentística medieval en España: Los Orígenes*. Zaragoza: Univ. de Zaragoza, 1980.

Lauchert, F., ed. *Barlaam et Iosaphat. Romanische Forschungen*. 1893, 33–402.

Menéndez y Pelayo, Marcelino. *Orígenes de la novela*. 3 vols. Santander: Consejo Superior de Investigaciones Científicas, 1948.

Perry, Ben. E. "The Origin of the *Book of Sindibad*." *Fabula* 3 (1960):1–94.

Tawney, C.H. *The Ocean of Story: Being a Translation of Somadeva's "Katha Sarit Sagara."* 10 vols. London: Charles J. Sawyer, 1924.

## Castigos e documentos

Anderson, Ruth Matilde. *Hispanic Costume, 1480–1530*. New York: Hispanic Society of America, 1980.

Foulché-Delbosc, R. *"Los Castigos e documentos de Sancho IV."* *Revue Hispanique* 15 (1906):340–71.

Gayangos, Pascual de. *Castigos e documentos del Rey Don Sancho*. Biblioteca de Autores Españoles. 51:79–228. Madrid, 1952.

Groussac, Paul. *"Le livre des Castigos e documentos* attribué au Roi Sanche IV." *Revue Hispanique* 15 (1906):217–339.

Rey, Agapito, ed. *Castigos e documentos para bien vivir ordenados por el Rey Don Sancho IV*. Bloomington: Indiana Univ. Press, 1952.

Serrano y Sanz, J. "Fragmentos de un códice de los *Castigos e documentos del rey Sancho IV*." *Boletín de la Real Academia Española* 17 (1930):88–95.

## El Cavallero Cifar

Bonilla y San Martín, Adolfo. *Libro de caballería*. Nueva Biblioteca de Autores Españoles, vol. 11. Madrid, 1908.

Burke, James F. "Names and Significance of Etymology in the *Libro del Cavallero Cifar*." *Romanic Review* 59 (1968):167–73.

———. "Symbolic Allegory in the Portus Salutaris Episode in the *Libro del Cavallero Cifar*." *Kentucky Romance Quarterly* 15 (1968):68–84.

———. "The *Libro del Cavallero Zifar* and the Medieval University Sermons." *Viator* 1 (1970):207–21.

———. "The Meaning of the *Islas Dotadas* Espisode in the *Libro del Cavallero Cifar*." *Hispanic Review* 38 (1970):56–68.

———. *History and Vision: The Figural Structure of the "Libro del Cavallero Zifar."* London: Tamesis, 1972.

Curtius, Ernst Robert. *European Literature and the Latin Middle Ages*. Translated by Willard R. Trask. New York: Pantheon Books, 1948.

Deyermond, Alan. *The Literary History of Spain: The Middle Ages*. New York: Barnes and Noble, 1971.

———. "The Lost Genre of Medieval Spanish Literature." *Hispanic Review* 43 (1975):231–59.

Diz, Marta Ana. "El mundo de las armas en el *Libro del Caballero Cifar*." *Bulletin of Hispanic Studies* 56 (1979):189–97.

Dutton, Brian, and Walker, Roger. "*El libro del Cauallero Zifar* y la lírica castellana." *Filología* 9 (1963):53–67.

González Muela, Joaquín. "Ferrand Martínez, mallorquín, autor del '*Zifar*'?" *Revista de Filología Española* 59 (1977):250–61.

———, ed. *Libro del Caballero Zifar*. Madrid: Clásicos Castalia, 1982.

Green, Otis H. *Spain and the Western Tradition: The Castilian Mind in Literature from el Cid to Calderón*. 4 vols. Madison: Univ. of Wisconsin Press, 1963.

Javier-Hernández, Francisco. "Sobre el *Cifar* y una versión latina de la *Poridat*." In *Homenaje universitario a Dámaso Alonso*. Madrid: Gredos, 1970.

Keller, John E., and Keating, L. Clark. *The Book of Count Lucanor and Patronio: a Translation of Don Juan Manuel's "El Conde Lucanor."* Lexington: Univ. Press of Kentucky, 1977.

Köhler, Eric. "Ritterliche Welt und *Villano*: Bemerkungen zum *Cuento del enperador Carlos Maynes e de la emperatris Seuilla*." *Romanisches Jahrbuch* 12 (1961):229–41.

Krappe, Alexandre Haggerty. "Le Mirage celtique et les sources de *Chevalier Cifar*." *Bulletin Hispanique* 33 (1931):97–103.

———. "Le lac enchanté dans le *Chevalier Cifar*." *Bulletin Hispanique* 55 (1933):107–25.

Menéndez y Pelayo, Marcelino. *Orígenes de la novela*. 3 vols. Santander: Consejo Superior de Investigaciones Científicas, 1948.

Piccus, Jules, "Consejos y consejeros en el *Libro del Cavellero Cifar*." *Nueva Revista de Filología Hispánica* 16 (1962):16–30.

Sánchez de Vercial, Clemente. *Libro de los exenplos por a.b.c.* Edited by John E. Keller. Madrid: Consejo Superior de Investigaciones Científicas, 1961.

Scholberg, Kenneth R. "A Half Friend and a Friend and a Half." *Bulletin of Hispanic Studies* 35 (1958):87–98.

———. "La comicidad del *Caballero Cifar*." In *Homenaje a Rodríguez Moñino*, 157–63. Madrid: Castalia, 1966.

Wagner, Charles Philip. "The Sources of the *Caballero Cifar*." *Revue Hispanique* 10 (1903):5–104.

———. *El libro del Cavallero Zifar*. Ann Arbor: Univ. of Michigan Press, 1929.

———. "The *Caballero Zifar* and the *Moralium Dogma Philosophorum*." *Romance Philology* 6 (1953):309–12.

Walker, Roger M. "The Unity of *El libro del cauallero Zifar*." *Bulletin of Hispanic Studies* 42 (1965):149–59.

———. "The Genesis of *El libro del Cauallero Zifar*." *Modern Language Review* 62 (1967):61–69.

——. *Tradition and Technique in "El Libro del Cauallero Zifar."* London: Tamesis, 1970.

——. "Did Cervantes Know the *Cauallero Zifar?"* *Bulletin of Hispanic Studies* 49 (1972):120–27.

### *La vida del Ysopet con sus fabulas hystoriadas*

Beardsley, Theodore S. *Hispanic-Classical Translations Printed between 1482 and 1699.* Pittsburgh: Duquesne Univ. Press, 1970.

*Fábulas de Esopo, reproducción en facsímil de la primera edición 1489.* Madrid: Real Academia Española, 1929.

Hervieux, Léopold. *Les Fabulistes latins.* Vol 4: *Eudes de Cheriton et ses dérivés.* Paris: Librairie de Firmin-Didot, 1869.

Hirschman, Joan. *Aesop's Fables.* New York: Dell, 1964.

Jacobs, Joseph. *History of the Aesopic Fable.* London: Nutt, 1889.

Keller, John E. *El libro de los gatos.* Edición crítica. Madrid: Consejo Superior de Investigaciones Científicas, 1958.

Komroff, Manuel. *Tales of the Monks from "Gesta Romanorum."* New York: Tudor, 1928.

Lenaghan, R.T., ed. *Caxton's Aesop.* Cambridge, Mass.: Harvard Univ. Press, 1967.

McKendry, J.M. *Aesop: Five Centuries of Illustrated Fables.* New York: Metropolitan Museum, 1935.

Menéndez y Pelayo, Marcelino. *Orígenes de la novela.* 3 vols. Santander: Consejo Superior de Investigaciones Científicas, 1948.

Perry, Ben E. *Aesopica: Greek and Latin Texts.* Vol. 1. Urbana: Univ. of Illinois Press, 1952.

Swan, Charles. *The Tales of the "Gesta Romanorum" Translated from Latin.* Revised by Wynnard Hooper. New York: Everest Books, 1958.

Wright, Thomas. *A Selection of Latin Stories from Manuscripts of the Thirteenth and Fourteenth Centuries.* Percy Society Publications, vol. 8. London: Richards, 1843.

# Index